LIBERATING SPIRITUALITIES

# Liberating Spiritualities

## REIMAGINING FAITH IN THE AMÉRICAS

*Christopher D. Tirres*

FORDHAM UNIVERSITY PRESS    NEW YORK 2025

Front cover image courtesy of Juan Sánchez, Guarikan Arts, Inc. This mixed-media collage, entitled "Poema Para Mami: Missing You," pays tribute to Sánchez's mother and is in the permanent collection of the National Museum of African American History and Culture in Washington, D.C. The upper half of the artwork features a photo of his mother's worn feet on cracked pavement, as well as a testimony—which mixes past and present tense—that Sánchez wrote in her honor. The bottom half of the collage calls attention to his mother's prayer card to Our Lady of Perpetual Help, which she kept by her bed. Directly underneath, a row of five cowrie shells invoke Afro-Caribbean spirituality. Born in Brooklyn, NY, to working-class parents who migrated from Puerto Rico, Sánchez is one of the most important Nuryorican Latinx visual artists working today.

An earlier version of Chapter 1 appears as "At the Crossroads of Liberation Theology and Liberation Philosophy: José Carlos Mariátegui's 'New Sense' of Religion," in *Inter-American Journal of Philosophy* 8, no. 1 (2017): 1–16. Different versions of Chapter 4 have been published as "Spiritual Activism and Praxis: Gloria Anzaldúa's Mature Spirituality," in *Inter-American Journal of Philosophy* 10, no. 1 (2019): 1–22; "Spiritual Activism and Praxis: Gloria Anzaldúa's Mature Spirituality," in *The Pluralist* 14, no. 1 (2019): 119–40; and "Spiritual Realities and Spiritual Activism: Assessing Gloria Anzaldúa's *Light in the Dark / Luz en lo Oscuro*," in *Diálogo: An Interdisciplinary Studies Journal* 21, no. 2 (2018): 50–64. An earlier version of Chapter 5 appears as, "Conscientization from Within lo Cotidiano: Expanding the Work of Ada María Isasi-Díaz," in *Feminist Theology* 22, no. 3 (2014), 312–23.

Fordham University Press has no responsibility for the persistence or accuracy of URLs for external or third-party Internet websites referred to in this publication and does not guarantee that any content on such websites is, or will remain, accurate or appropriate.

Fordham University Press also publishes its books in a variety of electronic formats. Some content that appears in print may not be available in electronic books.

Visit us online at www.fordhampress.com.

Library of Congress Cataloging-in-Publication Data available online at https://catalog.loc.gov.

Printed in the United States of America
27 26 25    5 4 3 2 1
First edition

*For my children,*
*Eloisa, Mateo, and Ana Luz,*
*con amor y esperanza*

# Contents

Introduction: Toward a Liberating Spirituality   1

1   A "New Sense" of Religion:
    José Carlos Mariátegui's Pragmatic Sensibility   21

2   Conscientization as a Spiritual Praxis:
    Paulo Freire's Implicit Spirituality   36

3   A Cosmic Vision from the Borderlands:
    Virgilio Elizondo's Evolutionary Cosmology   51

4   Spiritual Activism as Conocimiento:
    Gloria Anzaldúa's Mature Spirituality   67

5   Subversive Everyday Knowledge:
    Ada María Isasi-Díaz's "Conscientized Cotidiano"   87

6   Ecofeminism and Relatedness:
    Ivone Gebara's Pragmatic Inheritance   100

Conclusion: Spiritual Praxis and the Fullness of Life   109

ACKNOWLEDGMENTS   125

NOTES   127

BIBLIOGRAPHY   157

INDEX   171

# LIBERATING SPIRITUALITIES

# Introduction:
# Toward a Liberating Spirituality

For five years, before the onset of COVID-19, I drove once a month to a detention facility about an hour from my home to sit with detained immigrants and listen to their stories. I did so as a volunteer with the Chicago-based Interfaith Community for Detained Immigrants (ICDI), an organization that provides support for immigrants caught in the immigration detention process. As its name indicates, ICDI is an intentionally interfaith organization. Founded by two determined Catholic Sisters of Mercy, the organization welcomes volunteers from all religious traditions—as well as those who claim no religious affiliation—to participate in the work of immigrant accompaniment and solidarity. The Jail Visitation program that I participated in was one of five outreach programs sponsored by the organization.[1]

Those of us who volunteered in the Jail Visitation program spent a little over two hours meeting with detained individuals, the vast majority of whom were men. We usually did so in three back-to-back sessions consisting of three to five individuals each. Many of the men who we met were young (eighteen to twenty-five years old) and had only recently been detained. All they had seen of the United States was a series of detention facilities, as they were often indiscriminately shuffled from one to the next. Some of the men were older (anywhere from twenty-five to sixty-five years of age) and had lived in the United States for years, if not decades. Many had spouses and children who are US citizens. More than anything, these longtime residents simply wanted to be reunited with their families. Most detainees were born in Latin America, but it was not uncommon to see others from Africa, Asia, and Europe. Accordingly, although the majority of our conversations were in Spanish, some volunteers also led discussions in English or French. In addition, one or two members of our volunteer group spent time in another part of the jail, meeting with a smaller group of detained women, mostly from Latin America.

Our role as ICDI volunteers was relatively straightforward: we were there to listen to these individuals and let them know that they were not forgotten. Sometimes, our conversations were filled with lighthearted small talk. On any given day, we might discuss their previous line of work (many men in detention formerly worked as cooks or construction workers), what they did for recreation in the detention facility (with limited options, many passed their time watching television), or what kinds of food they most looked forward to eating again once they were released (everyone disliked the jail's largely soy-based diet). Other times, our conversations would turn to weightier topics. Recently arrived detainees often expressed great worry about returning to their place of birth, given the threat of gang violence in their home countries. For example, "Edwin" from Honduras (this and subsequent names are pseudonyms, to protect privacy) explained how both his father and brother had been killed by a cartel in his small hometown and, if he returned, he would surely be next. Many longtime US residents expressed concern over no longer being able to support their families, and many appeared visibly shaken by the prospect of not seeing their family again in the United States. Such was the case with Bertín, who was born in Mexico but had been living in the Midwest for over twenty-five years with his wife and five children (ages fourteen, twelve, ten, six, and three), all US citizens.

Without exception, everyone with whom I spoke found the experience of being in detention fiercely disorienting. Referencing his encounters with detention officials and other officers from US Immigration and Customs Enforcement (ICE), Jacinto from El Salvador noted that "they treat us as if we were animals." This sentiment was expressed frequently among those in detention. With minimal exercise options, many were also often bored and, in some cases, depressed. As Luis from Mexico told me, "Sometimes after breakfast, I return to bed and try and go back to sleep." Making matters worse, many individuals had no clear sense of how long they would be in detention, especially if their case was being appealed. While most were typically detained for three to six months, it was not uncommon to encounter immigrants who had been detained for more than a year. Unlike traditional prisoners, immigrant detainees are not guaranteed a public defender under US law. As such, most individuals could not afford a lawyer and were left to navigate the labyrinthian court system almost entirely on their own.

As unpleasant and disorienting as these experiences were, many detained persons nevertheless approached their time in detention as an opportunity to engage in significant forms of reorientation. Many reflected deeply on their life, their priorities, and their relationship with God. While some looked to the past, others focused on their present circumstances and the underlying social forces that brought them to this point in their life. Many said that they had become disillusioned with the "American Dream" and tired of the myriad ways in which they were looked down upon because of their language, economic status, and/or the color of their skin. "If I do end up back in my home country," Israel from Mexico shared, "at least I know I will be treated like a human being."

I, along with my fellow volunteers, found it striking that despite the tremendous hardships that these men faced, they often expressed a profound gratitude for the very little they *did* have—be it as simple as their health, the safety of their family members, another day of life, or the gift of the present moment. These individuals often connected their gratitude to their faith in God, often adding to their comments phrases such as "si Dios quiere," "con el favor de Dios," or "gracias a Dios." It is worth noting that many of the individuals with whom I spoke had only loose ties to religion in its formal sense. While most considered themselves Catholic or Christian, a majority acknowledged attending church infrequently, even in the best of times. That said, it is fair to say that these men were deeply spiritual, given the reverence and gratitude they expressed for the small blessings in life. Many pointed out that their time in detention had afforded them opportunities to pray more, read the Bible, and grow more deeply in their faith. As Juan from Guatemala shared, "Before [detention], I didn't read the Bible. I didn't have time for God. Now, my situation has made me think; I have come to analyze things ["Me ha puesto pensar; llegué a analizar"]. And I have asked for forgiveness for the way I used bad words and didn't respect people." Toward the end of his comments, he added, "God is good. God does not fail us."

The more time I spent with detainees, the more I came to see how important faith was to their journey. This word "faith," however, can carry multiple meanings. Oftentimes, we use it to reference a particular religious tradition, such as "the Jewish faith," "the Christian faith," or "the Islamic faith." In such cases, the concept directs us to a particular institutional religion. Other times, the word suggests a more diffuse sense of "spirituality" that may—or may not—have a particular connection to institutional religion. It is very common these days, for example, to hear someone say, "I'm spiritual, but not religious." As this position suggests, although one may not belong to a formal faith tradition, one may still *orient* oneself in the world in a way that is deeply religious or, as many today prefer to say, "spiritual." Those who identify as "spiritual but not religious" might, for example, approach the world with reverence, awe, and

gratitude—traits that are commonly valued within institutional forms of religion—without actually participating in an organized religion. A similar dynamic
may be seen among Native American communities for whom faith has less to
do with adherence to specific religious traditions and more to do with cultivating a comprehensive outlook on life. Accordingly, it is rare to hear the phrase
"Native American religions" and more common to hear "Native American
spirituality."[2]

Examples like these help to illustrate that the meaning of faith is, indeed,
malleable, a fact that I saw firsthand through my time with detained immigrants. In many cases, detainees spoke of faith in connection to their ties—
however loose or tight—to institutional religion. Whether they identified as
Católico, Cristiano, creyente, or nonbeliever ("no soy religioso," some said),
they often described faith in terms of their proximity to (or distance from)
organized religion. At other times, however, detainees expressed faith through
their everyday *habits and actions*, as well as their general *attitude* toward life.
For many, faith was an ongoing process of making sense of and affirming one's
basic humanity. We can see this, for instance, when Juan described how his
experience in detention "made [him] think," prompting him "to analyze
things" more. As distressing as immigrant detention is, the experience of being
confined for months on end afforded detainees like Juan opportunities to
reflect deeply on their circumstances, take stock of the injustices they have
faced, and create new patterns of instilling hope in themselves and each other.
By creating these new habits of mind, detainees reoriented themselves in
fundamentally new ways. Such cases invite us to reimagine faith and spirituality in a new light.

We can certainly learn much from people who have been systematically
pushed to the margins of society. Through their example, they show us that
faith and spirituality, at their root, have less to do with self-enclosed doctrines
that human beings "import into" their lives; rather, they have much more to
do with the manner in which human beings *actively engage* experience
through reflective action, or praxis. As I and other ICDI volunteers saw firsthand, these individuals activated their faith *through* their praxis. This is not
to diminish the fact that many drew on traditional religious language, symbols, and doctrines as resources for their reflective action. Indeed, many
found solace and guidance in the grammar of institutional religion. That
said, the full meaning of faith is not exhausted by the parameters of institutional religion. A deeper exploration of faith requires us to also inquire into
how human beings *actively transact* with their world, both materially and
imaginatively.

## Liberating Spirituality: A Decolonial, Qualitative, and Functional Approach

This book explores this more robust sense of spirituality through the ground-breaking work of six exemplary twentieth-century liberation thinkers for whom spirituality, intelligence, and social activism are tightly connected. These figures are Peruvian Marxist philosopher José Carlos Mariátegui (1894–1930), Brazilian educator and philosopher Paulo Freire (1921–1997), Mexican-American constructive theologian Virgilio Elizondo (1935–2016), Chicana cultural and feminist theorist Gloria Anzaldúa (1942–2004), Cuban-American mujerista theologian Ada María Isasi-Díaz (1943–2012), and Brazilian ecofeminist theologian Ivone Gebara (1944–).

Some readers may immediately wonder: Why these six thinkers? After all, there is an abundance of liberationist voices in the Spanish- and Portuguese-speaking "Américas" that could merit our attention, beginning with key historical figures like Bartolomé de Las Casas, Antonio Montesinos, and Sor Juana Ines de la Cruz, all the way up to more contemporary figures like José Martí and Gustavo Gutiérrez.[3] Additionally, and staying within the ambit of the twentieth century, there are lesser known—yet equally important—voices like Rubem Alves, María Pilar Aquino, Dom Hélder Câmara, and Marcella Althaus-Reid, to name a few. In earlier drafts of this book, I considered including major sections or chapters on many of these historical and contemporary thinkers.

Ultimately, however, I decided on a handful of parameters to guide my study. First, I wanted a healthy balance of socially engaged thinkers from both North America and South America as well as an even split between men and women. Accordingly, featured here are three voices from North America and three from South America, and three men and three women. Second, although the book is very much written with liberation theology in mind, I wanted a representative mix of theologians and nontheologians, of theists and nontheists. As the reader will find, the six intellectuals featured in this book demonstrate varying commitments to institutional forms of religion. Some identify as practicing Catholics, while others have long left the church. A central premise of *Liberating Spiritualities*, however, is that regardless of their particular religious orientation, all recognize the socially transformative power of human spirituality. Along these lines, and given the book's historical focus, I decided to narrow the study to the twentieth century—not only because liberation theology stands as one of the twentieth century's most significant social movements, but also because the book reflects how liberationist approaches can address issues of intersectionality and religious pluralism, which are part and parcel of our

contemporary moment. Finally, I wanted to foreground six creative and courageous voices who have been somewhat understudied but are eminently worthy
of our attention.

As this book will make clear, three underlying traits connect these six thinkers: each is highly critical of colonial forms of Christianity; each understands
spirituality as an integral quality of human experience; and each champions
the potentially liberating function of spirituality as a powerful tool for social
transformation. Given that these are *Liberating Spiritualities'* anchoring themes,
a brief word about each is in order.

First, all of the figures in this book reject colonial Christianity. As is well
known, the Americas—both North and South—have been marked by colonial
violence. For the tens of millions of Indigenous peoples living on the continent
before the arrival of Columbus and the more than ten million African slaves
who were brought to the "New World," the discovery of America was hardly
a harbinger of a propitious future. Rather, the European desire for gold
and other natural resources unleashed cultural and physical structures of
oppression that resulted in genocide.[4] Five hundred years later, we continue
to grapple with what Peruvian sociologist Aníbal Quijano refers to as a noxious
"coloniality of power."[5] Although colonialism may no longer exist in the form
of distinct colonial administrations, its underlying logic persists on many
levels. Indeed, it is not difficult to see how European colonialism remains
stubbornly embedded in our continent's social fabric: one need only look at
how Indigenous communities and other communities of color continue to
experience disproportionate levels of poverty, unequal access to high-quality
educational opportunities, and ongoing systemic racism. The historical period
of colonialism may have passed, but its lingering logic, which is closely tied
to racialized hierarchies, continues to perpetuate needless forms of human
suffering.

The six intellectuals in this book understand that any significant account
of spirituality must wrestle with Christianity's imperial and colonial legacy.
Like all religious traditions, Christianity has a complex and, at times, paradoxical history that reveals internal tensions and disagreements. Even before
Christianity became the official religion of the Roman Empire in the fourth
century, early Christians varied greatly in terms of their teachings and practices, and they had a complicated relationship with imperial rule, at times
denouncing it, yet at other times embracing it.[6] Furthermore, one should keep
in mind that early Christianity was in many ways indistinguishable from Judaism in the first three centuries of the Common Era.[7] All of this goes to say
that Christianity has been—and continues to be—a fluid and contested tradition. Perhaps nowhere is this better seen than in the perennial battle between

Christianity's prophetic and apocalyptic influences, on the one hand, and its imperial, or "Constantinian" manifestations, on the other. Whereas prophetic and apocalyptic versions of Christianity draw on Hebraic ideals of social justice (as seen in the mandate to care for widows, orphans, and the poor) and the hope for a new future where "justice run[s] down like water, [a]nd righteousness like a mighty stream" (Amos 5:24), more imperial, or "Constantinian" versions emphasize theological orthodoxy and the consolidation and institutionalization of church power. Needless to say, these two versions of Christianity represent radically different visions of the tradition, oftentimes resulting in what can rightly be deemed as an "insidious schizophrenia."[8] In the Americas, this doubleness of mind can be seen in myriad forms, from sixteenth-century justifications of conquest ("we conquer for God *and* gold") to more recent—yet equally troubling—expressions of state-sanctioned Christianity, such as white Christian nationalism.

In response, all of the figures in this book critique the imperial, authoritarian, and colonial manifestations of Christianity, and some move well beyond a Christian framework. Such is the case with Mariátegui and Anzaldúa. Others raise the critique from within the tradition by reclaiming Jesus's prophetic message of love for all and his preferential option for the poor and oppressed. We see this in the work of Freire, Elizondo, Isasi-Díaz, and Gebara. Regardless of their particular take on institutional Christianity, all six thinkers know that any honest discussion of spirituality in the Americas must directly address the damage perpetrated by colonial Christianity. In doing so, they all approach spirituality from the perspective of "the least of these."

Second, the central figures featured in this book appreciate spirituality as an integral quality of human experience that reflects a core dimension of what it means to be human. Whereas a century ago, spirituality was thought to refer primarily to the interior life of the Christian, today the term has much wider applicability, reflecting a fundamental dimension of our lived experience at large. As noted scholar Sandra Schneiders observes, the term *spirituality* has "undergone an astounding expansion" in recent decades and is being "gradually adopted by Protestantism, Judaism, non-Christian religious, and even such secular movements as feminism and Marxism, to refer to something that, while difficult to define, is experienced as analogous in all of these movements."[9] In no small measure, the idea of spirituality has grown to include "the life of the person *as a whole*, including its bodily, psychological, social, and political dimensions."[10]

Many US Latine scholars of religion resonate with this expansive understanding of spirituality.[11] Anita De Luna, for example, writes that "[s]pirituality is about how a person relates to the totality of life." While spirituality may certainly surface in worship, it can also manifest itself "in the practical and concrete ways of how one lives the communal values that ground one's life and are transmitted through culture."[12] Similarly, Edwin Aponte describes spirituality as "that daily mix of practices, beliefs, and rituals small and large in diverse contexts, that point to an abiding and overarching sense of compelling impulse and desire."[13] By framing spirituality in light of the "the totality of life" and as an "abiding and overarching sense" of impulse and desire, De Luna and Aponte, echoing Schneiders, make clear that spirituality has to do with "the life of the person as a whole." As such, it is a pervasive *quality* of human experience rather than a self-contained *type* of experience that exists unto itself.[14] Whether they invoke the term *spirituality* or *faith*, all six thinkers in this book approach spirituality as a pervasive quality of human experience.

One further way to appreciate what I mean here by spirituality as a "quality" of experience is to consider the difference between dogmatic and anthropological approaches to spirituality. As Schneiders explains, whereas a dogmatic approach understands spirituality "only by way of extension or comparison" to the Christian tradition, an anthropological approach holds that "the structure and dynamics of the human person as such are the locus of the emergence of the spiritual life."[15] Accordingly, within an anthropological frame, spirituality is not confined to a single religious tradition like Christianity; instead, it is "an activity of human life as such." As Schneiders suggests, if this fundamental form of activity is open to engagement with the Absolute, then its character may be described as "religious." Likewise, if this activity makes special appeals to the person of Jesus Christ, then we can identify its character as "Christian." The important point is that in an anthropological approach, spirituality may assume many forms and is not limited to traditional religious or Christian imaginaries or doctrine. Rather, "[i]n principle, it is equally available to every human begin who is seeking to live an authentically human life."[16] Spirituality can emerge, for example, through the arts, nature, physical activity, meditation, intimacy, friendship, and other expressions of everyday experience.

Roger Haight approaches spirituality in a similar anthropological light, emphasizing it as a pervasive and fundamental quality of human experience. Although Haight is best known for his work in theology, he readily acknowledges that, methodologically speaking, spirituality always precedes religion and theology. As Haight explains, "religion, church, and church structure have their source and ground *in* spirituality."[17] Like Schneiders, De Luna, and Aponte, Haight appeals to spirituality as a basic anthropological reality—or quality—that all humans can possess, regardless of creed. Accordingly, he affirms the viability of both religious *and* secular forms of spirituality. In a most helpful way, Haight defines spirituality as "the logic, or character, or consistent quality of a person's or a group's pattern of living insofar as it is measured before some ultimate reality." Whether one is religious in a traditional sense or spiritual in a more secular sense, Haight underscores how an appreciation for the transcendent (or "ultimate") aspects of human experience can emerge organically within human experience, at large.[18] As he persuasively argues, the term *spirituality* can function as a useful bridge concept between religious and nonreligious imaginaries, and it is largely for this reason that *Liberating Spiritualities* will lean a bit more on the term *spirituality* than on other related terms like *faith* or *religion*.

Third, spirituality as a quality of human experience is closely tied to its active function. As we have just seen, contemporary scholars like Schneiders, Haight, De Luna, and Aponte affirm spirituality as a pervasive quality of human experience. But if we look closely at their work, we see that spirituality also functions as a form of human action itself. It is a form of "lived experience" (Schneiders), a "pattern of living" (Haight), and a "daily mix of practices, beliefs, and rituals" (Aponte).[19] Or, as De Luna puts it, spirituality is "*how* one lives the communal values that ground one's life."[20] All of these cases point in the direction of spirituality's active function.

Ronald Rolheiser, another prominent scholar of spirituality, captures well the active and functional character of spirituality. Rolheiser likens spirituality to a kind of unceasing desire—which he describes as an internal "fire"—that marks human experience at large. He writes:

> Long before we do anything explicitly religious at all, we have to do something about the fire that burns within us. What we do with the fire, how we channel it, is our spirituality. Thus, we all have a spirituality, whether we want one or not, whether we are religious or not. . . . Irrespective of whether or not we let ourselves be consciously shaped by an explicit religious idea, we act in ways that leave us healthy or unhealthy, loving or bitter. What shapes our actions is our spirituality.[21]

For the purposes of this book, I find Rolheiser's formulation especially helpful because he shows that spirituality is not only a dimension, or quality, of human experience but is also itself a form of *human action,* or *praxis.* Accordingly, spirituality is much more than a simple account, or mere "reflection," of what we undergo in experience. Rather, as with any meaningful experience, we also actively *refract* spirituality.[22] As Rolheiser makes clear, spirituality is "what we do" with our internal fire, and *how,* exactly, we channel it is what gives spirituality its meaning. Such considerations help us to see the ways in which spirituality is an active and ongoing function of our experience. Seen in this light, spirituality *is* what spirituality *does*, or better yet, spirituality is what we, as the initiators and drivers of spirituality, *actively make* of it.

Some readers may find it helpful to know that I am drawing here on insights gleaned from both philosophical pragmatism and liberation theology.[23] As pragmatism makes clear, to fully understand the meaning of something, we must inquire into its function and its conceivable practical effects.[24] This emphasis on what an idea *does* is echoed in liberation theology's claim that faith ultimately has less to do with orthodoxy (which etymologically means "right-belief") and more to do with orthopraxy (or "right-action"). For both liberation theologians and pragmatists, therefore, a truly faithful person *is* what a truly faithful person *does*. Within Christianity, this sentiment is captured well when Jesus tells his followers: "A good tree cannot bear bad fruit, nor can a bad tree bear good fruit. . . . Thus you will know them by their fruits" (Matthew 7:18–20). A similar pragmatic sentiment is captured in the English-language phrase "the proof is in the pudding," which is a shortened version of the earlier idiom, "the proof of the pudding is in the eating." In both of these examples, the meaning and value of something is best known through its actions and effects: a tree *producing* fruit, a person *eating* a particular dish. So, too, with spirituality. To grasp fully what spirituality *is*, we must therefore attend to the ways in which it functions in experience.

This last phrase, "in experience," is another major touchstone within pragmatism and liberation theology. Both traditions take actual experience—and, more specifically, *problematic situations* that arise in actual experience—as their methodological starting point. The task for both is how best to reconstruct and resolve problematic situations. Naturally, these two traditions express the transition from problem to resolution in different ways, but in both there is a sense of experience being "fulfilled." We see this, among other places, in John Dewey's sense of "consummatory experience" and liberation theology's invocation of "the fullness of life."

For all six figures that we will explore here, spirituality is a matter of actively engaging experience. It is not a *sui generis*, or self-standing, "thing"; nor is it something that we simply inherit; nor is it something that we should blindly accept. Rather, spirituality is an encounter that we qualitatively *undergo* and actively *do*. Seen in this light, spirituality is very much like intelligence, broadly understood: both draw on the many capacities available to us—including our bodies, imagination, senses, and language—to help us make sense of the world so that we can understand and engage it better. This forward-looking and action-oriented approach, which begins and ends in experience, is a hallmark of both pragmatism and liberation theology.

Thinking of spirituality in this way may feel unfamiliar to some readers, and this is understandable given our modern/colonial philosophical and theological inheritance. For centuries, we have been taught to see the world in terms of binaries, such as subject/object, mind/body, life/death, sacred/profane, male/female, human/nature, straight/gay. With respect to the subject/object and human/nature dualisms in particular, we tend to think that human experience is comprised of things "in" experience. As a result, we often understand ourselves as knowing subjects that are inherently different from the objects around us.

But what if we approached human experience not so much in terms of static and discreet things and more in terms of our ongoing encounters and interactions with a world that is itself always in motion? In other words, what if we approached the things of the world as themselves constantly changing, interacting, and evolving? The difference between these two approaches is akin to the distinction between a photograph and a video. When we see a photograph, our tendency may be to focus, at least initially, on the distinct things that are captured, frozen-like, in that moment. Consequently, when we see a photo, our first question might likely be: *Who* or *what* are we seeing? In contrast, when we watch a video, movie, or any other "moving picture," we are likely more inclined to ask: What is *happening*? or What are the figures on the screen *doing*? Whereas photos may prompt us to see things primarily *as* things, videos invite us to dwell on the *active* dimensions of figures and objects as they move through time and space.[25]

Given our largely dualistic philosophical and theological inheritance, we have been conditioned to see spirituality as if it were a picture or a static thing among the many other things in our experience. The six thinkers featured in this book, however, invite us to consider an alternative path. Each uniquely approaches spirituality as if it were more like a video, that is, as an ever-shifting form of human action that must constantly adjust to a world that is itself perpetually changing. Furthermore, like videos—especially ones that have circular narratives or disparate sequences that are dynamically stitched together to form new meaning—spirituality does not always make logical, narrative sense, yet it is no less meaningful.[26]

Crucially, all of the thinkers presented in this book take this insight one step further by homing in on its ethical implications. Each understands that if spirituality is intimately tied up with human action, then it is, in fact, our responsibility to guide and shape spirituality in ways that address needless forms of human suffering and lead to human growth and fulfillment. For all of the figures in this study, then, it is not enough simply to observe human spirituality at work or in motion. Rather, the thinkers featured herein remind us that we human beings have an active role to play in shaping our world. For this reason, all of them believe that spirituality should be married to critical forms of intelligence. Whether this is interpreted in terms of Freire's idea of "conscientization" or Anzaldúa's concept of "conocimiento," these six thinkers believe that a critical consciousness, rooted in a commitment to justice, is a sign of a mature spirituality. Accordingly, the burning question for all of them is not so much "What does it mean to be 'spiritual but not religious'?" (a question that would be well suited for Mariátegui and Anzaldúa) or even "How is it possible to be 'spiritual *and* religious'?" (which could pertain nicely to Elizondo, Isasi-Díaz, and Gebara). Rather, the central and animating question for all is: "What is required of us, both practically and imaginatively, to be *spiritual activists*?"[27] As *Liberating Spiritualities* will show, when we foreground this question—which takes human action, purpose, and intelligence seriously—we may gain significant insights into the meaning and function of human spirituality.

## Spirituality, Meaning-Making, and Human Intelligence

As I have already suggested, critical intelligence is a central concern for each of the six thinkers in this book. Indeed, each would support the claim that human intelligence, broadly understood, is a—if not *the*—primary means by which human beings transact with the world and through which spirituality is, in fact, "activated." Given how fundamental this claim is to this study, the reader may find it helpful to know what I mean by the phrase "intelligence, broadly understood."

Oftentimes, we envision intelligence as a high-order capacity of the mind that helps us to acquire some form of knowledge. We might think of an intelligent person, for example, as someone with a vast or deep expertise in a particular area. In this book, I approach intelligence in a more expansive and functionalist light: at its core, intelligence is the manner in which we transact with our environment in order to address particular problems. When seen this way, knowledge is less like a fixed state in which we definitively "possess" certain bits of information and more like an *emerging process* that is forged through our encounter with—and ongoing adaptation to—the ever-changing situations around us. As philosopher David Hildebrand puts it, within a functionalist and pragmatic model of inquiry, knowing is an "adaptive activity" that involves a dynamic process of doubt, belief, inquiry, and judgment.[28] This approach to knowledge and intelligence is reflected in the work of both Paulo Freire and John Dewey, two thinkers who substantially inform this book.

Seen in a more functionalist and pragmatic light, intelligence is part and parcel of *all* forms of human problem-solving and meaning-making, from high-order forms of reasoning, as seen in science, to more intuitive and creative forms of human imagining, as seen in the arts. For liberation theologian Ignacio Ellacuría and his philosophical mentor, Xavier Zubiri, *both* science *and* art involve an engagement with our "sentient intelligence." For them, sentient intelligence—which seeks to overcome modernity's pernicious body/mind dualism—involves three modes or phases of intelligence: 1) a primordial *apprehension of reality* (as when a baby *senses* light, warmth, or hunger without yet having the language, categories, or capacity to name them as such); 2) a process of *explanation or reasoning* that distinguishes how things experienced in reality are different from each other (as when a toddler begins to use language to differentiate a red ball from, say, a red apple); and 3) a wider form of *understanding* that helps to explain why things are what they are (as when the maturing toddler repeatedly asks "Why?").

One should note that these "phases" of intelligence need not be understood solely in developmentalist terms, that is, as phases of human maturation. Rather, these modes of intelligence may reflect how we "think" at any given moment. Consider, for example, that within the course of our daily lives, we encounter situations that we intuitively sense as blurry, inchoate, or problematic, such as when we encounter an unfamiliar sound, a moment of unease, or a perplexing passage of poetry. But even before we identify and name a situation as "unfamiliar" or "uneasy" or "perplexing," we first have a primordial *sense* of the experience. In other words, we "apprehend" the reality in a visceral, immediate, and emotional way, prior to our logically making sense of it.[29]

Of course, just as soon as we undergo these types of immediate experiences, higher-order processes of reasoning and understanding kick in almost instantaneously, thanks to the incredible power of human intelligence, an evolutionary adaptive activity that has been in the making for billions of years. Through our active use of reason, we know how to sort out the problem's component parts, and we are compelled to inquire more deeply: "*Why* am I experiencing perplexity or unease?" Through experimental processes of questioning and testing, we address and attempt to overcome our initial troubled sense.[30]

Such a broad conception of human intelligence allows for rich understandings of spirituality and religious faith. At first glance, Zubiri's three modes of intelligence may seem to privilege reason and understanding—which are often associated with science—over our more primordial apprehension of reality. But as one interpreter of Zubiri notes, "[L]ong before science as we know it existed, people sought explanations of things. And they found them in myths, legends, plays, poetry, art, and music—which are indeed examples of reason in the most general sense: they all seek to tell us something about reality."[31] Seen in this light, faith and spirituality—just as much as science—are logical extensions of our human drive to make meaning in our lives.

Moreover, we can add a most interesting insight when discussing Zubiri's three modes of human understanding: contrary to what many might believe, primordial apprehension (the first phase of intelligence)—and not reason (the third phase)—is arguably the most important. Why? For Zubiri, primordial apprehension is "the product of our somatic structures, and it puts us into direct contact with reality." As such, primordial apprehension "comprises the foundation for all other knowledge."[32] In other words, without primordial apprehension, there would be no higher-order levels of "knowledge." Primordial apprehension is the foundation that gives rise to all significant forms of human meaning-making.

As a student of Zubiri, Ellacuría took this insight to heart, which accounts for his theologically rich "open materialism" and his constant return to "historical reality" as the proper starting point for doing theology.[33] It also accounts for the ethical significance that Ellacuría ascribes to intelligence at large. As Ellacuría makes clear, intelligence exists to promote life. He writes, "The first human utilized intelligence to keep on living, and this essential reference to life . . . is the primary 'what for' of intelligence and, correctly understood, also the primary purpose of all intelligent apprehension. . . ." Indeed, so important is intelligence for Ellacuría's theological method that he connects intelligence to the New Testament's life-giving message of God's promise of new life in the here and now. As he suggests, intelligence is a powerful means by which people "might have life and have it more abundantly." Ellacuría is referencing here John 10:10, a biblical passage that is often cited by liberation theologians. In tying his discussion of intelligence to this "secularized version of the formula so essential to the Christian faith," Ellacuría helps us to appreciate the fact that spirituality and faith are themselves potent forms of intelligence, broadly conceived. I resonate with such an approach, and I offer this book as my own attempt to shed light on the ways in which liberating spiritualities function as critical epistemologies.

## Plan of the Book

Readers may use this book in a number of ways. For those with a more theological bent, the chapters on Elizondo, Isasi-Díaz, and Gebara may be of particular interest. Conversely, for those drawn to liberation philosophy and decolonial thought, the chapters on Mariátegui and Anzaldúa may be good starting points. In both cases, the chapter on Freire can serve as a helpful bridge between theological and nontheological authors.

For readers interested in feminist and/or intersectional perspectives, I especially recommend the chapters on Anzaldúa, Isasi-Díaz, and Gebara. These chapters plumb the pragmatic dimensions of these exemplary scholar-activists, and readers may also find useful the chapter on Freire, especially the last section where he discusses his own process of conscientization regarding gender.

Ideally, of course, *Liberating Spiritualities* is best read as a whole so as to illuminate the myriad ways in which liberationist and pragmatic impulses have fueled the work of all six authors. Reading its entirety will help readers see how these diverse thinkers share an approach to spirituality that is much more contextual, pluralistic, and socially engaged than more traditional and orthodox approaches. Although some biographical details are provided for each author, this work is not primarily focused on individual biographies. Rather, it is a study of their significant intellectual contributions, with a nod to the how their particular social location informs their thinking.[34]

To help the reader see this, I now offer a brief snapshot of each of the book's six core chapters, which move in chronological order by the authors' dates of birth. Chapter 1 explores the revolutionary thought of José Carlos Mariátegui and lays the groundwork for imagining what a "new sense" of religion might look like. I unpack what this phrase meant for Mariátegui, how it influenced later traditions like liberation theology and decolonial thought, and how Mariátegui drew on pragmatic sources, both implicitly and explicitly. Chapter 2 explores Paulo Freire's idea of conscientization, a central motif for the book as a whole. Although the concept is pivotal to liberation theology, Freire, an educator, writes surprisingly little about the connections between conscientization and spirituality. This chapter makes these connections explicit. Chapter 3 transitions to the thought of Mexican-American theologian Virgilio Elizondo, who is often read as a theologian of culture and/or a liberation theologian. While both of these frameworks encapsulate key aspects of his work, I argue that a fuller understanding of Elizondo must take into account his fascination with the evolutionary cosmology of scientist, theologian, and philosopher Teilhard de Chardin. In reading Elizondo in a Teilhardian light, we gain valuable insight into Elizondo's own cosmic vision and his deep appreciation for religious pluralism.

Chapters 4–6 turn to the inspiring and trailblazing work of three female intellectuals. Chapter 4 looks at the mature work of Chicana theorist Gloria

Anzaldúa and her articulation of "spiritual activism." As Anzaldúa makes clear, spiritual activism is a form of conocimiento, a category that is akin to Freire's understanding of conscientization insofar that it can help to redress pressing social problems like racism, sexism, and heteronormativity. I argue that this concept, and Anzaldúa's posthumous work at large, makes significant gestures in the direction of a functionalist and pragmatic idea of spirituality. Chapter 5 turns to the work of Cuban-American mujerista theologian Ada María Isasi-Díaz. I examine Isasi-Díaz's productive, yet underdeveloped, idea of a "conscientized cotidiano," and I show how the pragmatic epistemologies of John Dewey and Agnes Heller, who foreground the role of habit and doubt in the process of knowing, can help to make explicit the ways in which a conscientized cotidiano actually operates in experience. Conversely, I explain how Isasi-Díaz's intersectional understanding of a conscientized cotidiano, which includes an approach to faith that is both critical *and* sympathetic, has much to offer Dewey's and Heller's more allergic approaches to religion. Finally, Chapter 6 delves into the groundbreaking work of Brazilian ecofeminist theologian Ivone Gebara, who has articulated one of the most creative responses to the implicit epistemological traps of Latin American liberation theology, a tradition that she both upholds and celebrates on the one hand, yet simultaneously questions and reconstructs on the other. This chapter looks at her concept of "relatedness," which is arguably at the very core of her thought. Gebara presents this term at face value, with almost no indication of its intellectual inheritance. I inquire into the likely sources of this idea and the ways in which it could be developed further through sympathetic discourses such as process thought and pragmatism.

In closing, I return to the example with which this Introduction began. Within the context of immigrant detention, faith emerged in a variety of ways. On the one hand, there were explicit institutional markers of faith: our work, after all, was spearheaded by an intentionally interfaith organization; at the end of each session, we offered inmates prayer cards, daily prayer booklets, and other print resources from various religious traditions; and many individuals in detention understood their own faith stance in terms of either their proximity to or distance from organized religion. On the other hand, we also witnessed a number of implicit and active expressions of faith. Most notably, many inmates embarked on a reflective process of making sense of, and affirming, their basic humanity. They reflected critically on their circumstances, creating new habits of mind that instilled hope in themselves and each other. In doing so, they transformed their profoundly disorienting situation by reorienting themselves in fundamentally new ways.

Such active processes of reorientation are shining examples of spirituality in action. Moreover, they are also deep forms of pedagogy, as the work of John Dewey and Paulo Freire helps to elucidate. As Dewey understands it, education is "that reconstruction or reorganization of experience which adds to the meaning of experience, and which increases ability to direct the course of subsequent experience."[35] Education, therefore, is not restricted to the classroom, nor is it simply an act of transmitting knowledge from the teacher to the learner. In fact, Dewey consistently argues against such a limited and routine view of education. As we will see in Chapter 2, Freire agrees with this position. Education, as it is traditionally conceived, reflects what Freire calls a "banking model of education" wherein experts "deposit" bits of knowledge into the passive minds of learners. Instead, Dewey and Freire argue for a much more robust and dialogical "problem-posing method" of educational encounter in which teachers and learners work together and learn from each other.[36] Through a process of mutual exchange and testing, not only is new knowledge created, but also experience itself is qualitatively expanded and transformed.[37]

I raise this point to suggest that such a robust, experience-centered conception of education can be a useful point of reference when approaching spirituality. If we take the core insights of our earlier discussion of spirituality and layer them atop Dewey's and Freire's understanding of education, then we arrive at an understanding of spirituality that can inform this study: *spirituality emerges when we reconstruct and reorganize experience in ways that form a consistent pattern of habit and action that is measured by some ultimate concern.* Furthermore, we are now in a position to say that a *liberating* spirituality is one in which this consistent and habitual pattern of living incorporates a *critical consciousness* and measures ultimate concern in terms of *redressing oppressive situations* and *promoting human flourishing.* Such an orientation gives experience not only new meaning, but also an intentional sense of direction, which may precipitate further experiences of freedom.

Through my work with detained immigrants, I witnessed on many occasions the seeds of a liberating spirituality germinating among the men I visited, particularly when they would accompany, encounter, and—in Dewey's and Freire's understanding of the term—"educate" *each other.* At no point did I see this more clearly than during a visit with inmates one wintry morning. Because of a heavy snowstorm, only two other volunteers and I successfully made it to the jail. We were confronted with a daunting task. Close to thirty men were expected in our first session. We knew instantly that we needed to change our usual format. Rather than meet with three to five individuals, as was our usual practice, we had no other choice but to break them up into their own small groups and have them discuss three questions among themselves: 1) How are you doing in this moment?, 2) What are you thankful for today?, and 3) What do you most look forward to when you are no longer in detention? As I wandered around the room, observed body language, and listened in on conversations, I was struck by the men's level of engagement. They listened attentively to one another, supporting others as they spoke. We then invited individuals from the small groups to share relevant insights with the larger group. Their responses were honest and real, and they affirmed each other's experiences. The men were clearly ministering to each other, and a palpable sense of goodwill permeated the room.

Bringing the session to a close, a fellow volunteer (a beloved Dominican sister who visited the men weekly) thanked them for sharing and underscored what a privilege it was for us, as volunteers, to hear their stories and learn from them. Normally, we would then pass around a handout featuring various interfaith prayers and recite one together. This time, however, we asked if any of them would be interested in leading the group in prayer. A young man in his mid-twenties rose to his feet and volunteered. (As it turns out, there is commonly at least one detained person—usually a self-identified "Cristiano," as opposed to "Católico"—who, independent of our ICDI gatherings, serves as an informal Bible study leader for detainees who are interested. This man was clearly someone who served in that role.) He invited the men to join hands, and with all the eloquence and grace of a seasoned preacher, he delivered one of the most heartfelt and moving prayers that I have ever heard. He spoke openly of the pain and difficulties that these men were undergoing, but he also framed these challenges within a larger matrix of gratitude, perseverance, and hope—and he did so in a way that was welcoming to all, Christians and non-Christians alike. With their eyes closed, the men listened attentively, and at least one became visibly emotional. In that moment, this young man's words and vision gave added meaning and depth to the group's shared experience, providing a framework of hope that the men could draw on when faced with the challenges that were most certainly to come. This prayer leader was not only a "compañero" who felt these men's pain firsthand; he was also a guide and a teacher who brought new life to those who acutely needed it. In this moment, spirituality emerged not only through the explicit means of religious language and imaginaries, but at an even more fundamental and implicit level, through the ways in which this compañero-teacher so artfully helped these men imaginatively reconstruct their current, dehumanizing experience and set it against a wider vision of the fullness of life.

The six thinkers featured in this book help us to appreciate the theoretical and practical heft of transformative and life-giving experiences like these.

Methodologically, they all approach spirituality from the starting point of actual experiences of suffering. For some who take a more traditional theological or philosophical approach, such a turn to experience might seem at odds with a sense of transcendence. Detractors might hold, for example, that spirituality points in the direction of that which exceeds experience. The figures in this book, both theists and nontheists alike, however, demonstrate otherwise. They invite us to consider how a sense of awe, reverence, and grace may organically emerge *in* and *through* experience.[38] Furthermore, they awaken us to the reality that such experiences of transcendence are not there for us simply to "have" or to "undergo." Rather, it is part of our ethical duty as humans to *engage, reconstruct, expand*, and *share* these experiences of transcendence with others. By focusing especially on the qualitative and functional dimensions of spirituality, this study makes such insights explicit.

Today, we live in a world rife with profound structural problems: economic inequality, racial hostility, gender discrimination, and ecological indifference are some of today's harsh realities. Such crises continue to be exacerbated by a pernicious modern/colonial mythos, to which many traditional forms of spirituality unfortunately adhere. Now more than ever, we need to rethink spirituality and reapproach it as one of humankind's most powerful tools. However, in order to avoid, or at least minimize, past traps, we must engage spirituality capaciously, in ways that are pluralistic, robustly empirical, and justice-centered. The exemplary spiritual visions featured in this book can aid us significantly in this task. They help us to see that new forms of meaning-making, healing, and freedom are still possible.

# 1

# A "New Sense" of Religion: José Carlos Mariátegui's Pragmatic Sensibility

Philosophy has long been an important conversation partner for theology. Daniel Pilario, a Filipino theologian and expert on the thought of philosopher Pierre Bourdieu, reflects on a long-standing interplay between the two disciplines: if theology is "classically defined as *fides quaerens intellectus*, i.e., faith seeking understanding," he writes, "then one must recognize that *intellectus* has been mediated by different sciences, mostly by philosophy, in the various moments of its history."[1] After all, there can be no St. Paul without Greek thought, no Augustine without Neoplatonism, no Thomas Aquinas without Aristotle, no Karl Rahner without Immanuel Kant and Martin Heidegger, and no Paul Tillich without existentialism. So, too, is the case with Gustavo Gutiérrez, the father of liberation theology, whose work is often (and all too easily) associated with the philosophy of Karl Marx.

Each of these pairings between philosophers and theologians, however, requires nuance, as there is never a simple one-to-one equivalence. Although prior philosophies no doubt "mediate" and "inform" new developments in theology, the genius of a St. Paul, Aquinas, Rahner, Tillich, or Gutiérrez ultimately has more to do with the ways in which these theologians creatively *transform and reconstruct* the significant philosophical currents of their day, intermixing them with other schools of thought.

Enrique Dussel underscores how Latin American liberationist approaches in the 1960s and 1970s drew on a rich diversity of intellectual traditions. Philosophers of the era engaged Levinas and Marx (Dussel), Indigenous hermeneutics (Rodolfo Kusch), popular wisdom (J. C. Scannone, Carlos Cullén), ideological deconstruction (Hugo Assmann), the critique of utopian reason

(Hinkelammert), intercultural exchange (Raul Fornet-Betancourt), a philosophy of erotic liberation and feminism (Vaz Ferreira and Graciela Hierro), and a pedagogy of liberation (Paulo Freire).[2]

Furthermore, Dussel notes that these liberation thinkers often utilized three interlocking methodological approaches: They emphasized a method of *empiricism* ("in the way that pragmatists did from the perspective of the process of *verification*," writes Dussel); they highlighted the need for *liberation* and not simply freedom (or revolution); and they sought to utilize a process of *conscientization* to help give rise to concrete historical projects.[3] Significantly, these three methodological foundations—which are all central themes of this book—are as relevant to liberation philosophy as they are to liberation theology. Historically, however, most interpreters have tended to give much more attention to the last two concepts—"liberation" and "conscientization"—than to the first theme—a pragmatic "method of empiricism."

Fortunately, a growing number of scholars have begun to reckon in earnest with the empirical and pragmatic dimensions of Latin American liberationist thought. Dussel's own work serves as a prime example, given his use of the foundational insights of Charles Sanders Peirce, the father of US pragmatism, in the development of his own liberation philosophy.[4] Other more recent philosophically-minded scholars who recognize and explore pragmatic imprints within various strains of liberationist thought include Eduardo Mendieta, José-Antonio Orosco, Gregory Fernando Pappas, Alexander Stehn, Lilian Calles Barger, Michael Raposa, Terrance MacMullan, and myself, among many others.[5]

Adding to this rich and growing body of work, this chapter looks at a pivotal, yet often overlooked, resource for both liberation theology and liberation philosophy alike: the contributions of Peruvian intellectual and social critic José Carlos Mariátegui (1894–1930). In what follows, I explore Mariátegui's own heterodox approach to religious faith. As I show, Mariátegui's conception of religious faith—which has some noticeable links to pragmatism—stands as a useful point of reference for ongoing conversations between liberation theology and liberation philosophy. Furthermore, whereas many critics often highlight the European influences on Gustavo Gutiérrez (in particular, the "two Karls": Karl Marx and Karl Rahner), I show that the Peruvian-born Mariátegui played perhaps the most significant role in shaping Gutiérrez's nondogmatic approach to Marx. Toward this end, the first section of this chapter offers a brief overview of Mariátegui's career, the second section highlights some of the central pragmatic features of Mariátegui's conception of religious faith, and the final section establishes key resonances between Mariátegui and Gutiérrez.

## José Carlos Mariátegui

José Carlos Mariátegui, who was born in 1894 in the southern part of Peru to a poor mestizo family, has been hailed as "undoubtedly, the most vigorous and most original [Marxist] thinker from Latin America."[6] Abandoned by his criollo father (of Spanish descent) and raised by his Quechua Indian mother, he was forced to leave primary school after a few grades and support the family through work. When he was eight, Mariátegui suffered a leg injury, crippling him for life. (His leg was eventually amputated in 1924.) Despite persistent problems with his leg and tuberculosis, the young Mariátegui apprenticed at a major newspaper business in Lima. He quickly worked his way up the ladder, becoming a respected journalist and editor. He did most of his writing for newspapers and political journals, including the cultural and political journal *Amauta* (1926–1930), for which he served as founding editor. As a reporter in Lima, Mariátegui became increasingly critical of Peru's social structures. These views eventually led to an exile in Europe from 1920 to 1923. While there, he befriended Italian idealist philosopher Benedetto Croce, who encouraged him to read the work of the French socialist Georges Sorel. Mariátegui also became enamored with the thoughts of the Marxist philosopher Antonio Gramsci, and he returned to Peru as a Marxist, remaining active in socialist politics until his early death at the age of thirty-five in 1930.

Before he turned to Marxism, Mariátegui grew up in a fervently Catholic household, owing largely to the influence of his mother. Mariátegui was greatly influenced by the examples of two sixteenth-century Spanish mystics, Saint Teresa of Ávila and Saint John of the Cross, founders of the Order of Discalced Carmelites.[7] In his late teens, he made a retreat with the Carmelites, which had a significant impact on him. Although his search for direct knowledge of God proved inconclusive, according to one interpreter, he nevertheless "became conscious of the need for what he called 'faith,' a belief in people's potential to create a new, more just social order. He understood the message of Jesus as both a call to interior conversion and social action incumbent on all, but particularly the poor."[8]

As Mariátegui became more politically involved in his twenties, he left the institutional church which, he believed, had betrayed its basic gospel value of serving "the least of these" in exchange for its own worldly power. Such a sentiment is conveyed, among other places, in Mariátegui's chapter on "The Problem of the Indian" in his most important work, *Siete ensayos de interpretación de la realidad peruana* (*Seven Interpretive Essays on Peruvian Reality*), published in 1928. Staying faithful to his Marxist roots, Mariátegui argues that the "problem of the Indian" is, at root, a material and economic one: Indigenous Peruvians do not have control of their own land. Instead, much like sharecroppers during the period of US Reconstruction, native Peruvians work the land for elite landowners, mainly of European descent, through a feudalistic land tenure system known as *gamonalismo*.[9] Any attempt that fails to address this core issue of land ownership will remain "superficial and secondary," Mariátegui writes, "as long as the feudalism of the *gamonales* continues to exist."[10]

Mariátegui critiques a number of these "superficial and secondary" approaches, including bureaucratic and administrative solutions, proposals for ethnic assimilation, moral and religious arguments that attempt to defend the rights of the Indians, and liberal forms of education that continue to operate within a feudalistic framework. All of these, Mariátegui argues, evade the central issue, which is the economic question of Peru's land tenure system.

At first glance, Mariátegui's assessment of religion appears especially harsh. He writes:

> But today a religious solution is unquestionably the most outdated and antihistoric of all [approaches]. Its representatives—unlike their distant, how very distant teachers—are not concerned with obtaining a new declaration of the rights of Indians, with adequate authority and ordinances. The missionary is merely assigned the role of mediator between the Indian and the *gamonal.* If the church could not accomplish this task in the medieval era, when its spiritual and intellectual capacity could be measured by friars like Las Casas, how can it succeed with the elements it commands today?[11]

In Mariátegui's estimation, representatives of the church serve as middlemen between the Indian and the gamonales, without calling into question the inherently unjust system of gamonalismo in the first place. As such, the church serves a largely bureaucratic function that keeps intact existing systems of power, including its own.

But a closer reading of this chapter also reveals some surprisingly salutary, perhaps even redeeming, aspects of the church. We see this in Mariátegui's passing phrase about modern-day representatives of the church who, "unlike their distant, how very distant teachers," are no longer "concerned with obtaining a new declaration of the rights of Indians."[12] Here, Mariátegui seems to be speaking somewhat longingly of a church that, at least at one point in time, vigorously defended the rights of the Indians, as seen in the case of Las Casas. In fact, Mariátegui believes that in comparison to the humanitarian teachings of liberal humanism (such as reflected in the important anti-imperialist efforts of Albert Einstein and Romain Rolland), the church took an even "more energetic or at least a more authoritative stand centuries ago."[13] Whereas liberal humanism "tried to make itself heard by a weak and formalist criollo liberalism," religious tenets appealed to "a noble and active Spanish Catholicism."[14] Again, one is left with the impression that Mariátegui longs for a form of Catholicism that is "noble and active," "energetic," and morally "authoritative" when it comes to the rights of the Indians. To be sure, Mariátegui's rhetorical question at the end reveals that he sees little hope for the church in the future. After all, if a friar like Las Casas, with all of his "spiritual and intellectual capacity," could not help to change the plight of the Indians, how can we expect the largely accommodationist church of today to do so? That said, the caveats that Mariátegui makes about religion provide new pathways for more nuanced and contemporary theological interpretations of his thought. As I will show momentarily, this can especially be seen in the groundbreaking work of Gustavo Gutiérrez.

All told, despite his harsh (but largely accurate) critiques of the institutional church of his day, Mariátegui never became fully anti-religious. Rather, he interjected his heterodox understanding of faith and myth into his version of Indigenous socialism. But what did Mariátegui's unorthodox approach to faith entail? Is it possible to discern a theory of religion in Mariátegui's philosophy? It is to these questions that we now turn.

## Mariátegui's "New Sense" of Religion

Perhaps the closest Mariátegui ever comes to addressing his distinctive approach to religious faith is in a chapter entitled "Literature on Trial" from his *Seven Interpretive Essays on Peruvian Reality*. In this essay, Mariátegui makes clear his intellectual debt to the Peruvian intellectual Manuel González Prada (1844–1918), who voiced deep concern for the condition of the Indigenous peoples of Peru and who criticized Peru's ruling elite for their inattention to the plight of the Indigenous poor. As part of this critique, González Prada attacked the Church as a political and social institution. According to him, this potentially powerful force for good had violated its own tenets and become a corrupting force in Peruvian society.[15]

Mariátegui shared González Prada's critique of the institutional church, but he did not go as far as González Prada to denounce religiosity altogether. In an illuminating passage from "Literature on Trial," Mariátegui writes:

> González Prada was wrong . . . to preach antireligiosity. Nowadays we
> know more about religion. . . . We know that a revolution is always

religious. The word "religion" has a new value, a new sense. It is more than a mere designation for a rite or a church. It matters little that the Soviets write in their propaganda, "Religion is the opiate of the masses." Communism is essentially religious. The remaining cause of the misunderstanding is the old connotation of the word.[16]

As Michel Löwy observes, however, Mariátegui does not make explicit a new definition of religion, one that goes beyond the "old connotation" and explains its "new sense." Accordingly, we are left to infer its meaning. Löwy suggests that Mariátegui's "new sense of religion" is likely related to humankind's "need of the infinite" and its quest for a heroic myth that provides meaning and "enchantment" to life.[17] Like Löwy, Ofelia Schutte comments on Mariátegui's fluid understanding of religion. As she points out, Mariátegui's Marxism is premised on three interactive levels: Marxism as a science, Marxism as an aesthetic impulse, and Marxism as a faith. Schutte argues that Mariátegui's concept of religiosity should be linked to his interest in the psychological dynamics of religious belief and to his aesthetics.[18] Like Löwy, Schutte maintains that Mariátegui's sense of religiosity is deeply enmeshed with other areas of his thought and is thus difficult to pin down.

Omar Rivera, another important interpreter of Mariátegui, adds to these insights. Although Rivera's recent study on Mariátegui does not address his religiosity at length, his attention to the aesthetic dimensions of Mariátegui's thought makes ample room for religious considerations. In particular, Rivera questions the narrowness of Aníbal Quijano's interpretation of Mariátegui. According to Rivera, Quijano reads Mariátegui through the lens of a "strict theoretical Marxism." For Quijano, "Mariátegui's Marxism is ultimately not infused and distorted by religiosity."[19] Rivera takes issue with this reading by drawing on the work of Alberto Flores Galindo who, unlike Quijano, finds value in what could be described as Mariátegui's "open Marxism." For Flores Galindo (and Rivera), Mariátegui's religiosity is a "connecting thread throughout his works that predates his Marxism, determining his Marxism in unorthodox ways."[20] Furthermore, and perhaps even more significantly, such an appreciative reading of Mariátegui's religiosity allows us to remain "sensitive to the way theoretical framings, including Marxism, will always lag behind the totality of phenomenon." For Rivera, Flores Galindo, and, indeed, Mariátegui, "this lag will fail to direct praxis unless infused by a faith and commitment to a myth that moves multitudes in political struggle."[21] In other words, an enclosed, strict, or scientific form of Marxism—which eschews questions of myth and utopia—is likely to come up well short of generating genuine forms of praxis. This is precisely why Mariátegui holds that authentic forms of revolution and communism "will always be religious."

I believe that Löwy, Schutte, Rivera, and Flores Galindo help to set us in the right direction for better understanding Mariátegui's new sense of religion. In what follows, I develop these promising insights further by way of three theses that I believe implicitly undergird Mariátegui's new sense of religion.

## Religious Faith Is a Quality, Not a Type, of Human Experience

The first implicit presupposition may be stated as follows: for Mariátegui, the religious dimension of human experience is a quality—and not a discreet type—of human experience. Whereas philosophers and theologians are often prone to treat "religious experience" as categorically distinct from other forms of human experience, Mariátegui was interested in showing how the religious dimension of human experience could color and shape all kinds of experience, be it political, artistic, or scientific. Mariátegui thus approached religion less as a noun—a church, a set of rites, an object of devotion—and more as an adjective or adverb—as in how we do things in a "religious way."

While it is clear that Mariátegui does not want to limit the meaning of religion to a particular institution, what would he say about the meaning of religious experience? How are we to understand an experience that someone refers to, for example, as mystical or ecstatic? While Mariátegui does invoke the term *mystical* with some frequency, I think it is instructive to note that he rarely, if ever, uses it to answer the question, "What is the essence of religious experience?" Rather, he invokes the term to show how the mystical is in continuity with human experience at large. "Revolutionary emotion . . . is a religious emotion," Mariátegui writes.[22] For him, religious faith is coterminous with revolutionary action. Ultimately, Mariátegui was less interested in the question of religious essence and more interested in the function of religion, which yields revolutionary praxis.

To underscore what is at stake here, we would be well served to note that around the turn of the twentieth century, mystical or ecstatic experience was often thought to be an experience unlike any other. Such an experience was believed to be entirely *sui generis*, as Rudolf Otto famously put it.[23] It was thought to exist well outside of the common experiential frameworks of the true, the good, or the beautiful. In such a case, religious experience is taken to be not so much a dimension *of* human experience as it is an experience that breaks itself off *from* everyday human experience. Indeed, this belief persists to the present day. It is virtually the antithesis of the kind of experience proffered by more contemporary relational and emergentist approaches to faith, such as is seen in process thought, pragmatism, and feminist theology. As I see it, Mariátegui's understanding of religion is best understood in light of traditions like these and not as a *sui generis* phenomenon.

## Religious Knowledge Is Not Rationalistic

If Mariátegui's approach to experience may be described as integral and unitive insofar as he connects religious, political, and ethical experience along a common continuum, so too may the same be said of his anthropology and epistemology, which are also intimately connected. As Ofelia Schutte incisively notes, the human being is, for Mariátegui, a "unity of thought and feeling rather than . . . a composite or combination of both."[24] Mariátegui understands actions like thinking, feeling, and struggling as equally indicative of what it means to be human.

Such an integral approach to anthropology and epistemology is significant in light of the Western tendency toward rationalism, which places reason over and above all other human faculties and activities. Traditional forms of both philosophy and theology have often "produced a divided (if not dualistic) view of the self and thus have contributed to the fragmentation of human consciousness," writes Schutte.[25] Feminist philosophy and theology have been especially insightful in showing the many limitations of such a position. As ecofeminist theologian Ivone Gebara argues, for example, we must now begin "to affirm relatedness as a primordial and foundational reality [that] requires us to eliminate dualisms and other forms of separation." Such an affirmation also requires us to affirm a new vision of human rationality, one that is "connected, integrated, independent, creative, open, and willing to engage in dialogue." Emotions, Gebara adds, "are as much rationality as analytical rationality is emotion."[26]

If the Western tendency has been to divorce reason from other forms of human consciousness—such as imagination, perception, feeling, emotion, passion—then Mariátegui moves decisively in the other direction, toward their integration. To forge a unity between knowing and feeling, Mariátegui first distances himself from overly rationalistic approaches to knowledge, such as are found in certain scientist and dogmatic versions of Marxism and positivism. Mariátegui does not oppose reason and science, but he does warn against their rationalistic manifestations, which he renders as "Reason" and "Science." Neither "Reason nor Science," he writes, "can meet the need of the infinite that exists in man."[27] Mariátegui laments bourgeois civilization's "lack of myth, of faith, of hope" which has resulted in the "crisis of bourgeois civilization." He shares Ernest Renan's melancholy toward positivism: "Religious people live in a shadow," observes Renan. "On what will those who come after us live?" This despairing question, writes Mariátegui, "still awaits an answer."[28]

If one were to take these comments out of context, one might very well be inclined to believe that Mariátegui would likely want to return to the "old myths" of religious belief, to the time when people "live[d] in a shadow," or to "the prestige of the ancient religions."[29] It is true that Mariátegui wants to re-store humankind's faith in myth, for "myth moves man in history" and "without myth, the history of humanity has no sense of history."[30] Yet, it should be equally clear that Mariátegui does not want to return to an "old" sense of religion. Rather, he wants to retain the direction and meaning that religion and religious myth offer without returning to a "single church" or a "single rite."

## Religious Knowledge Is Instrumental to the Enrichment of Experience

As we have seen, Mariátegui understands religious experience as a quality of experience rather than a *sui generis* type of experience. I noted that Mariátegui makes room for religious knowledge and expression by pointing to the inherent limits of rationalism. If we are to make Mariátegui's newer sense of religion even more explicit, we may note a third crucial building block, which is Mariátegui's instrumentalism. For Mariátegui, the religious dimension of human experience functions as a regulative guide for our actions. Embedded in this insight are two related considerations: Mariátegui's voluntarism and his desire to overcome the dualism between the material and the ideal. Significantly, both are connected to Mariátegui's interest in pragmatism.

Let me unpack these ideas by first turning to Mariátegui's anti-foundationalism, which is articulated well in his 1925 essay "Pessimism of Reality, Optimism of the Idea." In this essay, Mariátegui expresses his appreciation for pragmatism as a philosophical approach that not only effectively moves people to action but also "is in fact a relativistic and skeptical school."[31] As Mariátegui notes, for pragmatists, "there are no absolute truths." However, Mariátegui adds, "But there are relative truths that govern people's lives as if they were absolute."[32] Mariátegui is drawing here on the philosophy of Hans Vaihinger, a neo-Kantian whose 1911 *Philosophie des Als Ob (The Philosophy of Either/Or)* was "imme-diately perceived as having similarities with pragmatism."[33] But Mariátegui could have as well drawn on *The Varieties of Religious Experience* by William James, whom Mariátegui cites elsewhere in his writings. As James argues in *Varieties*, while words like "soul," "God," and "immortality":

. . . cover no distinctive sense-content whatever, it follows that theoreti-
cally speaking they are words devoid of any significance. Yet strangely
enough they have a definite meaning *for our practice*. We can act *as if*
there were a God; feel *as if* we were free; consider Nature *as if* she
were full of special designs; lay plans *as if* we were immortal.

When we do so, "we find then that these words do make a genuine difference
in our moral life."[34] For James, as for all pragmatists, the meaning of an idea
is to be determined not by its antecedent causes but by its conceivable practical
effects.

Mariátegui is clearly drawn to this idea, and he offers his own summary of
the pragmatic position, which I quote here in full. "This philosophy," Mariátegui writes:

. . . does not call us to abandon action. It only seeks to deny the Absolute. But it recognizes in human history the relative truth, the tempo-
ral myth of each time, the same value and the same effectiveness as an
absolute and eternal truth. This philosophy proclaims and confirms
the need of the myth and the usefulness of the faith.[35]

Mariátegui's discussion of anti-foundationalism and regulative ideals provides
some important clues to his new sense of religion. Mariátegui does not take
refuge in any *a priori* understandings of God, "the sacred," or "the divine." He
is not convinced that faith is primarily about the search for "the Absolute."
Rather, Mariátegui understands that faith is first and foremost an *active* endeavor, a complex process of constructing, honoring, and giving oneself over
to ideals and myths. Like Marx, he is interested not merely in describing experience but, rather, in changing it.

This emphasis on human praxis is taken up explicitly in Mariátegui's discussion of a poem written by Henri Franck in 1912 called *La danse devant
l'arche* (*Dance in Front of the Ark*). In many ways, the poem mirrors Mariátegui's
own faith journey. Like Mariátegui, the poet is in search of a faith. He does
not find it in the faith of his Jewish forebears, nor in any absolute idea of infinity
or eternity. But just when the poet is on the brink of full-blown skepticism and
relativism, he realizes that although there may be no truth outside of humankind, we may nevertheless carry truth inside ourselves. Moreover, we must
willingly activate this truth. Mariátegui ends his discussion of Franck's poem
by quoting its most evocative line: "If the Ark is empty where you hoped to
find the law, nothing is real but your dance."[36]

Mariátegui's point here seems to be this: although we may no longer find
truth in the conventions of institutional religion, we may well find it in our

creative acts, which are guided by their own myths and ideals. Faith, then, is not limited to the churches. Rather, it is constitutive of human action and imagination at large. Mariátegui's voluntaristic faith is indeed a faith that has more to do with orthopraxy (right-action) than orthodoxy (right-belief). While there is good reason to be pessimistic about the social realities that we have created, Mariátegui reminds us that our unrest and dissatisfaction with this reality are fueled by a deeper optimism—a melioristic faith in our ability to change reality through the aid of powerful ideals and heroic myths. In no small measure, Mariátegui helps us to see that our creative praxis is made possible through our faith in these things.

## Mariátegui's Influence on Gutiérrez's Theology of Liberation

Mariátegui no doubt deserves special recognition within the field of liberation philosophy. But equally noteworthy is his significance for liberation theology, beginning with his notable influence on the father of this tradition, Gustavo Gutiérrez (1928–), a fellow Peruvian.

For many theologians, Gutiérrez's watershed 1971 text *Teología de la liberación* stands as one of the most creative applications of the theology of Karl Rahner to the Latin American context. In this work, Gutiérrez emphasizes some of the central tenets of Rahnerian theology, such as the intrinsic connection between nature and grace, as well as salvation and history. Gutiérrez builds on Rahner's insights by moving beyond Rahner's generalized anthropological subject to look at the concrete subjects of Gutiérrez's own place and time—the Latin American poor. Furthermore, Gutiérrez moves beyond Rahner by concretizing what it means to approach salvation in history. For Gutiérrez, this task involves a tangible commitment to accompany the poor.

As noted at the outset of this chapter, for better or worse, Gutiérrez's groundbreaking work is also commonly associated with the philosophy of Karl Marx. Gutiérrez affirms the need to use the social sciences to "read the signs of the times," and he turns to the sociological contributions of Marx to explain the persistent inequalities between social classes. Gutiérrez does indeed gesture in the direction of a Latin American socialism, but he is very careful to avoid any uncritical or dogmatic use of Marx. "As in the case of Mariátegui," writes Gaspar Mártinez, "Gutiérrez argues it must be a Latin American socialism, able to take into account the complex reality of the continent."[37] For Gutiérrez, as for Mariátegui, the telos toward which human praxis points is not so much a new political order as it is a fundamentally new society and a new way of being human. This is why Gutiérrez continually highlights the theme of "integral liberation" instead of mere political revolution.[38]

While the influence of European thinkers like Rahner and Marx (and, one could add, Ernst Bloch) on Gutiérrez are readily apparent, what is often underappreciated are the specifically Peruvian influences that shaped Gutiérrez's thought. Around 1920, a group of intellectuals (often referred to as the "Generation of 1919") emerged in Peru that sought to overcome class divisions and forge a more inclusive society in order to "Peruvianize Peru." Exemplary figures of this generation include political figures like Víctor Raul Haya de la Torre (1895–1979), poet César Vallejo (1892–1938), novelist and anthropologist José María Arguedas (1906–1969), and Mariátegui. "The influence of this generation on Gutiérrez can hardly be overemphasized," writes Gaspar Mártinez. Gutiérrez is "clearly heir to [these thinkers] and the one who has established a most fruitful dialogue with that generation."[39]

Of all the European and Peruvian figures mentioned above, Arguedas and Mariátegui are the most important for Gutiérrez. As Kurt Cadorette unequivocally states, "Gutiérrez studied primarily in Europe, yet no one has influenced his thinking more than two fellow Peruvians: José María Arguedas and José Carlos Mariátegui. . . . Their ideas and words are part of Peru's intellectual heritage and constantly surface in Gutiérrez's theology giving it a unique pathos and frame of reference."[40]

What, exactly, was Mariátegui's influence on Gutiérrez? In a 1980 interview in the Peruvian journal *Quehacer*, Gutiérrez directly addresses this question. "Mariátegui is especially significant for Peruvian culture," Gutiérrez notes. "It is he who, for the first time, tries to think out of the Peruvian historical process and the Peruvian reality of his time with new and distinct categories which have had an enormous impact on the way we understand our society." Although Gutiérrez does not state so explicitly, the "new and distinct categories" are no doubt a reference to Mariátegui's use of Marxist analysis. Gutiérrez adds the following:

> I have had the opportunity to work through Mariátegui for academic reasons. For several years at the University [Pontificia Universidad Católica del Perú] I taught a course dedicated entirely to Mariátegui's ideas. . . . In my opinion he combines many qualities. He is significant because his action and thought arise from his experience of the popular classes.[41]

In *A Theology Liberation*, Gutiérrez further elucidates Mariátegui's contributions. In Latin America's "search for indigenous socialist paths," Gutiérrez writes, Mariátegui is "the outstanding figure" who "continues to chart the course." Gutiérrez quotes this famous passage from Mariátegui:

We certainly do not wish for socialism in America to be an exact copy of others' socialism. It must be a heroic creation. We must bring Indo-American socialism to life with our own reality, in our own language. This is a mission worthy of a new generation.[42]

Gutiérrez then offers his own analysis:

For Mariátegui, as for many today in Latin America, historical materialism is above all "a method for the historical interpretation of society." All [of Mariátegui's] work, thought and action—although not exempt from understandable limitations—was characterized by these concerns. He was loyal to his sources, that is, to the central intuitions of Marx, yet was beyond all dogmatism; he was simultaneously loyal to a unique historical reality.[43]

As Gutiérrez makes clear from passages like these, the nondogmatic nature of Mariátegui's Marxism was one of his greatest strengths, not weaknesses. Like other nondogmatic Marxists of his time such as Georges Sorel and Antonio Labriola, Mariátegui did not let his use of Marxism overtake his commitment to remain true to the specific historical reality of Peru at that time. Economic inequalities between Peru's social classes were indeed a major problem. But Mariátegui also knew that issues of race and ideology compounded Peru's most intractable problem—namely, the problem of the land tenure system, or gamonalismo. As he explains, the term *gamonalismo* "designates more than just a social and economic category. . . . It signifies a whole phenomenon. *Gamonalismo* is represented not only by the *gamonales* but by a long hierarchy of officials, intermediaries, agents, parasites, et cetera. The literate Indian who enters the service of *gamonalismo* turns into an exploiter of his own race."[44]

Stepping back a moment from these two thinkers, we may note several commonalities. First, both Mariátegui and Gutiérrez are critical of colonial forms of Christendom, while remaining appreciative of more authentic and liberating forms of faith. Second, both are consummate contextualist thinkers insofar as they ground their theoretical reflections in specific historical circumstances. This applies not only to contextualist (i.e., Indigenous) forms of socialism, but also to native forms of religious expression. Both thinkers therefore appreciate the integrity of what has become known as "popular religion," or simply, "lived religion." Third, both remain committed to the plight of the Indigenous poor. In their own ways, they espouse what Gutiérrez refers to as "a preferential option for the poor."

Regarding his thoughts on revolutionary faith, Mariátegui has not been without his critics. Within his own lifetime, the Communist International discredited Mariátegui for his nationalism and for refusing to identify his own socialist political party as "communist." No doubt, Mariátegui's unorthodox religious views, along with his unwavering attention to questions of race, added to the Comintern's suspicion of him. A second possible critique arises when looking at Mariátegui's faith in revolutionary myth. The problem is one that Sorel faced: What was to guard against revolutionary myth being used for fascist and other right-wing purposes? After all, fascist leaders in the 1920s, such as Mussolini, put into practice Sorel's belief in the need for a deliberately conceived myth to sway the masses. Although Sorel himself believed that the "energizing myth" of the general strike would promote a sense of solidarity and class consciousness among the working class, fascists would appeal to the same myth to bolster ideas of race, nation, or people, as defined by the state.

Philosopher Kim Díaz offers a third critique of Mariátegui's use of myth. Although she praises Mariátegui for working tirelessly to secure the rights of Indigenous peoples, she argues that Mariátegui is "ultimately inconsistent in the way he relates to Indigenous people." "On the one hand," Díaz writes, "he believes Indigenous people are human beings, deserving of recognition as rational autonomous agents. On the other hand, Mariátegui also believes that Indigenous people are not sophisticated enough to understand scientific and philosophical subtleties."[45] Díaz bases this critique on a passage in "Man and Myth" in which Mariátegui states that "relativist language [of the philosophers] is not accessible or intelligible to the common people." Unlike Díaz, I read this passage less as an indictment of common people and more as a lament on the shortcomings of philosophy's prosaic use of language. Such an interpretation is corroborated, I believe, by Mariátegui's subsequent insight: "Professional intellectuals will not find the path of faith; the masses find it."[46]

This difference of interpretation notwithstanding, I believe that Díaz raises some points worthy of consideration. To what extent, if at all, does Sorel's willingness to "deceive" the proletariat figure into Mariátegui's own thinking? Moreover, how much trust is Mariátegui willing to place in revolutionary forms of education? Díaz's own work on the potential contributions of Paulo Freire to Mariátegui's thought are utterly salient.[47] If nothing else, this pairing helps to make more explicit the need for authentic forms of conscientization within any revolutionary struggle. Indeed, this is also precisely the pairing that Gustavo Gutiérrez makes in his *A Theology of Liberation*. Having discussed Mariátegui, Gutiérrez turns almost instinctively to Freire: in order for liberation to be "authentic and complete," Gutiérrez writes, "it has to be undertaken by the oppressed people themselves and so must stem from values proper to these people. Only in this context can a true cultural revolution come about." He continues, "From this point of view, one of the most creative and fruitful efforts which has been implemented in Latin America is the experimental work of Paulo Freire."[48]

As worthy as all of these criticisms are, the larger question still remains: What can be gleaned from Mariátegui's new sense of religion for our own time? As I have shown, Mariátegui has already played a notable role in the development of Latin American liberation theology through the work of Gutiérrez. Mariátegui's philosophical contextualism and his overriding concern for the Indigenous poor are two hallmarks that can be easily seen Gutiérrez's writings. But as I have also underscored, Mariátegui's significance for liberation theology and liberation philosophy can extend even further, particularly when we approach his new sense of religion through a nonreductive, pragmatic lens.

# 2

# Conscientization as a Spiritual Praxis: Paulo Freire's Implicit Spirituality

Since the 2000s, Latin American philosophy has gained a growing audience among North American philosophers. A number of recent anthologies have opened up Latin American philosophies to a North American readership, including, most recently, Kim Díaz and Mathew Foust's *The Philosophies of America Reader: From the Popul Vuh to the Present* (2021), Robert Eli Sanchez, Jr.'s *Latin American and Latinx Philosophy: A Collaborative Introduction* (2020), and Carlos Alberto Sanchez and Robert Eli Sanchez, Jr.'s *Mexican Philosophy in the 20th Century: Essential Readings* (2017). These works follow on the heels of several other important collections.[1] Similarly, significant single-authored works like Terrance MacMullan's *From American Empire to América Cósmica through Philosophy: Prospero's Reflection* (2023), Enrique Krauze's *Redeemers: Ideas and Power in Latin America* (2011), and Ofelia Schutte's *Cultural Identity and Social Liberation in Latin American Thought* (1993) offer incisive interpretations of key Latin American figures.

One prominent theme among many, if not all, of these contributions has been that of liberation, with special focus given to the tradition known as Latin American liberation philosophy. Schutte's book stands as a landmark work in this regard, and other more recent essays have contributed substantially to the discourse.[2]

With a few exceptions, nearly all of these treatments of Latin American liberation philosophy give little, if any, attention to Latin American liberation theology, a tradition in which the theme of liberation is also central. While it is difficult to pinpoint causes, lingering forms of positivism, both in philosophy and the social sciences, likely have something to do with this. Just as many scholars in Chicano/a Studies have curiously sidelined discussions of religion, so too have many philosophers overlooked the philosophical significance of religion, leaving matters of faith to the purview of theology and religious studies. Fortunately, however, some philosophers are entering the fray. Among others, Nicolás Panotto offers a rereading of Latin American theology from the perspective of decolonial philosophy, and Alexander Stehn, Iván Márquez, and Antonio González have explored the thought of key thinkers like Enrique Dussel, Ignacio Ellacuría, and Xavier Zubiri, who may serve as useful bridge figures between liberation philosophy and liberation theology.[3]

In an effort to bridge these traditions further, this chapter focuses on the work of Brazilian educator Paulo Freire (1921–1997), whose work has proven significant for liberation theologies and liberation philosophies alike. Freire's guiding and anchoring theme is conscientization, a process of developing a critical awareness of one's social reality through reflection and action. As Freire explains, conscientization "refers to learning to perceive social, political, and economic contradictions, and to take action against the oppressive elements of reality."[4] It is humankind's way of becoming better aware of our reality—particularly, the structural aspects that are often hard to see—so that we can use this knowledge to change the world for the better.

As is widely known, Freire's understanding of conscientization as a form of critical education was a central pillar in the development of Latin American liberation theology. As Lilian Calles Barger notes in her rich intellectual history of liberation theology, "Freire's influence was both deep and broad. During the 1960s and 1970s, Freire maintained relationships with educators, intellectuals, and theologians throughout the Americas. The 1968 Latin American Bishops Conference endorsed the process of *conscientization* as indispensable for pastoral action, encouraging political education in lay-led base ecclesial communities (BECs)."[5]

Yet, while it is clear that Freire had a tremendous impact on liberation theology, one may still wonder: In what ways, if at all, was Freire's vision of faith—or spirituality more broadly—connected to his understanding of conscientization? What are the spiritual dimensions of conscientization itself? Even though Freire's work has clearly informed liberation theology, Freire himself writes surprisingly little about his own understanding of spirituality and its direct connection to conscientization. In fact, as Irwin Leopando notes, Freire was reticent about discussing his faith in personal terms. "I do not feel very comfortable speaking about my faith," admitted Freire. "At least I do not feel as comfortable as I do when speaking about my political choice, my utopia, and my pedagogical dreams."[6]

A recent commentary on Freire by James Kirylo and Drick Boyd suggests that Freire's idea of conscientization points to an "implicit spirituality."

Borrowing from Daniel Schipani's insight that Freire had an "implicit theological foundation or infrastructure of his pedagogy,"[7] Kirylo and Boyd argue that "in regard to his views on conscientization, Freire also had an implicit spirituality. In other words, Freire does not link his description of conscientization explicitly to an interaction with God, but we get hints from his writings what his underlying assumptions are."[8] I find Kirylo and Drick's work significant and helpful. They discuss important touchpoints for Freire's approach to spirituality, including Freire's interest in the personalism of Emmanuel Mounier and various forms of secular and Christian humanism. Furthermore, they are correct in noting that "[w]hile Freire has been criticized by those who would wish him to have a more mainstream Christian theological view, it is clear that the essence of Freire's spirituality is rooted in a dialectic between a God present and involved in history, and human beings who are called to be the primary actors in and on that history."[9]

Among other things, this chapter attempts to tease out further how, exactly, this dialectic works. Although I retrace some of the same ground that Kirylo and Boyd cover in their work, I aim to make even more explicit the philosophical and pedagogical significance of Freire's implicit spirituality, and I do so by looking at conscientization through a functionalist and pragmatic lens. Toward this end, I focus on the three interlocking and spiritually significant factors in Freire's concept of conscientization: the human desire to become "more fully human" (which Freire describes as "humanization"); the centrality of authentic dialogue and communion in bringing forth new forms of humanization; and the ongoing process of conversion. As I will show, conscientization carries spiritual significance, not only because of Freire's own religious inclinations and influences but, more importantly, because the inner dynamics of conscientization, captured by these three foci, already point to a rich spirituality-in-action. We see this best, I believe, when we approach conscientization as an indispensable tool for transforming hope into action and ideas into practice. In this light, conscientization may itself be described as a "practice of spirituality," broadly conceived. It is a powerful spiritual technique or technology (in the original Greek sense of *tekhnē*, which is "art" or "craft"), insofar that its "thought dimension" effects changes in thought patterns and behavior, and its "behavioral dimension" points to active participation in the world, both in terms of reflecting critically on one's reality, as well as changing existing structures.[10]

Before we look at these three interlocking factors, it is important that I address two interpretive knots. The first has to do with how we read Freire. For some, he is best read as a revolutionary Marxist, and for others, as a Christian activist. On the one hand, the "revolutionary Marxist" interpretation could very well be supported by the attention that Freire gives to the necessity of objective outcomes, as seen in his preoccupation with human action and revolutionary structural change. On the other hand, the "Christian activist" interpretation could be defended in light of the subjective (and, by extension, quasi-religious) dimensions of Freire's thought, including his thoughts on hope, utopia, and love. As one prominent commentator points out Freire's substantial interest in psychoanalysis and the work of Eric Fromm may, in the end, be more central to Freire than the work of Marx.[11]

I believe that both of these readings may be persuasively defended. But as I suggest, the deeper question has to do with the *means* by which one moves from subjective considerations like hope, utopia, and love to more concrete and objective considerations like tangible forms of human action and revolutionary change. As I will show, the process of conscientization serves as the indispensable bridge that links objective and subjective considerations. To put the matter another way, Freire often describes the relationship between hope and social transformation, ideas and action, and subjectivity and objectivity as a "dialectical" one. Part of the contribution here is to make explicit the ways in which conscientization functionally mediates this dialectic.

A second interpretive knot has to do with how we are to assess the spiritual dimensions of conscientization. One possible route forward might be to identify Freire's "outward" commitment to conscientization as an expression of his own "inward" spiritual commitments. Such is a path that is adopted by Kirylo and Boyd in their study of Freire's implicit spirituality.[12] Undoubtedly, having some awareness of Freire's own Catholic upbringing, his faith in the reforms of Vatican II, and his particular reading of the Bible all contribute to a more complete picture of this spirituality. But as to the more specific question regarding the spiritual dimensions of the process of conscientization itself, additional lines of convergence may be discovered when we bring into focus certain parallels between Freire's liberating spirituality and his understanding of conscientization. Thus, rather than start with a discussion of what Freire "believed" and then apply that to his idea of conscientization, I would like, instead, to point out structural similarities between his understanding of conscientization and his approach to spirituality. As such, my primary aim is not so much to show that Freire's faith (understood here as a reference to his personal religiosity) "informed" his pedagogical work (which I take as a given) as it is to make the stronger claim that conscientization is, for Freire, a spiritual praxis in the widest sense of the phrase.

While Freire's spirituality may be understood as an extension of his Roman Catholicism, I believe that Freire would have also defended spirituality in a more expansive sense. As I outlined in this book's Introduction, I understand spirituality as an existential pattern of living that is guided by some ultimate value, and it can be explicitly religious in character or not.[13] Freire would no doubt understand spirituality as a human being's unceasing quest to become more authentically human, which he describes as a process of humanization. For Freire, authentic humanization is realized when human beings take responsibility for the various forms of oppression that they have created and actively work to overcome these dehumanizing relationships.

With these two interpretive caveats in mind, let us now turn to the three aspects of conscientization that help to shed light on its spiritual character.

## Humanization: A Constant Search

Keeping in mind the aforementioned expansive definition of spirituality, we may begin to appreciate how conscientization, as a form of humanization, is itself a spiritual praxis. As Kirylo and Boyd point out, Freire's approach to humanization is heavily indebted to the personalism of Emmanuel Mounier (1905–1950). Although Mounier drew broadly from existential and phenomenological thought, his approach differed from more individualist approaches to personhood that often typify these traditions. Influenced by his Catholic faith, Mounier "promoted a personalism that looked to the interiority of the person, the spiritual being in which human beings are active subjects of history." Furthermore, his concept of personalism, "while realizing the self in personhood, is a constant dynamic to move outside of the self to therefore provide the opening to enter into the challenges that cause human beings to struggle and thus work toward 'humanizing' humanity."[14]

Carrying echoes of Mounier, Freire's groundbreaking *Pedagogy of the Oppressed*, first published in Portuguese in 1968, begins with these lines:

> While the problem of humanization has always, from an axiological point of view, been man's [sic] central problem, it now takes on the character of an inescapable concern. Concern for humanization leads at once to the recognition of dehumanization, not only as an ontological possibility but as an historical reality. And as man [sic] perceives the extent of dehumanization, he asks himself if humanization is a viable possibility.[15]

In these opening lines, we see the seeds of several of Freire's core themes: the need for *humanization* amidst prevailing forms of *dehumanization*; the fact that humanization may be understood as both an *ontological* and *historical* reality; and the latent *hope* that humanization is indeed still possible. As Freire explains, conscientization is rooted in hope, and hope, in turn, is "rooted in men's [sic] incompletion, from which they move out in constant search—a search that can be carried out only in communion with other men [sic]."[16]

These ideas of "incompletion" and "search" help to explain what Freire means by humanization as both an ontological and a historical reality. In *Pedagogy of the Oppressed*, Freire makes clear his phenomenological debt to philosopher Álvaro Borges Vieira Pinto who, as Freire mentions elsewhere, was part of the original group in Brazil who began to use the term *conscientization*.[17] Freire adopted Vieira Pinto's concept of "limit-situations" and "limit-acts." Because we are conscious beings who are aware of both ourselves and the world, humans "exist in a dialectical relationship between the determination of limits and their own freedom," writes Freire. As human beings separate themselves from the world, that is, as they step momentarily out of their own shoes and look in, they begin to "overcome the situations which limit them."[18] Rather than rely on Karl Jaspers's idea of the limit-situations as "impassable boundaries where possibilities end," Freire leans on Vieira Pinto's understanding of the limit-situations as "the real boundaries where all possibilities begin." For Vieira Pinto, the boundaries of limit-situations are not "the frontier which separates being from nothingness, but the frontier which separates being from being more."[19]

In having the capacity to identify and name limit-situations, human beings "respond to the challenge" with limit-acts, which are actions that are "directed at negating and overcoming, rather than passively accepting, the 'given.'"[20] As such, Freire's phenomenology already implies an ethics. The ethical moment of the dialectic between limit-situation and limit-act rests not only on a *conscious recognition* of a real boundary that separates being from being more, but also on an *active commitment* to rectify that which limits humanization. As Freire puts it, conscientization is not simply a *prise de conscience*, or a basic awareness of reality that comes about naturally as a result of our human situatedness in the world. Rather, conscientization also demands concrete action and historical commitment. The more that human beings historicize and demystify their limit-situations, the more pronounced the ethical dimensions of conscientization become. Thus, conscientization proves ethically significant not only because it demands ethical intention in a general sense (individuals, after all, must have the courage to face up to limit-situations), but also, more significantly, because it demands very specific limit-acts that respond to the challenges of particular times and places. In doing so, conscientization helps human beings overcome what is often uncritically accepted as simply "the way things are."

Fortunately, Freire's discussion of limit-situations and limit-acts does not stay on an abstract level of ontology and phenomenology, focusing generically, for example, on questions of consciousness, intentionality, and sensory qualities.

Rather, Freire, from his very earliest writings, historically contextualizes the fundamental limit-situation of our day. The "fundamental theme of our epoch," he writes, is "that of *domination*—which implies its opposite, the theme of *liberation*, as the objective to be achieved. . . . In order to achieve humanization, which presupposes the elimination of dehumanizing oppression, it is absolutely necessary to surmount the limit-situations in which men [sic] are reduced to things."[21] As such, conscientization involves not only a reflective, or noetic, moment of apprehending reality, but also an ethical moment of praxis, which requires intentional commitment and concrete historical action.

As mentioned, although Freire is widely recognized as having enormous influence on liberation theology, his writings on religion and theology are somewhat scant. What he did write on these topics, however, proves highly illuminating, revealing the centrality of humanization. In 1970 and 1977, Freire wrote two letters to theology students. In the first, "Letter to a Young Theology Student," Freire makes a connection between the Word of God and the task of humanization. He writes:

> The true humanization of man [sic] cannot be brought about in the interiority of our minds; it has to take place in external history. If objective reality keeps man [sic] from being humanized, then he [sic] should change that reality. I am convinced that we as Christians have an enormous task to perform, presuming that we are capable of setting aside our idealistic myths and in that way sharing in the revolutionary transformation of society. . . .[22]

Freire then goes on to make explicit the link between the Christian witness and the task of humanization. The "first requirement for knowing how to hear the Word of God (and not only hearing it but putting it into practice) is, in my opinion, a willingness to dedicate oneself to the liberation of man [sic]," he writes. "Such a process . . . demands of us a historical commitment, it requires a transforming activity, one that will embolden us to challenge the powerful of the earth."[23] As Freire suggests here, the Word of God has everything to do with liberating humankind, which is to say, moving from situations of dehumanization to humanization.

In another letter written to four young German seminarians in 1977, Freire echoes these sentiments by drawing a connection between the Word of God and the pedagogical witness of Christ, a witness that demands that the Gospels be actively lived rather than simply passively heard. Freire begins this letter this way: "I am accustomed to say, independently of the Christian position that I have always attempted to hold, that Christ will always be, as he is for me, an example of the Teacher."[24] The two parenthetical caveats that Freire uses here provide valuable insight into his multilayered approach to Christianity. In the first phrase, Freire attempts to bracket his own "Christian position" as somewhat "independent" from the thoughts that are about to follow. Read in this way, Freire's ensuing thoughts on Christ may be seen less as a reflection of his own personal commitments to Christianity and more as a meditation on what a truly humanizing form of education can look like. In the second parenthetical clause ("as he is for me"), Freire seems to acknowledge that his thoughts on Christ are nevertheless shaped by his own experience of Christianity. Freire is well justified, I believe, to hold both positions in mutual tension: no doubt his Christian outlook informs his pedagogy, yet, at the same time, his pedagogy should not simply be reduced to his Christian outlook. Both point equally, and somewhat independently, to an authentic form of humanization.

In this letter, Freire suggests that a variety of pathways are available to Christians. He laments that it is all too easy for Christians to talk "about the *Good News* without denouncing the evil that places obstacles in the way of realizing the Good News." It is also regrettably convenient for Christians to separate (other-worldly) salvation from (this-worldly) liberation, and to bury themselves in traditionalist or modernist forms of Christianity without taking a truly prophetic position.[25] Freire admits that he experienced such contradictions as a child:

> In my long ago childhood, in catechism classes, when a dear, but ingenuous priest spoke of the everlasting damnation of lost souls in the fires of an eternal hell, in spite of the fear which filled me, what really stayed with me was the goodness, the strength to love without limits, to which Christ witnessed.[26]

The essential point here is that, for Freire, Christ is an example of a humanizing teacher *par excellence*. Christ does not shirk from the oppressive limit-situations of his day. Instead, he fully leans and lives into them through prophetic limit-acts of denunciation and annunciation. Christ loves without limits and humanizes humanity by actively living out God's word, showing how other human beings can do the same. [27]

## Authentic Dialogue and Communion

As Freire makes clear, conscientization, as a constant and hopeful search for authentic forms of humanization, is not merely an individual process. Rather, it is a "search that can be carried out only in communion with other men [sic]."[28] Because conscientization emerges as a response to dehumanization, it

is necessarily relational; it discloses a fundamental connection between oppressor and oppressed, between teacher and learner. In the case of the oppressor-
oppressed relationship, Freire observes that the process of conscientization
frees not only the oppressed but the oppressor as well. If oppression is that
which prevents human beings from being more fully human, then it stands to
reason that both parties will inevitably suffer from situations of oppression.
"The pedagogy of the oppressed is an instrument for [the] critical discovery
that both [the oppressed] and their oppressors are manifestations of
dehumanization."[29]

In the case of teacher and learner, Freire is most concerned with pedagogical
processes that dehumanize learners, particularly "banking models" of education that treat learners as passive depositories of knowledge and teachers as the
depositors. "In the banking concept of education, knowledge is a gift bestowed
by those who consider themselves knowledgeable upon those whom they consider to know nothing."[30] This system of education is inherently oppressive,
argues Freire, because students remain "alienated like the slave in the Hegelian
dialectic" and "accept their ignorance as justifying the teacher's existence—but,
unlike the slave, they never discover that they educate the teacher."[31] For Freire,
educators have a choice to make. They can either educate students to maintain
the status quo, thus keeping in place systems of dehumanization, or they can
educate for freedom, so that students become active agents in their own ongoing process of humanization. When an educator chooses the path of humanization and conscientization, they are choosing a path for both their students
and themselves. In this sense, conscientization is a *cointentional* affair between
teacher and student. Both become active subjects, not only in the task of unveiling reality and thereby knowing it more critically, but also in the task of
creating new knowledge. "As they attain this knowledge of reality through
common reflection and action, they discover themselves as its permanent re-
creators."[32] As Eduardo Duarte points out, this aspect of cointentionality may
be seen as a further advancement upon more traditional and individualistic
approaches to phenomenology, since, as Freire puts it, the "pursuit of full humanity . . . cannot be carried out in isolation or individualism, but only in
fellowship and solidarity. . . ."[33]

In his more explicit religious writings, Freire reworks the theme of communion around the question of humankind's communion with God. For Freire,
God is not an abstract being who lives in the heavens and controls humankind's
fate. Freire asks: How do peasants in desperate situations in northeast Brazil
make sense of their reality? What reasons do they attribute to their dehumanizing situation? Very often, Freire points out, human beings look for causes in
things "higher and more powerful" than themselves. "One such thing is God,"

who is often seen as "the maker, the cause of [human] conditions." The trouble with this position, however, is that if "God is responsible, man [sic] can do nothing." Freire continues:

> Many Christians today, thanks be to God, are vigorously reacting against that attitude, especially in Brazil. But as a child, I knew many priests who went out to the peasants saying: "Be patient. This is God's will. And anyway, it will earn heaven for you." Yet the truth of the matter is that we have to earn our heaven here and now, we ourselves. We have to build our heaven, to fashion it during our lifetime, right now. Salvation is something to achieve, not just to hope for. This latter sort of theology is a very passive one that I cannot stomach.[34]

Freire then goes on to describe God as "Absolute Love" and concedes that if Absolute Love were to abandon humanity to constant victimization, this would indeed be the type of palliative God that Marx described.

Freire instead holds out for a God who is reflective of limitless love and a God who intercedes in history. Furthermore, Freire's God does not control humanity but rather "invites" humankind "to re-create the world, not for my brother's [sic] domination, but for their liberation."[35] Freire understands, however, that human beings can only approach God through their finite and contingent experience of being human. "[J]ust as the Word became flesh," Freire writes, "so the Word can be approached only through man [sic]. Theology has to take its starting point from anthropology."[36]

All told, authentic dialogue and communion between human beings help to enable authentic communion with God. For Freire, however, communion does not refer to a strict identity between one human being and another wherein real differences collapse. Nor does it imply that "individuality must take on a subordinate position to the spirit of the whole group," as Schutte suggests.[37] Rather, Freire's understanding of communion grows out of his cointentional and dialogical phenomenology. Stretching this further, we could also say that Freire's understanding of community is richly semiotic, wherein human selves are conceived as "living streams of semiosis, continuously engaged in reading themselves, interpreting other persons, and struggling to create or find meaning in a world so thoroughly pervaded by signs."[38] For Freire, all of existence is relational, and the self is always socially constituted. Part of Freire's great contribution is not so much to highlight these things as set "facts of existence," but rather, and more importantly, to show how conscientization, as a method and process, can help us to interpret and reconstruct reality dialogically. Significantly, this process of dialogical encounter has spiritual implications, for it helps human beings move beyond themselves to ever wider frames of meaning.

## Ongoing Conversion

Conversion is a third element in Freire's understanding of conscientization that carries spiritual significance. At key junctures in his writing, Freire describes conscientization as a painful birth and a conversion. In one of his earliest essays, Freire writes that conscientization "involves an excruciating moment, a tremendously upsetting one, in those who begin to conscientize themselves, the moment they start to be reborn."[39] Such is the case, Freire explains, because conscientization demands a fundamental and deep-seated level of conversion, which he describes as an Easter experience.

It should be noted that Freire goes well beyond conventional understandings of conversion and rebirth. Typically, conversion refers to a basic change in formal religious affiliation, wherein one moves from one religion to the next. For example, someone may convert from Christianity to Islam or from Judaism to Buddhism. For its part, rebirth, particularly in more fundamentalist Christian circles, commonly refers to a process of "fully accepting faith in Jesus Christ," and this often happens after an intense religious experience. In such cases, the act of "fully accepting" faith in Jesus usually implies an assent to the "inerrant truths" of scripture and doctrine. One accepts faith in Jesus Christ by accepting what the tradition deems as true and right.

Freire understands conversion and rebirth in very different ways. For Freire, conversion has less to do with a formal assent to doctrine after having a single and/or solitary religious experience and more to do with critically questioning what is often accepted as given or natural. This process of critical questioning and "consciousness raising" naturally leads to engaged action that seeks to transform unjust and oppressive structures. Put another way, Freire connects both conversion and rebirth to a dialogical posture in life that engages a never-ending process of reflection and action. Furthermore, this process is always tied to addressing "the fundamental theme of our epoch," which is domination. Rebirth, for Freire, thus requires social awareness and a social consciousness, and it should happen not just once, but continually.

Such viewpoints enable Freire to hold that conscientization, in fact, "*demands* that we die to be reborn again." He adds, "Christians must live their Easter, and that too is a utopia. Those who don't make their Easter, in the sense of dying in order to be reborn, are not real Christians."[40] Freire then continues with this remarkable passage:

> This is why Christianity is, for me, such a marvelous doctrine. People have accused me of being a communist, but no communist could say what I have just said. I never had any temptation to cease being, to stop

existing. The reason is that I am not yet completely a Catholic; I just
keep on trying to be one more completely, day after day. The condition of being is to go on being. I have never yet felt that I had to leave
the church, or set aside my Christian convictions, in order to say what
I have to say. . . . I just feel passionately, corporately, physically, with all
my being, that my stance is a Christian one because it is 100 percent
revolutionary and human and liberating, and hence committed and
utopian. And that, as I see it, must be our position, the position of a
church that must not forget it is called by its origins to die shivering in
the cold. This is a utopia; it is a denunciation and an announcement
with a historical commitment that adds up to heroism in love.[41]

In another early essay, Freire adds that "[t]his Easter, which results in the
changing of consciousness, must be existentially experienced. The real Easter
is not commemorative rhetoric. It is praxis; it is historical involvement. The
old Easter of rhetoric is dead—with no hope of resurrection. It is only in the
authenticity of historical praxis that Easter becomes the death that makes life
possible."[42]

For some, Freire's toggling back and forth between explicitly "religious"
language (like conversion, Easter, and resurrection) and more "secular" themes
(like communism, historical commitment, and existential experience) may
seem jarring. Indeed, as I discussed earlier, it may be much easier to compart-
mentalize Freire's existential, practical, and "objective" pedagogy from what
may be presumed to be his religious, idealist, and "subjective" theology. Such
a bifurcation becomes problematic, however, when we see that both sides of
this thought are equally reliant on acts of becoming.

To put the matter another way, there is an unmistakable emergentist thrust
to all of Freire's work that is expressed not only in terms of "becoming," but also
in terms of potentiality, possibility, and hope. In so many words, Freire's main
contribution may be seen as an attempt to shed light on *how* conscientization—as
a critical and dialogical pedagogy—may serve as a powerful *tool*, or *instrument*,
for authentic humanization. Because it must be constantly applied and reap-
plied, conscientization opens itself to *ongoing* forms of conversion.

When we put front and center the question of *how* human beings may become more fully human, perhaps quibbles over the particular kinds of language
that Freire uses (i.e., is it objective or subjective? idealist or practical? philosophical or religious? pedagogical or spiritual?) will seem increasingly beside
the point. Whether we characterize Freire's thought as a secular "critical pedagogy" or a religious "spiritual praxis"—or, indeed, whether we appreciate it
as both—one point remains true: "The pedagogy of the oppressed is an

*instrument* for [the] critical discovery that both [the oppressed] and their op-pressors are manifestations of dehumanization."[43] It is precisely the *instrumentality* of conscientization that reveals its power as a spiritual praxis.

Although my own method of analysis has, in part, drawn certain parallels between Freire's pedagogical work on conscientization and his more explicit religious writings, I reiterate that the overriding goal here is not simply to say that Freire's personal spirituality "informs" his pedagogy or that he can easily "translate" his ideas of conscientization into more spiritual language. In both cases, spirituality has a somewhat limited connotation having to do with Freire's particular religious affiliation with Roman Catholicism. Instead, I have attempted to show that conscientization itself may be understood as a spiritual praxis, if we take spirituality here in a more expansive light. As I have suggested, Freire would likely understand spirituality, in its most profound sense, as referring to the unceasing quest on the part of human beings to become more authentically human. This requires us to take responsibility for our historically conditioned relationships and to transform them actively when they prove dehumanizing.

I would like to close with an example from Freire's own life that he would have likely found profoundly spiritual. The reader may have noticed that throughout this chapter, I employed the Latin adverb *sic* after Freire's use of male-specific pronouns to acknowledge a general shift toward nongendered pronouns since the time Freire was writing. Tellingly, Freire recalls his own painful birth in coming to terms with his masculinist use of gendered pronouns. In what follows, I reproduce almost in its entirety Freire's 1983 reflection on this difficult process:

> I have a fantastic debt to women in [the US]. *Pedagogy of the Oppressed* came out [in English] September, 1970, and I began to receive letters from women all over the United States. It gave me the impression that there was a kind of conspiracy, but it was not. In all the letters they said to me, "How is it possible to say that you believe in the ability which men have to transform, and not women, too?" I wrote to all of them, thanking them for the lesson, and saying "Look, the only explanation I could give you, I right now can no longer give, because the only explanation I could give you would be a kind of ideology tract of *machismo*. And the explanation would be that when I say 'men' I include 'women.' And it is a lie."
>
> You cannot realize how the first letter I opened was a kind of explosion of light for me. That suddenly such a thing, so clear and obvious, which I spent years without understanding and perceiving, came up

suddenly. It was also one moment in which I became angry, not because of the women, but because of my past. I said to myself, "Is it possible to have lived such a quantity of years, ideologized in this way, explaining, giving classes on syntax, and lying like this?" This is not a question of syntax; it is a question of ideology, ideology through language. Then I wrote to all of them: "This is an explanation I never gave after receiving your letter. Then what can I say to you? First of all, thank you very much again, and second, that I will stop today writing the way I have written." In Portuguese it is difficult. Our languages are machistic. I say "her/his," or "human beings," and so on.

After reading the letters I came home, invited our two sons to have a private conversation in one of their rooms, and I said, "Look, sons, I have something very serious to tell you. We are exploiting the women of this house. And the women of this house are your mother and your two sisters. We don't cook. We don't clean house. We don't make our beds. This is impossible. We must start anew!" I've become an excellent dishwasher. Before the arrival of the letters from the American women, I used to ideologize and justify and rationalize in this way: Elza washes and cleans the house, the girls do the dishes, and I write! It's an absurdity! But in spite of my attempt and intention, it was not possible for me to cook. I do just eggs, coffee. But I tried one day to cook. I bought one kilo of filet, enormous, and in Geneva tremendously expensive. It was absolutely lost. I don't know what I did to that meat. It became plastic material. Even Elza was not able to restore it. But I am convinced that my lack of ability to cook is just ideology. There is resistance, machist resistance. I am sure of that . . .[44]

This passage beautifully exemplifies Freire's own ongoing process of conscientization. Clearly, the women who wrote to Freire were writing to confront their own dehumanizing situation of systematic erasure as a result of widespread male privilege, and they challenged Freire to address this reality. Through their letters, these women were becoming active agents in shaping their own history. Freire, the renowned teacher of freedom, became painfully aware of his own complicity as an oppressor of women. He became angry, not at the women, but at his past—for he, too, had been living in a system built around an ideological lie. He recognized that there has been "resistance, machist resistance" to change in his own life. His male-centered ways of thinking needed to die so that new ways of relating to women could be born. His conversion entailed not only a cognitive recognition of his folly, but also a concrete gesture that helped to restore the humanity of his critics: he wrote letters to the women, thanking them for what they had taught him. Moreover, in his own household, he moved the process of conscientization forward through a dialogue with his sons that concretely named the ways in which all of the males of the house were exploiting the females. As he took on new household chores, like washing the dishes and cooking, Freire's critical consciousness became an embodied praxis. In no small measure, daily life in Freire's household was concretely changed through the many ripple effects of conscientization.

Does this example of conscientization count as a spiritual praxis? Again, much rests on how narrowly—or expansively—we choose to envision spirituality. Freire, I believe, would have approached the question very generously. Although his own religious imaginary was no doubt shaped by formal religious affiliation, Freire did not limit his faith to the mere ideas and words of formal religious doctrine. Rather, he found more value in *activating* faith through the ongoing process of conscientization. Furthermore, he believed that conscientization and spirituality are most deeply rooted in embodied acts of love, as seen in the example of Christ and everyday human interactions. That said, Freire would most certainly remind us that loving "is not only a free act, it is an act *for* freedom."[45] The corollary here is that conscientization is not only a kind of spiritual boundary or crossroads (which is to say, a place, or a stage), but is itself the means by which we encounter new horizons. In this light, conscientization is a powerful summons to ourselves, an invitation to die willfully so that we are reborn again into fuller experiences of freedom.

# 3

# A Cosmic Vision from the Borderlands: Virgilio Elizondo's Evolutionary Cosmology

Virgilio Elizondo (1935–2016) is widely recognized as the father of US Latine theology, a close cousin of its Latin American counterpart, liberation theology. Both of these traditions are highly contextual and empirical discourses that take as their starting point human experience in concrete social and historical settings. Both champion liberative and praxis-based approaches that underscore how human action, when guided by critical reflection, may prove socially transformative. Part of Elizondo's genius was to marry a US Latine emphasis on cultural context with a Latin American emphasis on liberative praxis. Indeed, these are the two primary and overlapping lenses that scholars have used to interpret his thought.

As useful as these two interpretive keys are, this chapter offers a significantly enlarged reading of Elizondo that underscores his indebtedness to the French Jesuit scientist, paleontologist, theologian, and philosopher Pierre Teilhard de Chardin (1881–1955), who sought to reconcile Darwinian evolution and Christian theology. As I show, Elizondo's early writings evince a clear interest in Teilhard's evolutionary cosmology, which, I contend, implicitly informs all of his subsequent work. By reading Elizondo in this way, we gain significant insight into the deeply evolutionary and emergentist thrust of his theology, which, in turn, allows for more functional, pragmatic, and process-oriented renderings of two key motifs of his work: spirituality and mestizaje.

This chapter is divided into three sections. In the first section, I look at the ways in which Elizondo's life and work reflect a dual emphasis on culture and liberation. Clearly, Elizondo was interested as much in the cultural dimensions of liberation as he was in the liberating dimensions of culture. The second section expands this interpretative framework by homing in on Elizondo's work from the early 1970s, which borrows heavily from Teilhard's evolutionary framework. I argue that Elizondo's early exposure to Teilhard's work provides us with an important clue for understanding his mature thought. The third section looks at the ways in which Teilhard's influence on Elizondo is still noticeably present in his later writings, particularly Elizondo's 1988 work, *The Future Is Mestizo: Life Where Cultures Meet*. While many interpreters read Elizondo in light of José Vasconcelos's highly racialized understanding of mestizaje, I show that Elizondo's understanding of mestizaje is actually much closer to Teilhard's evolutionary cosmology. Such a reading helps us better appreciate the true novelty of Elizondo's understanding of spirituality and mestizaje alike.

## Culture and Liberation

Virgilio Elizondo's life and scholarship reflect his abiding interest in issues of culture and liberation. Born and raised in San Antonio, Texas, Elizondo describes growing up in a largely Mexican-American community that was infused with life and love. "Looking back, I can see that [my family] was not rich or even middle class," he writes, "but we never lacked anything, especially a lot of personal care and affection. . . . In fact, I think we were truly of a privileged class—one in which tender, loving concern was the ordinary rule of the day and in which hard work was intermingled with many good times."[1] Elizondo's father, who never studied beyond the third grade, endured many hardships, including "long working hours, poor living conditions, [and] harsh treatment because he was a working nephew and not one of the sons of the family." But these hardships, Elizondo writes, "did not embitter him or dampen his enthusiasm. . . . His constant sense of humor and his great generosity toward those in need are still legendary among those who knew him."[2]

By contrast, Elizondo's mother came from a more privileged background, born to a wealthy family in Mexico City. However, with the unexpected death of her father, coupled with a situation of great political unrest in Mexico, the family dropped from wealth to poverty almost overnight. Fortunately, Elizondo's great-aunt (his grandmother's older sister) had married a man from the United States who brought the family to Texas. The family had to adjust quickly from a life of privilege to a life of struggle and hard work, including exposure to various racial and class inequities. Elizondo recounts, for example, the experience that his mother had at a Catholic college for young women: "My mother never forgot when one of the nuns asked her to give her class work to one of the wealthy girls in the class because the wealthy girl's parents would never understand her low grade!" For Elizondo, this situation was emblematic

of larger social dynamics and reflected an "unwritten law of so many civilizations": those with "little or nothing" are expected to give what little they have
to those who "already [have] too much."[3]

This example is also telling because it takes place within a religious context. Notably, Elizondo never shies away from pointing out how the church
itself has perpetuated injustice. Elizondo describes two very different experiences of church. On the one hand, some of his earliest experiences of school
and church were, in fact, joyful. He describes his Mexican-American church
as "the center of life." It was "the community living room where we all met
and enjoyed each other. From birth to baptism to the last anointing and fu-
neral it permeated our lives and gave us the experience of being a united
family."[4] Similarly, Elizondo speaks fondly of his earliest schooling experience
in his local parish kindergarten, which was operated by Mexican nuns. For
Elizondo, kindergarten was "simply an extension of the home." The sisters
"did their shopping in [our family's] grocery store as did the parish priests.
They frequently visited our home, and all the families from the area felt
welcome in the convent and kindergarten. . . . We had a wonderful experience of belonging."[5]

On the other hand, however, these positive experiences of church and
schooling quickly changed when Elizondo transferred to a Catholic grade
school operated by German nuns. The "paradise existence" of his neighborhood
"came to a halt." At the new school, the pastor "still told Mexicans to go away
because it wasn't their church." At best, "Mexicans were tolerated but not very
welcome."[6] Elizondo describes his years at the school as a "real purgatory." The
sisters and lay teachers were strict disciplinarians. "I don't think I ever saw them
smile," he wrote, "but I remember them well hitting us frequently with a ruler
or a stick. They were the exact opposite of the Mexican sisters around our home
who were always happy, joking, and smiling and formed us carefully through
counsels, suggestions, and rewards."[7] Even mass was different: Elizondo found
it "orderly and stern," and people "seemed to be in pain and even afraid of
being there." To him, mass in this new church was "recited but not celebrated."
It was "a church of discipline, but it was not one of joy." Elizondo sums up all
of these contradictions in a telling sentence: "It seemed like a totally different
religion."[8]

Years later, Elizondo attended St. Mary's University in San Antonio, Texas,
where he majored in chemistry, with the hopes of becoming a medical doctor
or psychiatrist. "Yet as university studies proceeded," he writes, "I became more
and more convinced that the best way to work with people—especially my
own people, many of whom were poor, uneducated, and unemployed—would
be through the church." In this regard, Elizondo was particularly impressed

by the archbishop of San Antonio, Robert E. Lucey, who was "an untiring champion of the rights of the poor and of the need to work for a just society."[9]

After college, Elizondo entered the local seminary "with very high expectations," but as he explains, these expectations "were soon very soon shattered." Not only was the level of teaching mediocre, but it was also evident that Mexicans were not welcome. As Elizondo recounts, "[t]here were always racial slurs and lots of laughter and ridicule about the stupid practice of Mexican Catholics. I hated it! Seminary for me was a bad experience."[10] Along with Elizondo, a few Mexican Catholics "managed to survive—probably because we saw the seminary more as an obstacle course to be conquered than a place for learning and development."[11]

Why then, one may ask, did Elizondo decide to stay in the seminary? As Elizondo acknowledges, the seminary experience was "not totally negative—just the classes and formation program." In fact, he developed many good friends among the faculty and seminarians. He recounts:

> Summers were good and we often visited one another. I started to become close friends with seminarians of German, Polish, and Czech backgrounds and would visit them in their ethnic communities. Some of the best times I ever had were with them. By their bringing me into their families and by my inviting them to become part of my family we were becoming a new family—our differences were no longer barriers to our friendship.[12]

Elizondo also notes that he continued to receive support from the Carmelite priests of his home parish, whom he describes as "hospitable, friendly, and encouraging."[13]

In many ways, Elizondo's seminary experience gave rise to a cultural awareness that was painful and, yet, also hopeful. He experienced firsthand the grief of racial, cultural, and class antagonisms, but he also learned how to embrace his "otherness" as a strength rather than as a deficiency. Furthermore, he actively formed new relationships across lines of racial difference, and he began to see the power of unity-in-difference.

Elizondo had a similar kind of awakening during the summer of 1968 while flying over Mexico City with one of his academic mentors, Professor Jacques Audinet of Paris. It was on that flight that Audinet told Elizondo how he had been captivated by the Plaza de las Tres Culturas in Mexico City, particularly by an inscription there that marked the site of the final battle between Hernán Cortés and the Aztecs. The inscription read, "Neither a defeat nor a victory, but the painful birth of the *mestizo* people that is Mexico today." This inscription resonated deeply with Elizondo because it recast the conquest as a form of new birth.[14] As he explained, it inspired him to discover "the new mestizaje of the Southwest that was pulling Anglos and Mexican-Americans alike into the formation of a new humanity. . . . As I consciously rewalked the historical pilgrimage, no longer through the categories of conquest but through the categories of birth, I saw the identity of the new being in a new light."[15] This newfound appreciation for categories like "new birth" and "new being" proved pivotal for all of Elizondo's subsequent work, especially his numerous books and essays on Jesus (whom Elizondo interprets as a Galilean "mestizo") and Guadalupe (whom he often describes as the "mother of the new creation").

As such biographical anecdotes help to illustrate, Elizondo learned how to reinterpret forms of cultural exclusion as catalysts to new forms of freedom. Such a reinterpretation was made possible by Elizondo's overall approach to theology. His theological method was not top-down and deductive, nor did he take *a priori* doctrines as his starting point. Rather, he approached theology as a bottom-up, inductive enterprise that begins in the ebb and flow of everyday life, in all of its social, cultural, and historical particularities. Furthermore, he understood that a major task of theology was to help redress social inequities to help usher forth the Kingdom of God in the here and now. In this sense, Elizondo was a consummate contextual theologian who had a clear dual interest in culture and liberation.

Along these lines, scholars often identify two types of contextual theology: ethnographic and liberationist. Whereas ethnographic approaches tend to focus on the nuances and complexities of cultural identity and social location, liberationist approaches emphasize social ills and the need for social change. Both privilege the wisdom and agency of minority cultures who undergo theological inculturation, and both provide important alternatives to older "translation" and "adaptation" models of inculturation, which either saw minority cultures as static or as mere reflections of dominant worldviews.[16]

In his scholarly work, Elizondo weaves together ethnographic and liberationist perspectives. As a good liberationist, he calls attention to structural injustice and mobilizes theology to redress needless forms of human suffering. But he also engages the process of liberation from the standpoint of one's own cultural and social location. In an exemplary passage, Elizondo explains:

> The beginning of liberation is the image of ourselves that we experience within the deepest recess of our hearts. . . . The realization that one has self-worth, fundamental dignity, radical equality, and love is the innermost and deepest beginning of liberation. It certainly does not stop there. But, on the other hand, there is no other authentic beginning.[17]

In this passage, liberation is clearly an overarching theme. Yet, for Elizondo, the *starting point* of liberation is always the recognition of one's self-worth and inherent dignity. Elizondo believes that for those on the underside of history, cultural awareness can be a powerful tool in affirming one's sense of individual and communal agency.

The twin lenses of culture and liberation help to illuminate Elizondo's significance for theology. But there are certain aspects within Elizondo's thought that call for an even wider angle of vision. How, for instance, do we make sense of Elizondo's cosmic sensibility, his deep appreciation for evolving forms of religiosity, and his inclusive and pluralistic understanding of human spirituality? Among other places, these questions are brought to the fore when Elizondo reflects on his twelve years serving as rector of the San Fernando Cathedral in San Antonio, Texas. As he observes, the "spirit energy of [faith's] living mystery goes far beyond the cathedral." "Where," he asks, "does this spiritual energy come from?" Then, in a most remarkable passage, he writes:

> As I celebrated the early pre-dawn daily Mass during any given day of the week, I felt always that we were energizing the entire city of San Antonio for one more day. As I offered the Holy Sacrifice, I felt that I was in continuity with Jesus who sacrificed himself to give us life, and with our Aztec ancestors who offered pre-dawn sacrifices to ensure that the sun would rise another day. I was in continuity with the generations from time immemorial who struggled and sacrificed to make this space of earth a more hospitable home for anyone who comes here. It was like "fueling up" the spiritual engines that give life to our city.[18]

I find it fascinating how Elizondo invokes his Aztec ancestors while celebrating daily mass in San Antonio. How, if at all, does an ethnographic and/or liberationist framework account for an experience like this, which is a radical expression of religious pluralism by a Catholic priest? In what follows, I argue that a question like this is best answered when we begin to account for the cosmic vision that Elizondo internalized from Teilhard de Chardin.

## A Wider Frame: Elizondo's Evolutionary Cosmology

Pierre Teilhard de Chardin was a French Jesuit philosopher, theologian, Christian mystic, and scientist who studied human origins. He had an equally passionate love for science and God, and his work attempted to show the compatibility between Darwinian science and Christian theology. During his life, he was prohibited by the Catholic Church from publishing any nonscientific works. As a result, his philosophical and theological writings were published only after his death in 1955, although they had been circulated clandestinely before. His two most celebrated books were *The Divine Milieu* (1957) and his magnum opus, *The Phenomenon of Man* (1955), which was subsequently republished, retranslated, and retitled as *The Human Phenomenon* (1999).

Teilhard saw evolution developing over billions of years through four levels or stages. "Cosmogenesis" represents the evolution of the *physical* universe; "biogenesis" describes the evolution of *life* in the physical universe; "psychogenesis" reflects the evolution of *consciousness* in biological organisms; and "noogenesis" captures the evolution of *reflective thought*, a characteristic that is unique to humans. Teilhard believed that with the evolution of humans, which began a mere 200,000 years ago, a "threshold of reflection" was crossed that fundamentally altered the very course of evolution, for evolution could now proceed more intentionally and rapidly through human intelligence. This led Teilhard to posit his most controversial idea: he believed that over time, human minds would eventually form a web of reflective consciousness that would envelope the earth, which he called the "noosphere." Teilhard believed that the noosphere would, at some point, reach an omega point where human consciousness would completely fuse with the God who created it.[19]

Philosophically speaking, Teilhard is an important contributor to the tradition known as "process thought." Like G. W. F. Hegel and Friedrich Schelling who saw development, process, and change as constitutive of reality, Teilhard upheld the notion of God's actual growth and dependence on the world. More directly, Teilhard was influenced by Henri Bergson's *Creative Evolution* (1907), which saw the world as deeply immersed in the process of evolution. In addition, like Alfred North Whitehead, Teilhard gleaned theological insight from this, positing that the world overflowed with the presence of the divine which made the world itself a cosmic and mystical "divine milieu." Ursula King, one of Teilhard's foremost interpreters, comments on the uniqueness of this vision. As she explains, Teilhard's phenomenology gives us insight into what reality not only *is*, but also *how it comes to be* through human coparticipation in the evolutionary process. As King explains:

> [Teilhard] emphasizes the study of all phenomena by relating outer
> to inner "seeing." Such seeing involves the correlation of scientific
> knowledge of the outer world with a unifying inner vision, whereby the
> world is seen as held together by "Spirit." This holistic approach leads
> to a profound transformation of the seeing person and the world as
> seen, for seeing more implies being more.[20]

Put another way, seeing is not simply an act of putting a mirror to nature to obtain a reflection of it. Rather, seeing is at once an interaction with and transformation of reality. Or, to use more pragmatic language, seeing is simultaneously a process of both "undergoing" and "doing."

Ideas like these had a significant influence on Elizondo. Teilhard's impact on Elizondo is most evident in his first book, *The Human Quest: A Search for Meaning Through Life and Death*, which was published in 1971, during a time when Elizondo was studying at a pastoral center in Manila, Philippines—in itself, a rich cross-cultural experience. Like Teilhard, Elizondo frames his approach to religion within the context of evolution; remarkably, of the book's thirty-two citations, more than half reference the work of Teilhard.

In this early publication, Elizondo draws on Teilhard in at least three ways. First, as already suggested, Teilhard gives Elizondo a useful framework for thinking about evolution as it has developed over billions of years through four evolutionary stages: cosmogenesis, biogenesis, psychogenesis, and noogenesis. Not surprisingly, Elizondo, like Teilhard, is especially interested in noogenesis and the ways in which humankind may further develop reflective thought and consciousness in the future. Second, Elizondo picks up on Teilhard's idea that God is always emerging. For both thinkers, God is not a divine power that exists above and beyond the natural world; rather, God is a life force that is part of the evolutionary process itself. In a passage that directly references Teilhard, Elizondo identifies a "certain consciousness within all matter" that, over the course of millions of years, "has been bringing about the development of the lesser forms into higher forms of existence." Elizondo then goes on to describe this process in terms of God's creative act. He writes, "We could say that there is only one creative act of God that has been going on for billions of years, is going on now, and will continue to go on."[21] Such a view of the divine clearly meshes with Teilhard's emergent and "cosmic" view of God that spans all space and time. Third, Elizondo is drawn to Teilhard's delicate balance between human action and divine insight. On the one hand, Elizondo resonates with Teilhard's insistence that Christians should never shirk from their responsibility to help actively build the Kingdom of God in the here and now. Both theologians reject Christian inaction and resignation in the face of evil, and Elizondo quotes Teilhard directly: "It is therefore of supreme importance for the Christian to understand and live submission to the will of God in an *active* sense which, as we have said, is the only orthodox sense."[22] On the other hand, both Elizondo and Teilhard recognize that there are always limits to our action and knowledge. As such, they acknowledge and accept certain types of Christian "resignation." Elizondo explains, "[I]n all human successes and failures, the Christian recognizes in faith a further dimension, suprasensible transformation and growth. The resignation of a Christian is not a psychological escape from reality. It is a trust that lifts the field of [their] activity above the zone of sensible reality."[23] Thus, as Elizondo explains, Christian "renun-ciation" must always satisfy two conditions: it must inspire development of this world, and it must afford human beings the space to go beyond everything in the world. In a most interesting way, Elizondo wraps up this discussion by paraphrasing the "Serenity Prayer" by Reinhold Niebuhr, who shared many of Elizondo's theological proclivities: "Give me the strength to change what has to be changed, the courage to accept what cannot be changed, and the wisdom to distinguish the two."[24]

Not many scholars have looked in earnest at Teilhard's influence on Eli-zondo, but two contributions stand out. In his introduction to Elizondo's *Spiritual Writings*, Timothy Matovina notes that, although Elizondo cites Teilhard "only occasionally" in his later writings, Teilhard's *The Human Phenomenon* grounds Elizondo's "deep convictions about God's cosmic design to redeem not only humanity but all of creation."[25] Alejandro García-Rivera similarly notes Teilhard's deep imprint on Elizondo. In an important essay entitled "Crossing Theological Borders: Virgilio Elizondo's Place Among Theologians of Culture," García-Rivera draws a connection between Latin American ec-clesial experience and Elizondo's early work regarding a sense of "the cosmic." García-Rivera argues that unlike other leading theologians of culture, such as Ernst Troeltsch and Paul Tillich, who "saw culture as separate from nature, Elizondo, like Teilhard, sees not a dichotomy but a mysterious unity. As such, Elizondo follows the intuition of the great religions that existed in the Americas before Christianity came."[26] Furthermore, García-Rivera convincingly argues that "[i]t is Teilhard who gives Elizondo the key 'New Creation' theme that will be heard in all his writings."[27]

Although Elizondo cites Teilhard less frequently in his later writings, one can nevertheless discern a clear and lasting imprint. It should come as no surprise, for instance, that Elizondo's remarks about invoking his Aztec ances-tors while offering daily mass sound strikingly similar to Teilhard's own cele-brated "Mass on the World," in which Teilhard, standing on the soil of China, makes the entire earth his altar. In both cases, we see two visionary priests reimagining the mass in ways that carry messages of renewal and new creation far beyond the institutional strictures of organized Catholicism. Indeed, one could argue that their cosmic visions are logical extensions of worldviews that are deeply "catholic" (small "c"), which is to say, radically universal.

## The Future Is Mestizo

In this section, I focus on Teilhard's lingering influence on Elizondo in *The Future Is Mestizo: Life Where Cultures Meet* (1988). Published nearly two decades after *The Human Quest*, Elizondo's book carries important echoes of Teilhard. The book is quintessential Elizondo: the first two chapters tell the story of Elizondo's own experience as a Mexican-American living in South Texas, which includes experiences of both cultural affirmation and cultural exclusion. Subsequent chapters touch on several key themes that Elizondo develops at length in other works. Such themes include reflections on racial and cultural oppression (chapters 3–4), Guadalupe (chapter 5), the Galilean (mestizo) Jesus (chapter 6), and a reflection on the possibility of "universal mestizaje" (chapter 7). For the most part, the first six chapters, with their focus on questions of culture and freedom, can be easily read as contributions to ethnographic and/or liberationist models of contextual theology. However, the final chapter, entitled "Towards a Universal Mestizaje," charts new territory, moving well beyond ethnographic or liberationist concerns. It is here that Elizondo breaks new ground in reconceptualizing spirituality and its relation to mestizaje. Not surprisingly, it is also here that Elizondo once again invokes Teilhard.

Elizondo explains what universal mestizaje is with a direct reference to Teilhard. He writes, "Following the categories of Teilhard de Chardin, it seems that we are witnessing the birth of a new phylum of human life, the breakthrough to a truly human family. As in any breakthrough, it will not come about without much pain, suffering, turmoil, and confusion, for the introduction of something truly new is not easily understood or appreciated." That said, Elizondo understands the "new mestizaje" as evidence of a partial breakthrough to "a new humanity."[28]

This perfunctory—yet significant—reference to Teilhard invites us to consider just how prominently the French Jesuit continues to shape Elizondo's thought. Indeed, when we step back and observe the principal moves that Elizondo is making in this last chapter, we can see insights that take inspiration from Teilhard's work and build on it. Two examples help to illustrate this point.

First, Elizondo begins his chapter on universal mestizaje with a discussion of the power of dreaming. He opens the chapter with these lines: "The future begins in the dream of what could and ought to be. When they are first announced, such dreams often appear as naive, simplistic, impossible, destructive of good order, and heretical. Yet dreams are the sparks of discoveries that allow us to transcend the barriers of present-day limitations of life."[29] Elizondo notes that just as the prophet Isaiah and Jesus of Nazareth dreamed of a future in which all would be one, so, too, did Simón Bolívar dream of "a united America without national borders" and Martin Luther King, Jr. dream of a future of racial freedom and economic justice. "We need to dare to dream," writes

Elizondo, "even when the dreams appear too optimistic or even unrealizable. . . . The dream is the spark that gives hope and the start of a new life."[30]

On the one hand, this passage may be read in light of Elizondo's eschatological Christian vision. Jesus's announcement of the Kingdom of God as already present in history, yet not realized in its fullness, is indeed an animating source for Elizondo's theology. On the other hand, one could also say that Teilhard gives Elizondo new insight into this idea by reframing it in the context of science and evolution. In such a frame, evolution itself is a sign of the in-breaking of God's kingdom that will continue to reveal itself more fully through the aid the aid of human hands and human intelligence, via conscientization.[31]

Elizondo's appeal here to dreams and hope is, admittedly, highly speculative. Such a mystical and cosmic approach has engendered criticisms of both Teilhard and Elizondo alike. Many "left-brain" critics who are drawn to analytical and logical forms of argumentation and derive meaning from existing thought patterns find it difficult to enter into the "right-brain" thinking of Teilhard and Elizondo, who favored more imaginative, intuitive, and generative modes of analysis and sought altogether new patterns of meaning. Fortunately, Teilhard and Elizondo would find common company with a host of thinkers within the traditions of pragmatism and process thought, from C. S. Peirce (who underscored the value of abductive, or hypothetical, reasoning) to the more recent work of John Cobb (who prioritized nonsensory forms of human experience, such as memory, as disclosive of God.)

Second, one can chart Elizondo's pluralistic approach to religions and his expansive understanding of spirituality alongside Teilhard's cosmic imaginary. As mentioned earlier, the first six chapters of *The Future Is Mestizo* are dedicated largely to a discussion of cultural mestizaje, particularly as it pertains to cultural mixture in the Americas. These chapters would surely lend credibility to an interpretation of Elizondo as a "cultural theologian." But in the final chapter of the book, Elizondo shifts, in a most interesting way, from a discussion of cultural mestizaje to a consideration of cosmic mestizaje, using religious mestizaje as his go-between.

What does he mean by these ideas, and how does he link them? Given Elizondo's role as a Catholic priest who must always keep in mind the dictates of official church doctrine, Elizondo, like Teilhard, moves boldly yet carefully toward a cosmic vision of spirituality that conforms to, but may still exceed, more traditional interpretations of faith.[32] Elizondo's first move in this regard is to show how some of the official decrees of Vatican II, such as *Nostra Aetate* and *Ad Gentes*, evince a clear appreciation for other religions. According to Elizondo:

[Vatican II] perceive(s) and proclaim(s) the gospel in its most dynamic and original way, no longer in terms of opposing peoples and their religions, but as the new unifying power capable of piercing through almost impenetrable boundaries and creating a new human fellowship. To many of us ordinary Catholics, this proclamation would not only have been unthinkable but would have sounded totally heretical before the Council.

Driving the point home even further, Elizondo adds: "A Copernican revolution in our official outlook toward other religions and our relation to them had been officially proclaimed by our church."[33]

With this doctrinal support in place, Elizondo then proceeds, somewhat gingerly, to discuss the implications that such teachings have for the creation of a new humanity. With a cautious and careful tone, he writes:

I suspect the deepest question, which we are even afraid to pose, is this: Is religious *mestizaje* possible? Given the fact that religion is the deepest and most unifying element of culture, can there be true cultural *mestizaje* without a corresponding religious *mestizaje*? I have no doubt that many would recoil at the thought of such a possibility. Yet can we speak of a true universal fellowship without addressing the question of religious *mestizaje*?[34]

The last five pages of *The Future Is Mestizo* attempt to unpack this question, and it is here that one can again see Teilhard's imprint on Elizondo. Elizondo explains what he means by religious mestizaje. He reminds readers that, like cultural mestizaje, religious mestizaje has been a source of both strife and new life. Such has been the case with Mexican mestizaje, which "although painful and negative at many moments of the process, can today play a positive role because its religious symbolism provides the synthesis of two apparently irreconcilable religions: Spanish Catholicism and the native American religions."[35] Elizondo goes on to give several other examples of what he calls "hyphenated-existences" including "Jewish-Christian, Gentile-Christian, Afro-Christians, Asian-Christians, *Mestizo*-Christians." Anecdotally, he also mentions a good friend of his who is a Catholic priest/Buddhist monk and who "says that his Buddhism has helped him to be a better Catholic and his Catholicism has helped him to be a better Buddhist."[36]

Examples like these may give readers the impression that Elizondo's understanding of religious mestizaje is premised on the coming together of two different religious traditions. After all, if cultural mestizaje represents the coming together of two or more different *cultures*, then it would stand to reason that religious mestizaje is the coming together of two more different *religions*. While this may be true in part, Elizondo also invites the reader to think about religious mestizaje in a much more profound, pragmatic, and cosmic way.

On my reading, Elizondo approaches religious mestizaje, first and foremost, in terms of the *actions and attitudes* that are required when encountering difference in the first place. Stated another way, Elizondo is not simply interested in how different religions can inform one another. Rather, he seems to be asking: In what ways might one's *active engagement* with difference and otherness qualify as religious or spiritual? Furthermore, what are the *effects* of this active engagement? In light of such questions, the proper starting point for making sense of religious mestizaje has less to do with one's particular religious identification and more to do with the practical outcomes of one's active encounter with difference and otherness. At root, Elizondo is interested in how one's *active encounter* with difference may *function* in life-giving and liberating ways.

We see this perhaps most clearly in Elizondo's discussion of the praxis of Jesus. In a pivotal passage, he writes:

> Jesus invites all to a conversion from their old ways to the way of the love of God, neighbor, enemy, and one another. And who are neighbors? In the story of the Good Samaritan Jesus makes it clear: not necessarily those who share the same religion and the same culture, but those who act on behalf of the other in need. For Jesus, love of the other allows us to go beyond all our barriers and even transgress our religious taboos if necessary for the sake of the other in need. Jesus does not destroy religion but he does defy its sacralized and absolutized limitations and barriers. His only absolute is the universal love of all people.[37]

In this passage, we hear echoes of Teilhard in Elizondo's reference to universal love as the only true absolute in the cosmos. Much like Teilhard (and, as we saw in Chapter 2, Paulo Freire), Elizondo believes that historical religions can indeed help guide humanity toward God's universal love, yet he acknowledges that they can be limited by their own hubris. This is clearly seen in the story of the Good Samaritan. In this story, a traveler is robbed, beaten, stripped of clothing, and left to die on the side of the road. In succession, two men who share the victim's religious and cultural background pass by and ignore him. Then, a man from the despised region of Samaria, a man who would have been a religious and cultural "outsider" to the victim in need, takes pity on him and makes sure that he is properly cared for. As the story shows, the true test of faith has less to do with how one identifies religiously and more to do with how one actively *responds* to the needs of others—especially those who are despised and discarded—even if this response appears to some as doctrinally taboo.

This passage is also significant because it shows how Elizondo maps onto his Teilhardian framework a clear preferential option for the poor. It is significant that Elizondo describes God's "universal love of all people" within the context of the liberating praxis of the Good Samaritan. The parable shows that it is precisely through one's active engagement with "the least of these" that God's cosmic love becomes manifest. In other words, Elizondo shows how human beings can help to bring about the new creation by accompanying the marginalized and seeing our lives and questions from their perspective. In so doing, Elizondo adds an important prophetic dimension to his Teilhardian cosmic imaginary. Ever mindful of the physical and psychic damage that was inflicted through New World colonization, Elizondo understands human evolution and spiritual advancement not only in terms of natural processes of evolutionary growth, but also in terms of humankind's ability—and ethical mandate—to respond to needless forms of suffering. For Elizondo, a preferential option for the poor and oppressed is therefore a core expression of God's ever-expanding evolutionary love.

Reading Elizondo alongside Teilhard allows us to appreciate his thoughts in new and creative ways. Such an interpretation helps to take Elizondo out of the sometimes-narrow boxes of culture and/or liberation. To be sure, Elizondo is indeed *both* a theologian of culture *and* a theologian of liberation, but he is also much more. If nothing else, a Teilhardian reading of Elizondo helps us to see that his concept of the new humanity may far exceed present-day notions of cultural and racial intermixing. For Elizondo, the new humanity is never static but, rather, always moving forward, emerging, becoming.

This emergentist vision of the new humanity offers a very different picture of mestizaje than the one that is often attributed to Elizondo. Scholars like Néstor Medina and Rubén Rosario Rodríguez have faulted Elizondo for subscribing to a notion of mestizaje that, to them, looks much like José Vasconcelos's understanding of the term.[38] As these authors rightly point out, Vasconcelos employs an essentialized, outmoded, and at times, racist notion of mestizaje, as seen in his book *La Raza Cósmica* (1925). In this work, Vasconcelos approaches mestizaje as a form of biological and cultural mixing that will lead to a new cosmic race. Vasconcelos believes that, in time, this new "fifth race" will morally and aesthetically transcend the racial differences of the previous four races, which he identifies as Black, Indian, Mongol, and white, thus yielding a racial type that is "infinitely superior to all that have previously existed."[39]

There is wide consensus among scholars that Vasconcelos's position is problematic on a number of levels. As Medina and Rosario Rodríguez correctly show, although Vasconcelos's aim is to call into question Anglo-Saxon notions of racial superiority, his appeal to static racial types, in which the Spanish play a redeeming role in history, ultimately reinscribes racial hierarchies that are both essentialist and deeply Eurocentric. Moreover, Vasconcelos naïvely believes that, unlike the Europeans, the Spanish did not conquer and destroy the native peoples of the New World but rather "fused" with them ethnically and spiritually. Such a position dangerously sugarcoats the violence that was inflicted on Indigenous peoples by the Spanish colonizers.[40]

As instructive as Medina's and Rosario Rodríguez's critiques of Vasconcelos are, we should nonetheless ask if Vasconcelos is really the right frame of reference for decoding Elizondo's understanding of mestizaje. Although Elizondo and Vasconcelos invoke the term *mestizaje* to describe biological mixing, there are notable differences. To begin with, Elizondo does not sugarcoat mestizaje. He is consistent in naming the conquest for what it was: a violent encounter that destroyed human bodies and ruptured—but never completely annulled— Indigenous worldviews. Even when Elizondo does speak of this violent encounter as a "new beginning," for him, these two realities are not mutually exclusive: as his ruminations on the Plaza de las Tres Culturas makes clear, 1492 marks a moment of *both* death *and* new life.

Furthermore, virtually nowhere in his writings does Elizondo discuss or cite Vasconcelos.[41] In fact, a 2004 interview with Elizondo in the *National Catholic Reporter* raises the point explicitly. After establishing that Teilhard was an early influence on Elizondo, the interviewer directly asks Elizondo if his understanding of mestizaje was influenced by Vasconcelos. "No, not really," Elizondo replies, adding: "Vasconcelos had the idea that the Europeans were going to improve the indigenous races through mestizaje. I see it as a meeting of equals."[42] As this statement suggests, Elizondo is not following an assimilationist model of mestizaje that privileges racial whitening. Rather, he is much closer to a transcultural and pluralistic model of cultural encounter that affirms the agency of colonized groups.[43] A Teilhardian reading of Elizondo brings this fact into better focus.

As the celebrated historian Gary Nash points out, there were *two* "utopian vision[s] of a thoroughly intermixed cosmic race" that were prevalent in North America between the two world wars: Vasconcelos's version *and* Teilhard's version.[44] If García-Rivera is correct that it is primarily Teilhard (and not Vasconcelos) who gives Elizondo his ubiquitous new creation theme, then we should make explicit the philosophical differences between these two thinkers.

When we do so, we see that, whereas Vasconcelos couched mestizaje's new creation theme within a Platonic framework of timeless universals, Teilhard approaches new creation within an evolutionary and pragmatic understanding of constant change.[45] As *The Future Is Mestizo* helps to show, Elizondo clearly picks up Teilhard's philosophical cues. For Elizondo, mestizaje is not a fixed, racialized state of being, but rather an open-ended experience of always becoming.

Ultimately, reading Elizondo through the lens of Teilhard allows us to see better the more process-oriented and pragmatic sides of his thought. For Elizondo, as for Teilhard, spirituality can no longer be understood as the sole purview of a single religious tradition (namely, Catholicism) but is, instead, an always-emerging quality and function of human experience at large. Spirituality in this sense is an ongoing and deep-seated response to one's ever-changing environment. To be sure, both Teilhard and Elizondo believe that the Catholic tradition has much to offer in nurturing this kind of spiritual orientation, and, indeed, they draw on insights from within the tradition that speak to this more pluralistic and evolutionary sensibility. At the same time, however, they also recognize that this kind of spirituality can never be exhausted by a single tradition, Catholicism included. In an ever-expanding cosmos that is continuously disclosing its own novelty, the future is just too open-ended for it to be otherwise.[46]

Part of Elizondo's great contribution is to show that cosmic emergence does not come without pain, confusion, intolerance, and at times, violence. Moreso than Teilhard, Elizondo is attuned to how these difficult experiences manifest themselves in the twentieth and twenty-first centuries, with special attention to his own Mexican-American community. Furthermore, Elizondo foregrounds how evolutionary growth can be significantly aided by a preferential option for the poor. For Elizondo, we help to cocreate the new humanity through our active responses to situations of suffering. All of this said, it is important to note that Elizondo's contextualism is not limited to present-day problems, nor is it held captive to static conceptions of culture or race. Rather, owing largely to the influence of Teilhard, Elizondo's spiritual orientation is expansive, forward-looking, and dynamic, remaining always open to the promise of new life in whatever new and surprising forms it may emerge.

# 4

# Spiritual Activism as Conocimiento: Gloria Anzaldúa's Mature Spirituality

Gloria Anzaldúa (1942–2004) has been hailed as one of most important cultural theorists of the past fifty years. Her work, especially her pioneering *Borderlands/La Frontera: The New Mestiza* (1987), continues to animate many contemporary discourses, especially those concerned with cultural and linguistic hybridity, intersectionality, and women of color feminism. Yet one may ask: What is Anzaldúa's distinctive contribution to contemporary discourses of spirituality and religion? In a 1993 interview, Anzaldúa herself lays bare the relative inattention that critics have given to her understanding of spirituality:

> One of the things that doesn't get talked about is the connection between body, mind, and spirit—anything that has to do with the sacred, anything that has to do with the spirit. As long as it's theoretical and about history, about borders, that's fine; borders are a concern that everybody has. But when I start talking about nepantla— as a border between the spirit, the psyche, and the mind or as a process—they resist.[1]

Building on the work of recent scholarship, I take up that challenge by reflecting on Anzaldúa's recently published, posthumous work, *Light in the Dark/Luz en lo oscuro: Rewriting Identity, Spirituality, Reality,* which stands as her most mature and explicit articulation of a *nepantla*, or "in-between" spirituality. I show that *Light in the Dark* offers us some important clues for understanding the intricacies of Anzaldúa's spiritual vision. In particular, I underscore the importance of the praxis- and process-oriented dimensions of her understanding of what she calls "spiritual activism." Anzaldúa urges us to confront the destructive and violent aspects of our world through conocimiento, a nonbinary and transformative mode of thinking. But, in doing so, she urges us "to respond not just with the traditional practice of spirituality (contemplation, meditation, and private rituals) or with the technologies of political activism (protests, demonstrations, and speakouts), but with the amalgam of the two: spiritual activism."[2] In many respects, Anzaldúa's understanding of spiritual activism significantly broadens her earlier forays into epistemology, which center around key concepts like mestiza consciousness, la facultad, and conocimiento.

I argue that Anzaldúa's articulation of spiritual activism in *Light in the Dark* helps counterpoise her somewhat conflicting stances on spiritual realism. Over the course of her career, Anzaldúa wrestled with the question "Are spirits real?" Before the publication of *Light in the Dark*, she appears most often to subscribe to one of two positions: a realist position (which assumes that spirits are indeed real) and a pluralist position (which affirms that spirits are both literally and imaginally present). While *Light in the Dark* continues to echo both positions, it also introduces a third functionalist and pragmatic option that sets Anzaldúa's understanding of spirituality in a new light: what really matters, Anzaldúa suggests, is whether the spiritual journey makes positive changes in a person's life. In light of these three positions, I show how the functionalist position meshes best with Anzaldúa's underlying commitment to spiritual activism as a nonreductive form of praxis, thus providing an important alternative to the cul-de-sacs of metaphysical realism.

The first section of this chapter offers a brief biographical sketch of Anzaldúa that serves both to contextualize her work and to provide a framework for understanding her own connection to spirituality. "Religion, whatever it is, is man's total reaction upon life," William James once wrote.[3] Having a sense of the totality of Anzaldúa's life is thus a helpful step in appreciating both her deep commitment to various forms of activism and her own heterodox experiences of spirituality. The second section looks at Anzaldúa's discussion of spiritual realism and some of the internal tensions within it. In the third section, I show how a pragmatic reading of her mature articulation of spiritual activism provides a key to help her readers adjudicate these incongruities.

## A Life Rooted in Activism

Gloria Evangelina Anzaldúa was born a seventh-generation Mexican-American on September 26, 1942, in the South Texas town of Raymondville. For the first seven years of her life, Anzaldúa lived on a ranch settlement that had no electricity or running water.[4] She learned at an early age how difficult farm labor could be, an experience that "instilled in her a deep respect for farm laborers."[5]

Adding to this hardship, Anzaldúa was diagnosed in infancy with a rare hormonal disorder that caused genital bleeding starting at three months old and monthly menses starting at age six. This condition caused her daily pain, which she lived with for thirty-five years until she had a hysterectomy at age thirty-eight.

Although farming was time-consuming, Anzaldúa found refuge in stories and storytelling. When everyone was asleep at night after a long day in the fields, she would pull the covers over her head, turn on her flashlight, and read into the early hours of the morning. When her sister discovered Anzaldúa's nightly habit, she threatened to tell their mother unless Anzaldúa told her a story. Thus developed Anzaldúa's gift for storytelling, a gift shared by many other members of her family, including her two grandmothers.[6] When she was eleven, Anzaldúa and her family moved to Hargill, Texas. For eight years, Anzaldúa grew up surrounded by Chicana/os in Hargill, having virtually no contact with Anglos. This changed, however, when she began high school. Because she had scored very well on a high school placement exam, Anzaldúa was sent to Edinburg High School, a predominantly Anglo institution. "I was the only Chicana in all my classes except P.E., health, homeroom, and study hall. That segregation, even more, cut me away from friends because the white kids didn't want anything to do with me and the teachers weren't used to having such a bright Chicana. To keep from being bored I'd have the textbook open, but hidden under it I'd be writing in my journal. I'd make up ideas about stories and plot them."[7] Although often ignored or overlooked by teachers and students alike, Anzaldúa nevertheless ended up graduating valedictorian of her high school class.

Throughout her early years, Anzaldúa learned to cope with a sense of being different, even within her own community. Three factors contributed to her experience of difference: her recurring menstrual bleeding, her voracious appetite for reading, and her disinterest in boys. As noted, Anzaldúa began menstruating when she was only six years old. Once a month, she would also experience fevers of 106 degrees and bouts of tonsillitis, diarrhea, and vomiting. "Sometimes it would go on for seven to ten days," she recounts. "So I withdrew all feeling from my genitals; from the time I was little it was always a smelly place that dripped blood and had to be hidden. I couldn't play like other kids."[8] Anzaldúa's mother made a special girdle for her to hide her breasts, which she began developing at the age of six, and her mother made sure that a rag was placed between Anzaldúa's legs in case of bleeding.

Anzaldúa's interest in books also set her apart from the other children. At an early age, she read "everything in the library. Everything: encyclopedias, dictionaries, *Aesop's Fables*, philosophy—I started reading all these heavy books.

I literally went through all the shelves, book by book."[9] Her love for books shed new light on the way that she looked at various cultures, including her own. From reading westerns, Anzaldúa saw that Indians and Mexicans "were portrayed like animals; we weren't really humans." But she also read books "from Europe and other races, which weren't as prejudiced against blacks and non-white cultures."[10] Anzaldúa read positive stories about Eskimos, and she was enamored with *Jane Eyre*, with whom she identified because, like Anzaldúa, Eyre "was short; she was little. She was stubborn and deviant."[11]

Anzaldúa's same-sex preference was a third factor that set her apart from children in her community. As she says in an interview, "[a] lot of the girls in my class were knocked up by the time they got to the sixth grade." Recalling her first experiences of masturbation and having an orgasm, Anzaldúa adds: "The sexual would make me feel different from the other girls because I wasn't out there fucking behind the bushes by the lake like they were. And I didn't really think men were all that great."[12]

In 1962, Anzaldúa enrolled at Texas Woman's University (TWU) in Denton, Texas. Her mother did not want her to go to a college so far away: the school was eight hundred miles—a twelve-hour bus ride—from Hargill. Yet Anzaldúa prevailed. At TWU, Anzaldúa began to question her own sexuality after seeing a number of homosexual relationships, among both lesbian women and gay men. After a year, financial difficulties forced her to return home. Upon her arrival, she worked for a year and then enrolled at the nearby Pan American University (now University of Texas Rio Grande Valley). Anzaldúa put herself through college by working during the day and taking classes at night. She graduated with a BA in English, art, and secondary education. Anzaldúa worked for several years in the public school system near her hometown, teaching grades from preschool to high school. This was difficult work. Her students faced not only tough economic and social situations at home but also rampant racism within the school system, which Anzaldúa experienced herself. (When she initially applied to teach high school, her job applications were rejected multiple times, likely because of her ethnicity.) She confronted this racism by committing herself to a study of Chicano culture and encouraged her students, who were mostly Mexican-American, to incorporate their personal experiences into their writing. Anzaldúa also became involved in the burgeoning Chicano movement in the United States; in the early 1970s, she attended meetings held by the Mexican-American Youth Organization as well as other political meetings. However, the more she attended these meetings, the more disenchanted she became "because it was all the guys." Women were simply not represented.[13]

During the summers, Anzaldúa attended graduate school at the University of Texas at Austin (UT Austin) and obtained a master's degree in English and education in 1972. Soon after, she moved to Indiana and worked as a liaison between the public school system and the children of migrant farmworkers. Anzaldúa was promoted to direct a bilingual migrant program for the state.[14] During this time, she also took her first creative writing course. In 1974, Anzaldúa decided that her work with the public school system did not enable her to make the kind of systemic changes she desired, nor did it allow her enough time to write. She thus returned to UT Austin to pursue a doctoral degree in comparative literature. Through her coursework, she explored feminist theory and esoteric literature, the latter which included a study of alchemy, astrology, the I Ching, and other metaphysical wisdom traditions. In light of her critique of the patriarchal nature of various Chicano social movements, Anzaldúa's encounter with both feminist and esoteric writings provided frameworks that enabled her to develop what one scholar fittingly describes as her "multipronged theory and aesthetics of social transformation and inclusive politics."[15]

In 1977, Anzaldúa committed herself to becoming a published author. She withdrew from UT Austin and moved to California. From 1977 to 1981, she lived in the San Francisco Bay Area, where she joined the Feminist Writers Guild and led a number of writing workshops. But after serving two terms of office at both the local and national levels, Anzaldúa quit because of the racism and alienation she faced from her colleagues, who refused to talk about Third World women, class issues, or oppression.[16] In 1979, she began working on what would become her first edited volume (with Cherríe Moraga), titled This Bridge Called My Back: Writings by Radical Women of Color (1981). This was a groundbreaking collection of essays, poems, letters, and personal narratives by an innovative group of thinkers who moved beyond the usual conventions of white middle-class feminism.

Between 1981 and 1985, Anzaldúa lived on the East Coast. During this time, she began working on a poetry manuscript that was later to become Borderlands/La Frontera: The New Mestiza (1987), her acclaimed book that continues to be widely anthologized, excerpted, and cited. Here, Anzaldúa interweaves history, contemporary issues, and myth, not only to shed light on her experience as a Chicana lesbian feminist but also to develop her theories of "new mestiza consciousness" and "the borderlands," exploring the therapeutic and transformative possibilities of embracing a hybrid, mestiza epistemology. These theories continue to be influential, especially for borderlands studies, intersectional studies, and decolonial thought. Similarly, her groundbreaking use of code-switching (or quick transitions between various forms of language, including standard English and Spanish, working-class English, Chicano Spanish, and Nahuatl) has influenced composition studies, literary studies, and Chicano/a/x studies.[17]

In 1985, Anzaldúa returned to Northern California, where she remained for the rest of her life. She published two multi-genre anthologies featuring the work of women of color feminists: *Making Face, Making Soul / Haciendo Caras: Creative and Critical Perspectives by Feminists of Color* (1990) and *this bridge we call home: medical visions for transformation* (2002). Both works document Anzaldúa's ever-expanding vision of social transformation, radically inclusionary feminism, and self-described spiritual activism. In addition to these edited collections, she published two bilingual children's books and a collection of interviews. Anzaldúa passed away in 2004 at the age of sixty-one from complications related to diabetes. When she died, she was within months of completing her doctoral dissertation in literature from the University of California, Santa Cruz (UCSC). In 2005, UCSC posthumously awarded her a PhD. Her doctoral dissertation has since been published as *Light in the Dark / Luz en lo oscuro: Rewriting Identity, Spirituality, Reality*, which represents the culmination of Anzaldua's mature thought.

## Spirituality and Spiritual Realities

Gloria Anzaldúa is broadly interested in the way that human beings come to know their reality and how they ascribe meaning to it. For Anzaldúa, knowledge is not limited, however, to the internal workings of the mind, nor is it always something that can easily be verified by science. While she would certainly acknowledge that we often engage our experience rationally through verifiable processes of deduction and induction (as seen, for example, in the scientific method), she is more interested in what can be called the "outer boundaries" of our knowledge. Her writings often broach questions such as the following: In what ways do our bodies—and not simply our minds—know? How may inferences, intuitions, dreams, and feelings be valid forms of knowledge? And, perhaps most crucially: In what ways can knowledge be creatively used to bring about social transformation?

These kinds of questions point to Anzaldúa's overriding interest in epistemology, or theory of knowledge. Later in her career, she developed the idea of conocimiento, which is central to her understanding of both epistemology and spirituality. For her, conocimiento is a nonbinary, connectionist mode of thinking that draws on nonrationalistic forms of knowing, such as sensing, intuiting, and dreaming. Conocimiento is "[s]keptical of reason and rationality," she writes. It "questions conventional knowledge's current categories, classifications, and contents."[18] Furthermore, it is deeply tied to spirituality:

> Those who carry conocimiento refuse to accept spirituality as a deval-
> ued form of knowledge and instead elevate it to the same level occupied
> by science and rationality. A form of spiritual inquiry, conocimiento is
> reached via creative acts—writing, art-making, dancing, healing, teach-
> ing, meditation, and spiritual activism—both mental and somatic (the
> body, too, is a form as well as site of creativity). Through creative en-
> gagements, you embed your experiences in a larger frame of reference,
> connecting your personal struggles with those of other beings on the
> planet, with the struggles of the Earth itself. To understand the greater
> reality that lies behind your personal perceptions, you view these strug-
> gles as spiritual undertakings.[19]

As this passage demonstrates, conocimiento in its highest expression *is* spirituality: it is a "form of spiritual inquiry" that offers a "larger frame of reference"
that gives us insight into "the greater reality that lies behind" our individual
epistemologies.[20] For Anzaldúa, conocimiento—which she describes elsewhere
as a "politics of embodied spirituality"[21]—should never be limited to the workings of subject-centered reason. Rather, its scope is more capacious and universal. Because experiences are embedded "in a larger frame of reference" that
connects "personal struggles with those of other beings on the planet" and to
"the struggles of the Earth itself," conocimiento begs cosmic and spiritual
questions, deepening our perception of what is real and ushering in new ways
of being in the world.[22] Also significant is the fact that Anzaldúa links conocimiento to her aesthetics: one reaches conocimiento through creative acts
such as writing, art-making, dancing, and teaching (and one could easily add
to this list ritual, prayer, and healing practices). In this sense, conocimiento is
not simply a form of knowledge that one passively possesses, but it demands
purposeful, creative, and skilled involvement that is constantly informed by
critical reflection.

Because Anzaldúa's idea of conocimiento is closely tied to her spirituality
and stands as one of her central post-*Borderlands* ideas, interpreters of Anzaldúa
would be well served to take note of her work in spirituality that predates her
discussions of conocimiento. In doing so, one sees that Anzaldúa's understanding of spirituality not only develops and matures significantly over the course
of her career, but also continues to be marked by certain unresolved philosophical tensions. While Anzaldúa herself noted that her views regarding spirituality
became "more solid" from the early 1980s to the late 1990s, a careful reading

of her work simultaneously reveals that, even in her mature writings, she continued to wrestle with competing ideas of spirituality.[23]

To see these lingering tensions, let us turn first to Anzaldúa's early writings. In some early interviews from 1982 and 1983, Anzaldúa does not yet speak of spiritual matters in terms of conocimiento, creative acts, or political engagement. Rather, she approaches spirituality more in terms of discreet paranormal events, drawing largely on her own heterodox spiritual experiences. She recounts, for example, her earliest spiritual memory:

> My awareness of a spiritual dimension started when I began differentiating between who I was as a little kid and who my mother was, what the table was, what the wall was. When I was about three years old, I was sitting on the floor and above me, on the table, were some oranges I wanted but couldn't reach. I remember reaching for the oranges; I could feel my arms getting really long. I really wanted them, and suddenly there were three bodies, like I was three of me. I don't remember if I really got the oranges or not. Right after that experience, I began to feel apart, separate from others. Before this point, I couldn't differentiate between myself and other things. I'd feel like I was part of the wall.[24]

In the interviews, Anzaldúa describes several other out of the ordinary experiences, such as the time she was tripping on mushrooms and discovered that she had multiple selves, the feeling of connecting her multiple selves through orgasm, the experience of being immobilized during meditation by a heavy vibration, and the ability to see "other worlds superimposed upon this one."[25]

Such accounts have proven to be a challenge for many interpreters. How does one assess such claims? If we momentarily leave aside the question of whether we can objectively verify them, it is first worth noting that Anzaldúa's insistence on sharing them proves significant in its own right. Knowing full well that many scholars will dismiss her for writing about her highly unconventional spiritual experiences, Anzaldúa nevertheless commits herself to the task. Her resolve becomes evident in the interviews from the early 1980s to the late 1990s. At the beginning of each interview, the editor of the collection, AnaLouise Keating, threads portions of a 1998–1999 interview that she conducted with Anzaldúa, to then allow Anzaldúa to return to and reflect on issues raised in the earlier interviews. The first chapter begins with this telling exchange between Keating (ALK) and Anzaldúa (GEA):

> ALK: You talk about some pretty wild stuff in this interview [with Linda Smuckler from 1982] and even more extensively in the

following interview with Christine Weiland [from 1983]—[about] an "extra-terrestrial spirit," different spirits entering your body, past-life regression, reincarnation, psychic readers, and more. How do you feel about these ideas being out there, in print?

GEA: I think it's about time for these ideas to be in print. I went to psychic readers and workshops in psychic development right after one of my near-death experiences, and these saved my life. It really helped me get in touch with who I was and what I wanted to do. I'm happy it's going to be in my interview book. People should know about this aspect of me and my life.

ALK: Don't you think it's going to make you less respectable and less reputable—because a lot of scholars don't believe in such things?

GEA: Tough shit! Once I get past my own censorship of what I should write about, I don't care what other people say. Some things were hard for me to reveal but my strong vocation for writing makes me more open. To be a writer means to communicate, to tell stories that other people haven't told, to describe experiences that people don't normally find in books, or at least in mainstream books.[26]

As Anzaldúa makes clear, her calling as a writer compels her to address such unconventional issues. She acknowledges that she will likely "be ridiculed." "[S]ome academics will lose their respect for my work," she writes, "while only a small number—one-half of one percent—will applaud me for talking about these things."[27] Aware of the politics of knowledge within institutions of higher learning, she notes that "[s]cholars connected to universities—what I call the 'dependent scholars,' dependent on their discipline and their school in order to survive—will object to this material, while independent scholars like myself who aren't tied up to any institution will applaud my discussions of spiritual realities, imaginal realities, and the inner subjective life."[28]

Anzaldúa's decision to share her heterodox spiritual experiences presents an important challenge to traditional academic disciplines, religious studies included, which tend to distance themselves from studies of esotericism and paranormal experiences. Although some leading scholars in the field such as Anne Taves and Jeffrey Kripal argue persuasively for the inclusion of such studies, the discipline as a whole tends to eschew such matters.[29] As Taves points out, under the influence of three leading theorists who distinguish among magic, science, and religion (Sir James George Frazer, Émile Durkheim, and Marcel Mauss), a disciplinary division arose around the beginning of the twentieth century among anthropology (which sets its sights on the study of primitive cultures, including animism and magic); folklore (which studies primitive survivals among the "folk" in the modern, civilized world); and religious studies (which, still very much under the sway of Christian theology, studies "civilized" religions).[30] With these divisions in place, serious studies of esotericism, the occult, and paranormal and psychical experience no longer had a disciplinary home. Against this backdrop, Anzaldúa's interest in esotericism and the occult may be seen as a challenge to these long-standing disciplinary divisions.

When seen through a disciplinary lens, there is much to learn from Anzaldúa's attention to "spiritual realities, imaginal realities, and the inner subjective life." But digging further, one may still ask: What, exactly, does Anzaldúa mean by these phrases? What are spiritual realities, and in what ways are they different from "imaginal realities" and "the inner subjective life"? Conversely, in what ways may a "spiritual reality" be coextensive with an imaginal reality? Furthermore, how are all of these concepts related to Anzaldúa's idea of spiritual activism?

On my reading, Anzaldúa was searching for a viable path that would allow her to approach spirits as both real and imaginative. At times, she seems to hold contradictory positions regarding these two possibilities. In a 1982 interview, she explains how she used to reject the ideas associated with folk healing in her community: "I'd hear people say that evil spirits, *mal aigre*, rode the wind, and that when a person got sick it was because the bad air had gotten in." In time, however, Anzaldúa came to see these experiences differently. "When I grew up I scoffed at these ideas," she notes, "but now that I'm older I know it's true. Bad vibrations come in the air; when someone is thinking bad about you—feeling envy, jealousy, or whatever and directing it at you—you get the evil eye; people really get sick."[31] Such a statement would seem to support a case for spirits as objectively real entities. A year later, however, Anzaldúa takes a different approach to the question. In light of situations in which she felt "totally isolated and totally alone," Anzaldúa explains that although she "was really fighting it," she needed to find "something outside myself that could sustain me." She then speaks of "la diosa" as "that spiritual help," but then she adds the following caveat: "or maybe it's imaginal help, as it all takes place in the imagination."[32] In light of these somewhat conflicting accounts, one may wonder: How can a spirit, like *mal aigre* or the evil eye, be real yet, at the same time, a creation of the imagination?

Written decades later, Anzaldúa's posthumous *Light in the Dark* continues to deal with similar quandaries around the "reality of spirits." In this work, Anzaldúa herself acknowledges that she struggles at times to provide an adequate framework for broaching this topic. One sees this both in her discussion of the archetypal "árbol de la vida" and in her musings on curanderismo.

## El Árbol de la Vida

Early on in *Light in the Dark*, Anzaldúa recounts her mystical experience of seeing the visage of the Virgen de Guadalupe in a cypress tree. A "severe winter storm broke off a section of the Monterey cypress one February several years ago," she writes, "and the park arborist sawed off the hewn branch and the trunk's damaged flank. That day, spirits flagging, I walked toward the cypress on West Cliff along the sea." She continues:

> In the mist and the fog and the stinging wind, I suddenly saw her
> coming out of the hollowed trunk: It was the Virgen de Guadalupe,
> head tilted, arms extended, halo spread all around. From a distance,
> the bright live tans and browns of the raw newly cut wood and dangling
> trunk fibers looked like the folds of her robe.[33]

Although the physical characteristics of the tree would change over time (the "bright live tans and browns" would eventually give way to a "weathered gray"), Anzaldúa would continue to apperceive what she took to be *la Virgen*. "[O]nce I *saw* la Virgen emerging from the tree," she explains, "my imagination picks her out every time I walk toward her, no matter how age, storm, or sea alters the cypress's trunk."[34]

In *Light in the Dark*, Anzaldúa returns several times to a discussion of the Guadalupe tree. At one point in the text, she explains how she has turned to the tree for inspiration to assist her as a thinker and writer. She beckons the tree to help her find "a paradigm, a framework or scheme for understanding and explaining" to her readers "certain aspects of reality":

> The tree is a link between worlds. Just as the cosmic tree connects
> under, middle, and upper world, I'll connect this essay's sections: from
> the roots to the ground and up its trunk to the branches and on to the
> sky, a journey from the depths of the underworld that ascends to the
> concrete physical world, and then to the upper realities of spirit, in a
> constant descend/ascend movement.[35]

Indeed, the organization of her chapter mirrors this journey. Taking a cue from the post-Jungian psychologist James Hillman, Anzaldúa interprets the underworld as "the mythological style of describing a psychological cosmos," and she describes at some length one of her own deep-seated archetypal figures, the Serpent Woman/la Llorona.[36] Anzaldúa's treatment of the middle world appropriately includes a discussion of nepantla, "the bridge between worlds," and the role of those who occupy this middle space, including "chamanas, curanderas, artists, and spiritual activists."[37] The chapter then moves to a discussion of "upper world" themes such as ensueños (fantasies), imagination, and the reality of spirits.

As much as this tripartite schema helps Anzaldúa organize her chapter, she acknowledges the theoretical limitations of the "tree of life" analogy. Immediately after introducing the three worlds as the guiding framework for her chapter, Anzaldúa concedes: "But the problem with this up/down, linear description is that these three worlds aren't separate. Interconnected and overlapping, they occupy the same place."[38] I return to this concession and its implications later.

## Curanderismo and the Reality of Spirits

A second *aporia* arises in Anzaldúa's discussion of curanderismo and traditional forms of folk healing. In *Light in the Dark*, Anzaldúa addresses head-on the question "Are spirits real?" "I've been asked this question many times," she writes, "and each time the question takes me back to my childhood when I learned, witnessing las curanderas de mi mamagrande, that the physical world is not the only reality."[39] Anzaldúa recounts a situation in which her grandmother believed that an older woman had bewitched her son (Anzaldúa's uncle), Rafa, into falling in love with her. Rafa was obsessed with this older woman. He could not eat or sleep and would walk around like a lost calf ("como un becerro perdido"). Anzaldúa's grandmother thus hired a curandera (healer) to heal her son. This curandera, who was from a small town across the border in Mexico, claimed to be an apprentice of the great folk healer Don Pedrito Jaramillo and was known for healing people all over South Texas "with a blend of shamanism, herbs, and invocations to Catholic saints."[40] Anzaldúa describes how the curandera proceeded to heal her uncle. After sweeping Rafa's body with small branches tied together with herbs, the curandera rubbed him with herbal tea and eucalyptus leaves to give him a proper limpieza (cleaning.) The curandera then took a fresh egg and rubbed it all over his body. "El huevo, [the curandera] claimed, would absorb the disease caused by the bad spirit invading him. She cracked open the egg into a bowl and examined it for spots or marks. The spots and condition of the egg, she said, helped her divine the cause and origin of the sickness."[41] The curandera then buried the egg in the backyard. As Anzaldúa recalls, Rafa slept very well that night and ate a huge breakfast the next morning. "He was back to his spritely self," writes Anzaldúa, "y yo empezé a tenerles fé a las curanderas [and I began to have faith in the curanderas] and the reality of spirits."[42]

Yet one may still wonder: In what sense did Anzaldúa have "faith" in curanderas, and what, exactly, does she mean by the "reality of spirits"? In a series of rhetorical questions, she sets up what seem to be two possibilities: spirits are either a psychological figment of one's imagination, or they are objectively real. Anzaldúa asks, for example, "Is the idea of chamanería real, or is it a work of imagination and therefore fantasy, not reality? When a chamana 'journeys,' does she move outward in her body around the Earth, or does she move inward into an altered state of consciousness where she experiences realities outside normal perception?"[43] Given the way that Anzaldúa asks these questions, one might surmise that there are only two possible answers for her: either spirits are figments of the imagination, or they are objectively real and occupy a place outside the body and mind. Anzaldúa's response, however, is telling. "Such questions keep cropping up, but their framework is too narrow."[44] What frameworks, then, does Anzaldúa propose?

## Three Frameworks

In *Light in the Dark*, Anzaldúa entertains three possibilities. First, she argues that "we must redefine the imagination not as a marginal nonreality nor as an altered state, but rather, as another type of reality."[45] Such a position seems to underscore Anzaldúa's defense of spiritual realism, but, unfortunately, she does not offer further elaboration.[46] Second, Anzaldúa points out that "the stories of nonliteral realities," such as stories of chamanas' flights to other worlds, are often invalidated by Western society and Western science. This point mirrors her earlier critique of traditional academic disciplines that tend to reduce spirits to mere mental images. In response, Anzaldúa draws on the work of anthropologist Edith Turner and Jungian developmental psychologist Mary Watkins to argue against Western forms of "intellectual imperialism" and to make a case for the self-determining and autonomous qualities of what Watkins refers to as "imaginal others." Anzaldúa quotes Watkins: "There is another force influencing our thoughts, emotions, movements, and actions," Watkins writes. "One can no longer say it is a god or a spirit and yet one has those ancient feelings of possession and movement by a force that does not answer to logic of common space and time."[47] Such a position seems to give credence to the power of spirits as imaginative projections, without reducing them to mere figments of the imagination.

Anzaldúa then offers a third, novel response to the "narrow framework" of her initial questions. She rehearses her key question again, this time with reference to dreams: "Are dreams real? Do they represent a separate reality? Do we make dreams, or does something outside us originate and orchestrate them? Is imagination's nonordinary reality real?"[48] She then responds rhetorically:

Does it matter whether the journey comes from a waking dream,
the unconscious in symbolic representation, or a nonordinary parallel
world? Who cares, as long as the information (whether metaphorical
or literal) gained from a shamanic journey makes positive changes in a
person's life. We must avoid the snares of literalism. Are spirits literally
present or are they imaginally present? They are both.[49]

I find these insights significant because they offer Anzaldúa, and those of us
who read her, some new interpretive pathways forward. Instead of circumscrib-
ing spirits, dreams, and shamanic journeying to the realm of either imaginative
fictions or objective realities, Anzaldúa offers two new interpretations here.
One may be termed "functionalist," and the other, "pluralist." Anzaldúa's
functionalism is apparent when she sidesteps the question of nonordinary
parallel worlds with the simple retort, "Who cares?" What matters, says Anzaldúa, are how these ideas work in practice and how they effect "positive changes
in a person's life." Anzaldúa's pluralism is evident in her defense of imaginal
journeys as both literally and imaginally present. Wary of intellectual imperialism, Anzaldúa does not want to have to decide definitively between one or
the other.

The functionalist and pluralist positions that Anzaldúa offers here represent
two of the most compelling responses to her central quandary, but, unfortunately, she does not develop these positions further. Instead, she seems to
return at times to a more realist position that asserts the objective reality of
spirits inhabiting different worlds. For example, just after making a case for
avoiding "the snares of literalism," Anzaldúa states that "for shamans the soul
parts live a parallel existence in nonordinary worlds."[50] Similarly, she defends
spirituality as "an ontological belief in the existence of things outside the body
(exosomatic), as opposed to the belief that material reality is a projection of
mentally created images."[51] Anzaldúa thus seems to defend, at times, a metaphysics of parallel realities that inhabit the world, an approach that is more
than likely attributable to her reading and use of Carlos Castañeda's idea of
"ordinary reality" and "nonordinary reality."[52] In my estimation, such an approach runs quite counter to her attempt to make a case for the interconnec-
tions and unity between all things.

As I develop in further detail in the next section, such appeals also draw
attention away from spirituality as an active process that unfolds through creative acts. In my reading of *Light in the Dark*, Anzaldúa often seems caught
between defending a kind of spiritual realism, on the one hand, and advocating
for a more functional vision of spirituality, on the other, which Anzaldúa simply
calls spiritual activism. Whereas her discussions of spiritual realism tend to

center around questions of being, or ontology, her understanding of spiritual activism points in the direction of spirituality-in-action, or praxis. Certainly, there are elements of both in her writing. How, then, should one adjudicate between the two?

## The Pragmatic Dimensions of Anzaldúa's "Spiritual Activism"

A strong case can be made for the centrality of praxis in Anzaldúa's concept of spirituality and spiritual activism. Although ontological musings about the reality of spirits pepper many of her writings, in *Light in the Dark*, one can see a clear pattern emerge in her line of thinking that culminates in the primacy of praxis. Early in the book, Anzaldúa insists that conocimiento urges us "to respond not just with the traditional practice of spirituality (contemplation, meditation, and private rituals) or with the technologies of political activism (protests, demonstrations, and speakouts), but with the amalgam of the two: spiritual activism."[53] Praxis, understood here as purposive action, undergirds both poles: With regard to "traditional practices of spirituality," it emerges as the act of imagination; with regard to "technologies of political activism," it surfaces as an intentional form of doing or making, which is seen, among other places, in craft-making and artistic performance (the ancient Greeks referred to this as "techne"). Both types of action make spiritual activism possible.

Anzaldúa's interest in the praxis of spirituality can also be seen in her nuanced critique of New Age spirituality. On the one hand, she is critical of scholars who dismiss New Age spirituality on the basis of what they take to be its "flaky language and Pollyanna-like sentiments."[54] Anzaldúa's long-standing interest in esotericism and theosophy—areas of study and practice that are commonly associated with New Age spirituality—suggests a basic affinity with New Age thought. On the other hand, however, Anzaldúa simultaneously laments the fact that many interpreters have reduced her work to a *mere* form of New Age spirituality. In one draft of "Flights of the Imagination," Anzaldúa writes in an abbreviated note to herself: "Why all people lump spirituality with new age—my position, stance," suggesting that she planned to explain further how her understanding of spirituality differs from New Age approaches.[55] As AnaLouise Keating argues, it is crucial "to distinguish Anzaldúa's spiritual activism both from the mainstream 'New Age' movement and from conventional organized religions." Whereas many mainstream New Age movements focus "almost, if not entirely, on the personal and thus leav[e] the existing oppressive social structures in place," Anzaldúa's holistic approach to spiritual activism "encompasses both the personal and the systemic."[56]

As a result, as sympathetic as Anzaldúa is to some forms of New Age spirituality, she is critical of the way in which it tends to take flight from the real
problems of the world. Anzaldúa is not surprised that New Age spirituality
strikes some of its critics as "disconnected from the grounded realities of people's lives and struggles." She squarely acknowledges that "[m]ost contemporary
practitioners in this country ignore the political implications and do not concern themselves with our biggest problem and challenge: racism and other
racial abuses." It is precisely in light of the social and political shortcomings of
New Age spirituality that Anzaldúa appeals directly to spiritual activism, which
she describes as an "activist stance that explores spirituality's social implications."[57] This emphasis on spirituality's social implications clearly puts Anzaldúa's
conception of spirituality on a different path from mainstream New Age
approaches.

In many respects, Anzaldúa's spiritual activism points to a more functionalist
and pragmatic approach to spirituality. Conocimiento, after all, "pushes us into
engaging the spirit in confronting our social sickness with new tools and practices whose goal is to effect a shift."[58] This emphasis on "new tools and practices"
that are used to "effect a shift" aligns with Anzaldúa's perennial commitment
to critical inquiry as a tool for social criticism.[59] This concern also aligns with
a more pragmatic approach to spirituality that is concerned with the *effects* of
spirituality rather than its primary *causes*. If spirituality indeed has more to do
with right-practice than right-belief (or "orthopraxy" rather than "orthodoxy,"
as liberation theologians might put it), then the question of how spirituality
functions becomes paramount. Whereas traditional understandings of religious
knowledge tend to emphasize the knowledge *of something* (such as the tenets
and doctrines of faith), more functionalist and pragmatic approaches tend to
emphasize the way that religious knowledge is *used* for, or toward, certain ends.
The "world of our experience is a real world," acknowledges pragmatist philosopher Larry Hickman, but the deeper question for pragmatists has to do
with the way that our world is "in need of transformation in order to render it
more coherent and more secure."[60] Seen in this light, religious knowledge is
more a mode of transformative engagement than it is a statement about static
truths about this world or the next. For Anzaldúa, spirituality and conocimiento
are valuable tools for the oppressed.[61]

Anzaldúa highlights the importance of praxis, not only in her approach to
spirituality, but also in her frequent discussions of the artist as *chamana*. As
mediator, healer, and teacher, the chamana literally embodies Anzaldúa's
functionalist approach, for it is the chamana who helps bring about positive
changes in a person's life. When speaking about the Guadalupe cypress tree,
for example, Anzaldúa explains her own role as chamana: "When I go for walks

with my friends, they don't see la Virgen until I call their attention to her. Later, they always see and point her out to their friends."[62] Here, Anzaldúa's physical presence as a walking guide serves as the conduit for her friends' new forms of knowledge. The new knowledge gained here is not merely epistemic; rather, it is a reorientation of the always-interconnected "body-mind." Anzaldúa's attention to embodied forms of knowledge echoes what Japanese philosopher of religion Yasuo Yuasa says about much of the Eastern philosophical tradition: "[T]rue knowledge cannot be obtained simply by means of theoretical thinking but only through bodily 'recognition' of 'realization' (*tainin* or *taitoku*), that is, through the utilization of one's total mind and body."[63]

Anzaldúa also understands herself as a chamana in light of her own role as a writer. Reflecting on her own vocation, Anzaldúa observes: "I struggle to talk from the wound's gash, make sense of the deaths and destruction, and pull the pieces of my life back together. I yearn to pass on to the next generation the spiritual activism I've inherited from my cultures."[64] The primary means by which Anzaldúa does this, of course, is through her writing. Referring to herself in the second person, she states: "Through the act of writing you call, like the ancient chamana, the scattered pieces of your soul back to your body. For you, writing is an archetypal journey home to the self, un proceso de crear puentes (bridges) to the next phase, next place, next culture, next reality."[65]

For some, a passage like this may suggest that Anzaldúa's purpose as a writer is to arrive at that "next place" or that "next reality." Such an interpretation would certainly fall in line with Anzaldúa's many discussions of ontology and realism. However, other passages, like the following, tell a different story:

> The aim of good writing is to decrease the distance between reader, writer, and text without "disappearing" any of these players. It's to involve the reader in the work as completely as possible without letting the reader forget that it's a work of art even as s/he interacts with it as if it were reality. In creating an identification or sympathy between reader and character and presenting an immediacy in the fiction's scenes and events, the writer allows the reader to create temporary unities and imagine/project possible wholes out of the given fragments. Both reading and writing are ensueños, willed interactions.[66]

In this passage, one does not find an appeal to spatial metaphors and other static notions of place like the "next place" or the "next reality." Instead, the passage hinges on the question of willed interactions. Significantly, these interactions are active ones: They "involve" the reader deeply so that she may "create temporary unities" of her own. In addition to being dynamic, the language here is also tentative and speculative, allowing for imaginative worlds to emerge and dissolve, much like the ebb and flow of experience itself. The reader interacts with the creative work and all the ideas inherent in it "as if it were reality." The unities and wholes created by the reader are "temporary" and "possible," not eternal and fixed. A pragmatist like William James would no doubt find resonance in Anzaldúa's position here for, as James reminds us, words like "soul," "God," and "immortality" "cover no distinctive sense-content whatever."[67] It would logically follow, then, that these words are devoid of any significance. "Yet strangely enough they have a definite meaning *for our practice*. We can act *as if* there were a God; feel *as if* we were free; consider Nature *as if* she were full of special designs; lay plans *as if* we were immortal." When we enter this subjunctive ("as if") mode of thinking, "we find then that these words do make a genuine difference in our moral life."[68]

Although most Anzaldúan scholarship has paid relatively scant attention to her conception of spirituality and spiritual activism, recent contributions by insightful commentators like Theresa Delgadillo, Tace Hedrick, AnaLouise Keating, and Laura E. Pérez, coupled with the publication of Anzaldúa's posthumous *Light in the Dark/Luz en lo oscuro*, are helping set the record straight: spiritual activism is both the impetus and terminus for Anzaldúa's literary production.[69] We glimpse this in one of Anzaldúa's earliest writings, "La Prieta" (1981), when she writes: "In short, I'm trying to create a religion not out there somewhere, but in my gut. I am trying to make peace between what has happened to me, what the world is, and what it should be."[70] The bookend to this statement may very well be this passage, written toward the end of her career, which speaks to Anzaldúa's sense of vocation and her emphasis on the ongoing practice of spiritual activism:

> In honoring the creative process, the acts of writing and reading, and border arte, I use cultural figures to intervene in, make change, and thus heal colonialism's wounds. I delve into my own mythical heritage and spiritual traditions, such as curanderismo and Toltec nagualism, and link them to spirituality, spiritual activism, mestiza consciousness, and the role of nepantla and nepantleras. I enact spiritual mestizaje— an awareness that we are all on a spiritual path and share a desire that society undergo metamorphosis and evolution, that our relationships and creative projects undergo transformations.[71]

As Delgadillo points out, Anzaldúa's theory of spiritual mestizaje—which is only momentarily touched on in *Borderlands/La Frontera*, yet which is so central to the text[72]—incorporates elements of both critical reflection and directive action. Spiritual mestizaje may be understood as "the transformative renewal of one's relationship to the sacred," which is achieved both "through a radical and sustained multimodal and self-reflexive critique of oppression in all its manifestations" and through "a creative and engaged participation in shaping life that honors the sacred."[73] In my reading, Anzaldúa's subsequent articulation of spiritual activism in *Light in the Dark* sheds further light on spirituality as a form of "creative and engaged participation." With its focus on spirituality as both an act of the imagination and as a concrete and intentional form of techne, spiritual activism illuminates the praxic dimensions inherent in Anzaldúa's earlier theory of spiritual mestizaje.

Yet, as I have shown, Anzaldúa's thoughts on spirituality in *Light in the Dark* also include various ontological appeals to spiritual realism, which may detract readers from the dynamic and emergentist thrust of her spiritual activism. As she makes clear in *Borderlands*, spiritual mestizaje is a "morphogenesis, an inevitable unfolding."[74] Anzaldúa's spiritual realism, with its appeal to discreet worlds and spiritual "places," tends to downplay spirituality as an unfolding and recursive process. In this respect, Anzaldúa's conceptualization of the "three worlds" of the árbol de la vida, which we saw earlier, can only get her so far. The spatial metaphor has its limits, as Anzaldúa herself recognizes. Her work on spiritual activism can be seen as an attempt to find a framework that helps bring her to an ongoing process of "inevitable unfolding."

Anzaldúa's functionalism therefore deserves a full hearing. Although she does not develop this position to the extent that she develops her spiritual realism, I believe that her forays in this direction actually afford her and her readers a more straightforward path to the kind of social change that she so desires, since the focus here is on the productive ways in which experience may be qualitatively transformed. Looking at the matter from another angle, we may ask: What is ethics for Anzaldúa? Is it a search for fixed solutions or criteria that are made objectively visible once and for all, or does ethics have more to do "with method, that is, with how we can become better prepared to obtain qualitative guidance in making good decisions in the difficult and complex situations we confront"?[75] For Anzaldúa, the answer seems clear: "There is never any resolution," she writes, "just the process of healing."[76] For Anzaldúa, conocimiento, spiritual mestizaje, and spiritual activism serve as the needed technologies to engage this process. They are the channels through which new forms of social transformation are born.

As a chamana, an artist, and a writer, Anzaldúa intuitively understands her role as an intermediary, a guide, a midwife, a "daimon." In ancient Greek religion, daimons served as intermediaries between heaven and earth who took prayers up to the gods and brought back rewards and commands. As philosopher Jim Garrison explains, the Greeks also believed that "at birth a daimon seizes each of us, determining our unique individual potential and mediating between us and our best possible destiny."[77] Anzaldúa understands herself as a daimon in two senses: both as an intermediary chamana who helps bring human beings to our best possible destiny and as a subversive and maverick "demon."[78] Like Jane Eyre, who was "stubborn and deviant," Anzaldúa bucks the conventions of traditional forms of religion (thus approaching "demonic" in the pejorative sense) while still performing a therapeutic and socially transformative function ("daimonic" in the salutary sense).[79] Both of these impulses give rise to an incredibly daring and socially conscious thinker.

As readers of Anzaldúa, we must choose how best to interpret her. Are daimons and spirits mere figments of our imagination? Or are they actual spirits? When we search for an answer, perhaps we would do well to turn to Anzaldúa as our guide, to hear her once again intone: Will we let the snares of literalism trap us? Does it really matter that we definitively know the origins of our spiritual journey? Let us focus instead on how the spiritual journey can heal us and our world and let us begin that journey by widening our perception of the world and transforming it through our embodied, creative actions.

# 5

# Subversive Everyday Knowledge: Ada María Isasi-Díaz's "Conscientized Cotidiano"

In his classic study, *Constructing Local Theologies* (1985), Robert Schreiter describes two types of contextual theologies: those that follow an ethnographic approach, which are particularly concerned with questions of cultural identity, and those that follow a liberationist approach, which emphasize the need for social change. For over three decades now, scholars working within the field of US Latine theology have honored and embraced both of these approaches. Without a doubt, the work of US Latina feminist and mujerista theologians has been pivotal in most effectively bridging both of these concerns.[1]

While never losing sight of Latin American liberation theology's commitment to a liberating praxis and the creation of concrete historical projects, or "proyectos historicos,"[2] Latina feminist and mujerista theologians have creatively expanded this discourse to include questions of culture, context, and gender. Although their insights have yet to be fully appreciated, there is a growing awareness that their contributions to theological method have been pivotal to the creative development of US Latine theology at large. Writing in 2000, US Latino systematic theologian Orlando Espín observes: "There is no question in my mind that one significant dynamic within Latina/o theology, over the last decade or so, has been the ever-increasing reception and incorporation of methodological concerns and issues raised by feminist critical theory." This being said, Espín adds the following:

> However, we would be daydreaming and lying to ourselves if we
> thought that this increased awareness and reception of feminist con-
> cerns and issues has occurred without tension, that it's a "done deal,"
> or that most of feminist critical theory has been understood, assimilated

or even read by most Latino/a theologians (who are males). Unfortunately, much Latino/a theology pays lip service to feminism, while ignoring it methodologically. We are certainly not where we were twenty years ago, but we are not even near where we should be.[3]

In the spirit of addressing this oversight and moving the conversation forward, I look now at the contributions of one of the leading figures within US Latine theology, Ada María Isasi-Díaz (1943–2012). Isasi-Díaz was a leading proponent of mujerista theology (she preferred the term "mujerista" over "feminist"), and her most important contributions include her ethnographic and inductive approach, her ruminations on mestizaje/mulatez, and her theorizing of "lo cotidiano," or daily life.

In this chapter, I explore the philosophical significance of Isasi-Díaz's understanding of lo cotidiano. In particular, I am interested in how she attempts to shift her discussion of lo cotidiano from a largely descriptive category (i.e., What *is* lo cotidiano?) to a more epistemological and engaged (i.e., How does one think critically from within the domain of lo cotidiano?). Isasi-Díaz begins to move in this direction when she speaks of a "conscientized cotidiano." I argue that this is a promising, yet underdeveloped, idea. As such, I expand this category further by drawing on the philosophy of Agnes Heller (a major influence on many Latin American and Latina feminists) as well as the philosophy of John Dewey. I show that Heller and Dewey may help to supplement Isasi-Díaz's work in two ways: (a) they help to reframe a conscientized cotidiano as a form of reflective judgment that arises through the encounter of problematic situations and the experience of doubt (scepsis); and (b) they underscore the continuity between abstract and intuitive forms of thought. Conversely, I show how Isasi-Díaz's sensitivity to issues of religion and gender adds significantly to Heller's and Dewey's philosophies.

## Lo Cotidiano

As an analytical category, lo cotidiano first emerged from feminist critical theory in the 1960s and 1970s in Eastern Europe and Latin America, areas that faced varying forms of ideological totalitarianism. Latina feminist theologian María Pilar Aquino notes that the aim of feminist critical theory during this period was "the reinvention of the ethical and political foundations of true democracy in social life."[4] Toward this end, feminist theorists turned to the category of lo cotidiano—or daily living—to expose problematic social hierarchies, patriarchy especially, that pervade people's daily living. Scholars like Agnes Heller, Teresita de Barbieri, Julieta Kirkwood, and Ana Sojo deployed the concept to highlight those aspects of daily life that have been passed over by androcentric theories, including questions of sexuality, culture, desire, and aesthetics.

From early in her career, Isasi-Díaz attempted to validate women's religious insights as organic expressions of lo cotidiano. In her earliest work, *Hispanic Women: Prophetic Voice in the Church* (1988), which she coauthored with Yolanda Tarango, Isasi-Díaz utilizes an ethnographic and narrative approach. This book was groundbreaking in that it was one of the first to give direct voice to the theological wisdom of grassroots Hispanic women.[5] Over time, Isasi-Díaz began to look more closely at the theoretical significance of lo cotidiano. As her later work makes clear, she understands it in terms of both a "what" and a "how." As a what, lo cotidiano serves as a descriptive category of experience; as a how, it sheds light on the function of everyday thinking.

As a descriptive category, lo cotidiano "constitutes the immediate space of our lives, the first horizon in which we have our experiences, experiences that in turn are constitute elements of our reality."[6] In saying this, Isasi-Díaz is interested in exploring experience in all of its many layers, nuances, and contradictions. Her empiricism is what I would describe as a "rich empiricism," for lo cotidiano is meant to cover all that experience has to offer, from its smallest details to its felt qualities to its latent possibilities. In this regard, I could imagine Isasi-Díaz finding much resonance with William James's *A Pluralistic Universe* or John Dewey's *Art as Experience*. For Isasi-Díaz, as for these pragmatists, experience is heterogeneous and messy; it is both actual and ideal.

Like many Latin American and Latina feminists before her, Isasi-Díaz takes this position a step further, arguing that everyday living is always intimately connected to larger structures of thought and power. While largely sympathetic to the project of Latin American liberation theology, Latin American and Latina feminist theologians have lodged two important critiques against Latin American theology, especially in its early years. First, they point out the obvious: early Latin American liberation theology (which, at the professional level, was mostly generated by male clerics) sidestepped questions of gender. Whereas early Latin American liberation theology does take as a central point of departure the poor and oppressed, it gives little to no attention to the concrete realities of Latin American women and the way that they are triply oppressed owing to their economic status, race, and gender. Second, and perhaps even more significantly, Latin American feminists point out that liberation theology tended to show a preference for structural forms of analysis at the expense of looking at the dynamics of everyday life. As we will see in Chapter 6, Brazilian ecofeminist theologian Ivone Gebara makes this point explicitly. For Latin American and Latina feminists, a new epistemology

demands that structural analysis be intimately tied to the realities of lo cotidiano. As long as lo cotidiano is ignored, processes of liberation will never gain
a real foothold.

Significantly, it is for this very reason that Isasi-Díaz pens one of her most
important essays on lo cotidiano. Writing in 2002, she argues that the previous
four decades have evinced "little change in structures of oppression." As she
explains, "Structural changes have not come about or lasted" because "structural change has not been seen as integrally related to *lo cotidiano*."[7]

## Isasi-Díaz's "Conscientized Cotidiano"

It is in this aforementioned 2002 article, "*Lo Cotidiano*: Everyday Struggles in
Hispanas/Latinas' Lives" (which was later included as a chapter in her 2004
book, *La Lucha Continues*: *Mujerista Theology*) that Isasi-Díaz introduces the
idea of a conscientized cotidiano. She writes:

> [*Lo cotidiano*] has to do with the practices and beliefs that we have in-
> herited, with our habitual judgments, including the tactics we use to
> deal with the everyday. However, by *lo cotidiano* we do not refer to the
> a-critical reproduction or repetition of all that we have been taught or
> to which we have become habituated. On the contrary, we under-
> stand by *lo cotidiano* that which is reproduced or repeated consciously
> by the majority of people in the world as part of their struggles for sur-
> vival and liberation. This is why this *conscientized cotidiano* carries
> with it subversive elements that can help us to question the reality in
> which we live.[8]

In this passage, Isasi-Díaz approaches lo cotidiano as an epistemological category: her goal is to call our attention to the ways in which it may function as a
critical mode of thought. Although she begins with a discussion of lo cotidiano
as a type of practical reason and habitual judgment, she underscores the fact
that, at its best, lo cotidiano does not speak to just any type of practical reason.
Rather, it refers to a practical reason that is thoroughly critical in that it is a
"conscious" practice undertaken by people in "their struggles for survival and
liberation." Here, we hear clear echoes of the critical pedagogy of Paulo Freire.

I find Isasi-Díaz's move toward the idea of a conscientized cotidiano significant because it attempts to take seriously the liberating potential of everyday
epistemologies. Perhaps more so than any other category within US Latino/a
theology, a conscientized cotidiano explicitly connects the two types of contextual theologies that Schreiter and others have identified—liberationist and
ethnographic. That said, Isasi-Díaz leaves this idea largely underdeveloped.

Furthermore, when describing a conscientized cotidiano and lo cotidiano, Isasi-Díaz often anthropomorphizes them, speaking of them as active subjects. As she phrases it, a conscientized cotidiano "carries with it subversive elements"; lo cotidiano "has an extremely important role in our attempt to create an alternative symbolic order"; lo cotidiano "plays a key role in [the] whole process" of "apprehending and facing up to reality." While this style of writing allows her to speak of what lo cotidiano does, it elides the question of how actual human subjects activate lo cotidiano in a functional way.[9] Along these lines, a more fundamental set of questions would be: How do grassroots individuals come to entertain subversive positions from within lo cotidiano in the first place? How do people construct an alternative symbolic order out of their experience of lo cotidiano? And finally, how can they apprehend and face up to reality in ways that stay true to the realities of lo cotidiano?

One helpful resource in answering these questions is the work of Hungarian philosopher Agnes Heller, who was one of the first theorists to write about "the everyday" as an analytical category and has proven to be a major influence on Latin American and US Latina feminists. As I see it, Heller's discussion of everyday knowing as a form of reflective judgment can help deepen our understanding of what a conscientized cotidiano is and what it does.

In one of her most important works, *Everyday Life* (first published in Hungary in 1970 and translated into English in 1984), Heller reflects on the dynamics of knowing. First, she establishes how perception, feeling, and thinking, while separable in theory, "form an indissoluble unity" in practice and in everyday life.[10] As she argues, we cannot engage one of these faculties in any meaningful way without the assistance of the others. Heller observes, for example, that there is no such thing as "pure" perception, save "certain extreme cases of no great significance," such as the perception of a sudden strong light. Rather, in most cases, "our perception is ordered by conceptual schemata: our way of perceiving is socially performed."[11] In saying this, Heller is underscoring the fact that we are creatures of culture. Our perception is guided by the knowledge we have taken over from previous generations. By the same token, perceptions and knowledge are shot through with feelings. "Can we possibly separate perception from feeling when we sink into a warm bath, or see a beautiful colour?" asks Heller.[12] For Heller, not only are knowledge and intelligence shaped by emotion, but also emotion can actually help to deepen our knowledge. As she notes, "The lover sees more in the face of his beloved than the casual onlooker."[13]

In much the same way, Isasi-Díaz underscores emotion and desire as a starting point for knowledge. She notes, for example, that desire is "a way of reaching out for what we believe is good for us." Desire also makes it possible for us to "break loose from oppression in order to resist, oppose, and transform," which, in turn, allows us to imagine differently. [14] As Isasi-Díaz makes clear, this "imagining differently is part of the process of conscientization that anchors our struggles to be self-defining, to become subjects of our own history, to struggle to make our utopian vision a reality." [15] On these questions of emotion, desire, and imagination, Isasi-Díaz and Heller share insights which, indeed, continue to be validated by recent scholarship in cognitive neuroscience and philosophy. [16]

Where Heller may begin to deepen Isasi-Díaz's understanding of a conscientized cotidiano is in Heller's second major insight, which is that all significant knowledge—whether everyday or abstract—comes about through an encounter with a problematic situation. "First and foremost," Heller writes, "everyday thinking is thinking concerned with solving the problems of the 'person' in his environment." [17] As long as there is no felt difficulty, no problem that presents itself to us, our thinking will proceed in a repetitive and habitual way. Although this type of thought may take the form of mere habit and custom, habitual thought, it should be pointed out, may also serve as a useful form of practical reason—folk wisdom being a point in case. Thus, the *sensus fidelium*, or "sense of the faithful," as described by Orlando Espín, would count as a significant form of practical reason since its truth can be communally verified over multiple generations. [18] It is not *mere* habit and custom but, rather, a form of habit and custom that carries with it its own forms of truth-testing.

Isasi-Díaz is attentive to both of these valences of habit and custom. On the one hand, she warns against appropriations of *mere* habit and custom, which often result in the "a-critical reproduction or repetition of all that we have been taught." [19] On the other hand, she wants to uphold a more intelligent and critical use of habit and custom as valuable forms of practical reason. However, the question that arises is: How does one get from one to the other?

As I have already indicated, it helps to keep in mind that all forms of reflective thought—whether everyday or abstract—emerge from the encounter of problematic situations. Isasi-Díaz seems to recognize as much when she makes a passing remark about lo cotidiano as a "problematized daily reality." [20] However, it is precisely at this juncture that we could dig more deeply. When we do, we find that problematic situations give rise to doubt, and it is doubt that fuels an alternative way of approaching reality.

Heller writes about doubt in her discussion of "scepsis." Scepsis is "what we might call a 'local' suspension of belief in relation to a certain event, an item of information, a person, a solution, an expectation." Heller makes clear that scepsis is not the same as skepticism since the latter is a way of life, a "mode of behaviour which sets out principally to suspend not a specific area of belief but belief, the 'feeling of certainty' in general."[21] Whereas scepsis is an everyday attitude that connects to certain events in life, skepticism is akin to a *Weltanschauung*, which is to say, a total philosophical outlook on life.

Heller sheds light on the significance of scepsis to our everyday lives when she writes:

> The importance of the part played by scepsis, by the suspension of the feeling of certainty, in our daily lives, should be clear to everyone. I believe in someone—as a friend, as a partner, etc.—until a piece of evidence comes my way, suggesting that my belief is not well-founded: I then suspend my belief and try to find certainty, that is, to reinforce my knowledge either way. I am told conflicting stories about life in a foreign country—so I suspend belief in my sources till one or another is proved right, etc. Scepsis can indeed be generalized in daily life.[22]

Heller's understanding of scepsis echoes a central tenet of pragmatism, which is that "real doubt" fuels inquiry. Real doubt is not doubting for the sake of doubting, as is the case with Cartesian skepticism; rather, it is doubting with an express purpose and reason, forged when our epistemic encounter with experience no longer seems "well-founded," as Heller would say. As C. S. Peirce, the father of US pragmatism, points out: "Doubt is an uneasy and dissatisfied state from which we struggle to free ourselves and pass into the state of belief. . . ."[23] Moreover, this struggle to attain a sense of belief is, at its core, representative of inquiry itself.

On my reading, Isasi-Díaz's articulation of a conscientized cotidiano could be deepened by taking account of the way in which critical forms of everyday knowing always arise from problematic situations and through an encounter with doubt.

## Expanding a "Conscientized Cotidiano"

In combining the idea of conscientization with lo cotidiano, Isasi-Díaz underscores the fact that everyday knowing has the potential to be a critical form of knowledge. She explicitly states, for example, that "the majority of people in the world" consciously and critically engage lo cotidiano "as part of their struggles for survival and liberation."[24] Elsewhere, Isasi-Díaz observes that "[a]ll those who work with grassroots people marvel at the way they use every possible minute and how they manage to bring something out of nothing."[25] For Isasi-Díaz, people on the underside of history know how to navigate their precarious lot in life, and they do so in a way that affirms their dignity, even in the face of tremendous struggles. With a nod to Antonio Gramsci, she writes that the poor and oppressed are "organic intellectuals." They are "admirably capable of understanding and explaining their experiences and beliefs."[26]

As I have argued, however, Isasi-Díaz never fully explains how this everyday critical epistemology works. To be sure, on more than one occasion, she does borrow from Ignacio Ellacuría's threefold understanding of knowledge as realizing the weight of reality (*"hacerse cargo de la realidad"*), shouldering the weight of reality (*"cargar con la realidad"*), and taking charge of the weight of reality (*"encargarse de la realidad"*). Ellacuría's discussion of epistemology, and how it intersects with questions of ethics, is no doubt a valuable resource. But even here, one is left wondering how these three dimensions of our knowing intersect specifically with lo cotidiano. Put negatively: How does knowledge that is rooted in lo cotidiano avoid what Isasi-Díaz describes as "the a-critical reproduction or repetition of all that we have been taught or to which we have become habituated"?[27] Put positively: How can everyday custom and habit prove critical and reflective?

As we have already seen, reframing the question in terms of a problematic situation and the way doubt functions within it marks one important step forward. A second major consideration, I would add, has to do with how one theorizes the relation between abstract forms of thinking and everyday forms of thinking.

As I read her, Isasi-Díaz seems, at times, to set up a divide between knowledge as a form of "common sense," on the one hand, and knowledge as a more abstract and deductive endeavor, on the other. She hints at such a split when she writes, first, that "Grassroots Hispanas/Latinas have a great capacity to pay attention to and to deal with a multitude of things at the same time. . . . Grassroots Hispanas/Latinas have the ability to see the connections that exist among things, elements, and people who are very different." Having established this point, however, she goes on to say that grassroots Latinas "would dull this ability if they were more methodical and dealt with things in a deductive and systematic way."[28]

I am not entirely convinced by this distinction. To be sure, there is no doubt a qualitative difference here between intuitive and deductive forms of thinking. For example, intuiting or sensing danger before it presents itself exercises a style of knowing that is distinct from more methodical forms of testing for danger, such as those seen in automobile crash tests, which are highly controlled. That said, pragmatism teaches us that whereas there may be qualitative difference between these kinds of knowing, there is no categorical difference. The same general process of knowing is operative in both situations.

To underscore this point, it might be helpful to turn to two interpretations of John Dewey's pragmatic theory of inquiry. In his influential 1910 work, *How*

*We Think*, Dewey identifies five "logically distinct steps" of inquiry: (a) a felt difficulty (which, we could add, gives rise to doubt); (b) the location and definition of this difficulty (the further concretization of this doubt); (c) the suggestion of a possible solution to the problem; (d) reasoned consideration of the proposed suggestion; and (e) further observation and experimentation leading to the acceptance and belief, or the rejection and disbelief, of the proposed solution. Presented as such, these steps may, no doubt, sound a bit mechanical and dry.

If seen solely in this light, Dewey seems to have much to say about how we deal with experience in a "methodical, deductive, and systematic way" (as Isasi-Díaz would put it) but less to say about the kind of intuitive knowing that emerges from lo cotidiano. Fortunately, however, contemporary Dewey scholars have done much to retrieve a more intuitive, aesthetic, and passionate side of Dewey's theory of inquiry.[29] They have reframed Dewey's theory of inquiry in light of his robust ruminations on the rich reality of the lifeworld, incorporating insights from his theory of aesthetics and theory of education. Their insightful work offers readers new ways of understanding knowledge from the perspective of lo cotidiano. It paints a much richer picture of Dewey's theory of inquiry, whereby the technical-sounding steps in *How We Think* can be reinfused with elements of desire, eros, passion, and creative imagination—the very lifeblood of lo cotidiano.[30] Thus, in this richer reading of Dewey, knowledge—at all levels, whether abstract or intuitive—demands that we (a) take in and *perceive* a felt difficulty; (b) define and *express* it; (c) *creatively imagine* and suggest a solution; (d) *artfully deliberate* and reason over this proposed solution; and (e) *skillfully act* and experiment on our best reasoning.

To bring the argument back to Isasi-Díaz, it would be appropriate to say that *not only* can Latinas practice a kind of creative and intuitive commonsense knowledge that helps them navigate the demands of "a multitude of things at the same time," *but also* they can engage this reality in a more "methodical, deductive, and systematic way." The difference here is one of degree, not of kind. After all, intuitive commonsense knowledge already implies a theoretical engagement with what Ernst Bloch calls "anticipatory thinking" or what John Dewey refers to as "ends-in-view." In both cases, and in Heller's words, thinking is always "directed towards a future object and towards action likely to bring this object about."[31] Although the epistemology of lo cotidiano may seem somewhat self-evident and obvious as it unfolds in real time, as an epistemic process, it actually involves a number of complex, emerging processes (which, as we have seen, includes perceiving a felt difficulty, working through one's doubt, weighing one's options, and forging a new way forward). Furthermore, the more deliberative one's engagement with lo cotidiano becomes, the more it will assume the character of "methodical, deductive, and systematic" analysis. In many ways, Isasi-Díaz's own scholarly trajectory is indicative of this relative shift between honoring the practical activity of lo cotidiano (as seen in her early ethnographic work) and critically assessing it in a more deductive and systematic manner (as seen in her later, more theoretical meditations on the subject).

To put the matter another way, illuminating the connection between intuitive knowledge and more abstract and deductive forms of knowledge need not be seen as a betrayal or a lessening of the unique epistemology of lo cotidiano. Rather, making this connection may be seen a consistent application of method. If lo cotidiano is indeed embedded in, and integrally related to, larger social structures, then it should follow that forms of knowledge associated with each are also integrally related. Although analytically distinct, intuition and abstract thinking are cut from the same epistemological cloth.

## Expanding Philosophy:
## Isasi-Díaz on Religious Faith and Gender

I have argued that Isasi-Díaz's articulation of a conscientized cotidiano could be enhanced by certain insights gleaned from pragmatic theories of knowledge, such as those articulated by Agnes Heller and John Dewey. In making this claim, however, I would be remiss were I not to add that Isasi-Díaz's conception of a conscientized cotidiano has much to offer both of these thinkers. Whereas Heller and Dewey are, at best, ambivalent about the redeeming aspects of religion, Isasi-Díaz appreciates the ways in which lo cotidiano may productively intersect with religion, as well as with questions of gender.

Heller's attitude toward religion is mixed. On the one hand, Heller recognizes that "[s]tructurally, religious thinking is akin to everyday thinking." She admits that "[w]here a corpus of religious knowledge has already crystallized, such elements of it as are indispensable for efficient everyday knowledge are propagated in the everyday knowledge of the adult segment in any one generation, thence to be transmitted to the successor generation."[32] One could easily connect what Heller says here to what US Latine theologians generally refer to as popular religion. Indeed, Latine popular religion may represent a "corpus of religious knowledge" that is "indispensable for efficient everyday knowledge" and passed down from one generation to the next. The problem, however, is that Heller gives scant analysis to the implications of such a grassroots type of knowledge. Instead, she is quick to focus on how everyday religious knowledge is taken over by a priestly class. Following Max Weber, she tends to speak of religion in terms of institutionalization and bureaucratization. Heller writes:

> [T]he institutionalized representatives of the religion in question (priests, soothsayers, the theocratic establishment, etc.) keep on "chipping in" and preventing the transmission of this knowledge from following its natural path: otherwise, as a result of the infusion of local idiom and particularistic knowledge, the corpus of knowledge as transmitted would gradually drift further and further from the original dogmatic system. This constant process of intervention and rectification aimed at "restoration" of the original doctrinal body, is particularly striking in the case of the great world religions.[33]

While I do not disagree with Heller's position here, I do find it incomplete. What would the transmission of local and particularistic (religious) knowledge look like were it to follow its "natural path"? One of the major contributions of US Latine theology is that it takes this question very seriously.

Like Heller, John Dewey also tends to reduce religion to a question of its institutional strictures. Although Dewey does offer significant insights into a type of religious knowing that grows organically out of our everyday experience (which Dewey labels "the religious"), he remains unimaginative when assessing how this type of knowledge can intersect with institutional religion. In fact, he tends to hold a sharp distinction between the two. At times, Dewey unwittingly betrays his own philosophical commitment to continuity—a touchstone of his thought at large—when dealing with questions of religion.

Isasi-Díaz, on the other hand, understands that lo cotidiano and religious faith—and, we could add, gender (a topic that is even less present in the work of Heller and Dewey)—operate on the same plane, affecting one another in both positive and negative ways. As Andrew Prevot observes, Isasi-Díaz "writes as a Catholic theologian who finds herself somewhat alienated from the [patriarchal] church and what she calls its 'traditional theology.'" "However," adds Prevot, " . . . this sense of estrangement does not prevent her from engaging with Christian scriptures, liturgies, and doctrines in creative and appreciative ways."[34] In my estimation, Isasi-Díaz's ability to keep in play all three of these considerations—everyday life, religious faith, and gender—should be seen as one of her greatest strengths.

Along these lines, there is perhaps no better way to close this chapter than with one of Isasi-Díaz's own stories.[35] In "La Lucha: My Story," she recounts how a friend of hers in the Women's Ordination Conference called her one day and said that she needed a break because she felt burned out. "What she said impacted me greatly," writes Isasi-Díaz. In fact, she adds, it "scared me out of my wits!" Although Isasi-Díaz herself did not feel exhaustion at that point in time, she observes that "I did not want to become so drained that I had to step away from my commitment to the women's movement."[36] She feared that her involvement with efforts to ordain women would leave her as psychologically spent as her friend. Then, in what I find to be one of her most telling and moving autobiographical passages, she writes:

> One day, as I drove home from work in the middle of a snowstorm, three things became clear for me. First of all, I realized that sexism was a category of oppression and that it did not exist apart from poverty but compounded it and vice-versa. . . . Second, as I slowly inched ahead on slippery roads, I could hear my mother saying the words with which she always ended her letters to me: as long as God gives us the energy we need for the struggle, we will be all right. Mamá has always insisted we should not ask God to free us from struggling but rather we should thank God we have something to struggle for. What we need to do is ask God to give us *fuerzas para la lucha*, strength for the struggle. (Years later I would work on developing *la lucha* as a category of social analysis and as a theo-ethical category.) Third, the snow-covered windshield of my car became like a movie screen where I could see my next-door neighbor in Lima, a woman who lived in extreme poverty yet never lost her sense of dignity and purpose of life. I remember the steadiness of her struggle: day after day she dealt with the reality of the present and survived that day in order to be able to face the next. (That reflection has led me to develop the category of *lo cotidiano* as the main site for struggle, as the site that reveals oppression at the same time it illuminates the preferred future.) . . . From that day forward I have never been scared of burning out, often singing to myself, "I ain't no ways tired. I've come too far from where I started from. Nobody told me the road would be easy." And, as to burning up, that is what life is all about, isn't it? For me life is about being passionate for justice! That is what fulfills me; that is what gives me energy and creativity.[37]

I am drawn to this passage for several reasons. First, it clearly underscores three of Isasi-Díaz's central themes: gender (as evidenced in her discussion of sexism), faith (as connected to her participation in the Women's Ordination Conference and her giving thanks to God for *la lucha*), and everyday living (as seen in her reference to lo cotidiano). One cannot fully appreciate the profundity of Isasi-Díaz's thought without seeing how these three themes interconnect and overlap throughout her writings. Second, I believe that Isasi-Díaz had these insights and visions within the context of her own problematic situation and process of doubt: Was she going to burn out like her friend? Her story provides insight into her own thought process, which took her from a situation of uneasiness to an outlook of resolute joy and hope. Third, I am drawn to the small but significant descriptions that she includes about the experience itself, namely, the fact that she had this realization while driving in "the middle of a snow-storm" as she "slowly inched ahead on slippery roads" and as the windshield of her car "became like a movie screen where I could see my next-door neighbor in Lima." These details no doubt reflect Isasi-Díaz's own experience of lo cotidiano. If taken out of context, they might seem mundane and insignificant. But when placed in the context of Isasi-Díaz's life and commitments, the par-ticularities of her story heighten what she argues all along: it is from the details of lo cotidiano that new forms of beauty and prophecy emerge. What she shares here is nothing less than a prophetic and mystical vision that emerges organ-ically out of the daily ebb and flow of her own engaged, passionate, and beau-tiful life.

6

# Ecofeminism and Relatedness:
# Ivone Gebara's Pragmatic Inheritance

Ivone Gebara (1944–) was born in Sao Paulo, Brazil, to Syrian and Lebanese immigrant parents who were disappointed that she was not a boy. Despite her parents' insistence that a "woman's place [was] in the home," Gebara pursued her education and chose philosophy as her undergraduate field of study.[1]

In 1967, at the age of twenty-two, and against her parents' wishes, Gebara entered the Roman Catholic order of Notre Dame, Canonesses of St. Augustine. As she explains, her choice to enter a religious order was a logical result of finding value in herself. "At first glance," she concedes, "that view may seem a contradiction, especially today when women's religious institutions are criticized for being patriarchal. But for me it was a path to justice and freedom, a place where I could live gospel values without the constraints of my native culture."[2]

In the early 1970s, Gebara began teaching theology, philosophy, and anthropology at the Theology Institute of Recife (ITER). This creative and socially committed school trained seminarians and lay pastoral leaders in the tradition of liberation theology.[3] Soon after she began teaching at ITER, Gebara decided that she needed to live in a poor neighborhood "in order to feel more directly the pains of the impoverished."[4] To this day, Gebara continues to live an intentional life of poverty in a favela in Brazil. Although Gebara has chosen to place herself in physical proximity to poor people, she has repeatedly recognized throughout her career that she is a "woman who lives in privileged conditions, conditions that give me enough space to reflect, to speak, and even to write."[5]

Such a recognition, however, did not dampen Gebara's commitment to those in need. Rather, it fueled it. With the help of both grassroots women and other female academics, Gebara came to acknowledge that her entire manner of thinking had been largely colored by male-centered concerns and did not adequately reflect the reality of the women she was trying to serve. One anecdote from Gebara's autobiography captures this reality especially well. In the late 1970s, in home meetings, Gebara provided theological training for a group of industrial laborers. During these meetings, she noticed that the homeowner's wife busied herself preparing coffee and bringing fruit to the participants. Although the woman was frequently invited to participate in the meetings, she repeatedly declined. One day, Gebara visited the woman to ask why she did not join, and she was shocked by her answer. The woman explained that she did not understand what was being discussed. She said, "This is not a language of my world—and you, Miss [Gebara], speak like a man." Baffled, Gebara explained that she was herself a woman. The homeowner's wife responded by noting that Gebara spoke only about the male reality of the industrial laborers, such as their need for better pay and their political struggles. She continued:

> I never heard you speaking about our children, about women, and about how much they struggle to feed their children. . . . You don't speak about the women industrial laborers' difficult life conditions, about their particular struggles during work hours when having their menstrual cycle, or when they have to breastfeed and work at the same time. You never speak about our sexuality and submission to men. You don't speak about our daily reality.[6]

The experience had a profound impact on Gebara and informed all of her subsequent thinking. Although Gebara does not invoke this word herself, one could say that she came to incorporate an "intersectional" approach to oppression that addressed not only economic and class inequality, but also various forms of gender, racial, and religious exclusions.

Having set herself on this new path of inquiry in the late 1970s, Gebara courageously confronted a series of professional and personal obstacles. She gained international notoriety in the mid-1990s for an interview that she gave in a Brazilian weekly news magazine where she publicly expressed her defense of women's right to abortion and critiqued the Roman Catholic Church for its patriarchal and androcentric assumptions around this topic. Gebara pointed out that the Church's view on abortion as a transgression against God is contradictory when set within the context of Brazil's poverty-stricken poor urban centers. In such a context, births often worsen life conditions for mothers and children, increase strain on natural resources, and decrease access to potable water. She was the first liberation theologian—and remains one of the few—to hold that abortion is not necessarily a sin.[7]

In a subsequent defense of her position, Gebara wrote: "For me, as a Christian, to defend the decriminalization and legal regulation of abortion is not to deny the traditional teachings of the gospel of Jesus and the church. Rather, it is to welcome them within the paradoxical reality of human history and to aid in diminishing violence against life." For Gebara, the legalization of abortion in Brazil was only one small aspect of a broader struggle in what she calls "an abortive society," that is, a society that does not offer jobs, health care, housing, or education to poor women.[8]

In response, the Vatican silenced Gebara for two years and ordered her to pursue further studies "to correct her theological imprecisions."[9] Gebara complied by completing a second doctorate in Religious Sciences at the Catholic University of Louvain in Belgium in 1998. Paradoxically, this process of theological "reeducation" only served to sharpen Gebara's core insights and critiques, which are articulated in key works like *Longing for Running Water: Ecofeminism and Liberation* (1999) and *Out of the Depths: Women's Experience of Evil and Salvation* (2002). Gebara is widely considered to be one of the most important liberation theologians alive today.

Ivone Gebara once described herself as a "naughty bee accused of producing a honey of a different flavor." Both her scholarly work and her personal example have inspired a number of scholars around the world to savor feminism in a new way. In the remaining sections of this chapter, I suggest that part of what makes her work so appealing is her implicit pragmatism, which is seen, among other places, in her concept of "relatedness."

## Ecofeminism and Relatedness

While highly sympathetic to the many advances of Latin American liberation theology, Gebara offers some of the most trenchant and productive critiques of the tradition. In her estimation, early proponents of liberation theology fell short of proposing a new epistemological framework, often falling back on more mechanistic and anthropocentric assumptions. As she writes, early liberation theology did not "in reality propose a new epistemology. All it did was to bring some aspects of the epistemology that characterizes the modern era into a theological perspective that sought the integral liberation of the Latin American poor."[10]

In response, Gebara develops an ecofeminist theology, in which the concept of "relatedness" is central. Ecofeminism is an inclusive style of thought that first emerged in feminist circles at the end of the 1970s. It is a combination of holistic ecology and social feminism that deals with the ways in which the exploitation of nature often overlaps with the exploitation of women.[11]

Ecofeminism therefore attempts to make explicit the shared logic between anthropocentrism (a human-centered view of the world) and androcentrism (a male-centered view of the world). Furthermore, it seeks to avoid modern dualisms between subject and object, human and nature, and immanence and transcendence.[12]

Key to Gebara's ecofeminism is her idea of relatedness. In *Longing for Running Water: Ecofeminism and Liberation*, she describes relatedness as the foundational reality of all that is or can exist. "It is the underlying fabric that is continually brought forth within the vital process in which we are immersed."[13] Relatedness, Gebara argues further, is significant for both anthropological and cosmological reasons. Anthropologically speaking, relatedness takes issue with individualist and egocentric conceptions of the self that draw a sharp line between self and community as well as between self and world. Instead, it points toward a collectivist understanding of "person" that underscores the inherent interconnectedness between individuals and their social and natural environments. Cosmologically speaking, relatedness relativizes human experience as just one among many significant expressions of evolution. As Gebara writes, relatedness invites us to "give up some of our anthropocentrism and some of our imperialism vis-à-vis the rest of the cosmos."[14]

While it is clear that the concept of relatedness is central for Gebara, she is somewhat elusive about its theoretical foundations. She writes:

In the first place, let me point out that the word "relatedness" is not taken from any particular philosophy, thought system, or school of spirituality. . . . [M]any of us who were working in an ecofeminist perspective suddenly found ourselves using a shared language that reflected our perceptions regarding the complex and extraordinary web of relationships that is called *life*. The term "relatedness" . . . has the advantage of not needing much explanation, because it is explained by everyday life itself and its innumerable circumstances.[15]

Although Gebara suggests here that relatedness has no specific intellectual inheritance, I will spend some time unpacking what some of these likely influences are. Such an explanation not only helps to give analytical clarity to Gebara's idea of relatedness, but it also opens up new methodological pathways for the future, especially when we put Gebara's work in conversation with pragmatism.

## Gebara and North American Pragmatic Feminist Theology

Gebara describes her work as "emphatically philosophical and theological," utilizing phenomenology and contemporary feminist theology as two of her most important theoretical resources.[16] From Paul Ricoeur (and also Edmund Husserl), Gebara approaches phenomenology as the attempt to understand concrete events from within. As such, she intentionally privileges the experiences and testimonies of women. Along with contemporary feminist theologians, Gebara seeks to dismantle Christianity's engrained patriarchal paradigm to create a more just and equitable world. Significantly, many of the contemporary theologians whom Gebara cites employ an implicitly pragmatic framework.[17] On my reading, Gebara is particularly indebted to the pragmatically minded work of Rosemary Radford Ruether and Sally McFague. Although Ruether's influence on Gebara is unmistakable,[18] for this chapter, I focus on the intersection between McFague's 1993 work, *The Body of God: An Ecological Theology*, and Gebara's *Longing for Running Water: Ecofeminism and Liberation*, which was published six years later.

Both McFague and Gebara use ecology as a primary point of departure. Similarly, both thinkers may be said to approach theology "not as a discipline that affords an objective view of the truth about God and the world, but rather as one that utilizes metaphors that enable us, in particular situations, to accomplish Earth-friendly and healing relationships with God and God's creation."[19] In *The Body of God*, McFague offers a model of God that postulates God's transcendence not in terms of traditional political models (God as a "ruler") or negative abstraction (God as "pure mystery"), but rather in terms of God's immanence within the universe.[20]

In *Longing for Running Water*, Gebara similarly argues for an immanentist and organic understanding of God, but her argument reaches further. Gebara shows how humankind's prevailing mechanistic understanding of ecology, which essentially estranges human beings from their inherent connection to their environment, shares a common logic with patriarchy and androcentrism. In one respect, then, Gebara's ecofeminism may be said to build on McFague's work in that it layers a feminist hermeneutic onto an ecologically minded theology.

I would like to drill down further to explore how McFague's articulation of an organic model of the cosmos may serve as an implicit and somewhat overlooked influence on Gebara's concept of relatedness. As McFague explains, although a mechanical and linear model of creation has dominated both science and theology for centuries, organic models have nonetheless survived through a variety of traditions. Significantly, McFague names several of these traditions, including (a) incarnational forms of Christianity; (b) Goddess and Native American traditions; (c) postmodern science; and (d) process thought. In naming these traditions, McFague helps to make explicit several resources that are available to Gebara in articulating her own concept of relatedness.

Throughout her writings, Gebara consistently draws on organic models that emerge from incarnational forms of Christianity. She is also sympathetic to Goddess and Native American traditions as well as African traditions. What remains somewhat underdeveloped, however, is how postmodern science and process thought might further lend validity to her ecofeminist project.

I believe that there is more to be gleaned from McFague's understanding of postmodern science than Gebara seems willing to admit. To see this, it is worth noting that McFague utilizes the work of Ian Barbour to disentangle three paradigms of science: the medieval, the Newtonian, and twentieth-century postmodern approaches. Whereas the medieval approach to science sought to explain the cosmos in terms of a fixed order based on natural law, the Newtonian model took up the question of change. The job of Newtonian science was to explain change in terms of causal relationships. It was largely an enterprise of reducing phenomena to their root causes. Both of these models assumed certain dualisms, whether between spirit and matter in the medieval schema or between the knowing subject and the passive object in the Newtonian era. In response, contemporary twentieth-century models of science offer another paradigm. Rather than succumb to a Newtonian determinism, twentieth-century evolutionary approaches underscore the emergent quality of all reality, which is characterized by both law and change, both structure and openness. Reality is what it is *through relations*. Experience, therefore, is a qualitative transaction, marked by its development over time, between an organism and its environment. Rather than reducing phenomena to primary causes, contemporary evolutionary approaches see reality in terms of dynamic systems of transactions.[21] Moreover, contemporary evolutionary approaches seek to avoid dualisms between spirit and matter, mind and body, human and nature. They understand matter and energy as mutually interdependent factors that transform each other over time. More important than the question of what these things *are* is the question of how these things *function* in relation to one another.

Although she does not name it explicitly, Gebara resonates deeply with McFague's organic and holistic model of the cosmos. Gebara approaches experience as a dynamic and always emerging transaction between an organism and its environment. Moreover, she understands human beings in terms of the ability of the cosmos to understand—and hence, ultimately, to transform—itself. That said, however, Gebara tends to focus her discussion of science on a negative critique of mechanistic and linear approaches without fully engaging the contributions of more contemporary, evolutionary approaches. In other words, Gebara lodges a vigorous and warranted critique against medieval and Newtonian models of science without fully developing the benefits of evolutionary models.

Why is this oversight worthy of our attention? If nothing else, it may unwittingly hide from our view some very helpful theoretical resources that attempt to do philosophy from the standpoint of an evolutionary model of science. McFague identifies one of these traditions as process thought. A second, related tradition that could also be explicitly named here is US pragmatism, which, like process thought, sees everything in the universe as being in motion.[22] In such a cosmos, every individual *thing* is really a spatially and temporally extended *event*. In addition, these events have no antecedent fixed meanings or essences; instead, meaning and essence emerge as a consequence of transactional processes.[23] For this reason, pragmatism puts a premium on how things and ideas function. The root question for pragmatism is not what something *is* "in itself" but, rather, how something *works* in a given environment. The "self," for example, is always functionally, and not "simply," located. When we begin to realize that our individual "selves" live by the grace of our sustaining relations, the meaning of our relations can accrue spiritual overtones.[24]

I mention all of this simply to reiterate that, contrary to what Gebara suggests about the origins of the concept of relatedness, there are, in fact, multiple resources that may both inform and amplify her concept. Such resources include not only incarnational forms of Christianity (as well as Native American, African, and Goddess cosmologies), but also evolutionary science and its philosophical offshoots, namely process thought and pragmatism.[25]

The study of pragmatism has traditionally implied both an engagement with canonical figures from the United States (such as Peirce, James, Dewey, Mead, Addams, Du Bois, and others) as well as a commitment to certain ways of thinking that pragmatists value (such as fallibilism, meliorism, pluralism, verification, and hope). Recent efforts to imagine "American" pragmatism as a deeply interwoven *inter*-American discourse, not only expands the canon significantly, but also sharpens pragmatism's core methodological commitments.[26]

Gebara models what a transhemispheric exchange of philosophical, theological, and feminist ideas can look like. While clearly influenced by Latin American male liberation theologians and Latin American feminists,[27] Gebara also expresses "a debt of gratitude" to many authors from North America. She laments that this is the same North "that has engaged in so many campaigns of domination and destruction, the North that keeps on subjecting people and regions to its greedy and exploitative projects." Yet, as she so graciously adds, "in the very midst of that empire of profit, prophetic voices have composed an alternative song, one that it is being heard also in the South."[28] The topics that all of these authors raise "belong not only to the North"—they are instead "key issues for all of humanity" and "they take on planetary significance . . ."[29]

As I have shown, Gebara and McFague remind us of the value of non-Western (and non-Christian) ways of knowing. Both authors actively work against the assumption that Christianity holds a deposit of eternal truth. That said, it is worth noting that Gebara's entry point is always the poor women with whom she lives and works. By listening to their voices, stories, and struggles, Gebara became aware of how central native forms of knowing are for these women. Even though she has lived among them for decades, Gebara makes clear that her own experience differs significantly from many of these women's realities.

For some, such disclaimers might seem to weaken Gebara's position since she herself cannot fully claim an "insider" position as a poor woman with an Indigenous inheritance, given the relative privilege she has as a woman religious who is supported by a religious order. On the contrary, I believe that such disclaimers actually strengthen her argument. Gebara shows us what it means constantly to decenter oneself for the purpose of lifting up the lowly. Moreover, like Jane Addams, one of Gebara's beautiful attributes is that she does this, not only through her philosophical and theological interventions, but also by living out her commitments in practice among poor women.

Although Gebara lodges one of the most important critiques against early liberation theology, one constant in her work is a preferential option for the poor and oppressed, which is indeed a hallmark of all liberation theologies. For Gebara, while philosophers and theologians may be well trained and equipped to lodge theoretical critiques against theories that mislead, obscure, and dehumanize, intellectual work is never enough. Gebara underscores her point when discussing current forms of feminism: "The challenging question for me is not the struggle among different ways of interpreting women's lives and the ecosystem, or the reductionism of theories, but the destruction of life while we are discussing the theories." For Gebara, socially committed academics should never lose sight of *actual* lived experiences of poverty, discrimination, oppression, or violence that so many women, children, and poor people face today. These experiences should serve as the starting point and the ending point of our work. Gebara warns that feminism should not "be tempted by masculine and competitive theories, which are in love with themselves." Rather, she insists that feminism should aspire equally to theories of structural reform as well as to concrete actions toward justice.[30]

Pragmatism has long been characterized as a tool for social criticism that takes lived experience as its starting point. Gebara, I believe, would urge pragmatists to push further. What are the actual problematic situations today that warrant the application of this "tool for social criticism"? Moreover, when we speak of lived experience, whose lived experiences do we care to privilege? Through her scholarly work and her own personal praxis, Ivone Gebara models what it means to use philosophy as a tool for social criticism and what it looks like to do so with a clear preferential option for the poor. For her, proximity to the poor and marginalized is essential both for grounding one's methodology and for centering one's ethical commitments. Those of us who care to sharpen pragmatism's social and political commitments would do well to learn from her example.

# Conclusion:
# Spiritual Praxis and the Fullness of Life

As I suggested in this book's Introduction, my time with detained immigrants taught me valuable lessons. As a volunteer, I had a firsthand opportunity to see how spirituality can function in life-giving ways, especially in light of the highly precarious situation of immigrant detention. Although it is easy to interpret immigrant detention in terms of what detainees lack (including access to high-quality legal representation and adequate mental health support), it is at the same time crucial to acknowledge the many resources that detained immigrants *do* bring to the table, including a dogged determination and an unceasing sense of hope. These assets point in the direction of a deep-seated spirituality. I had much to learn from the fortitude and faith of these exemplary human beings.

I started working on this book around the same time that I began volunteering with detained immigrants. I quickly came to see just how connected these two tasks were. The six thinkers featured in this book helped deepen my understanding of what I was experiencing in the detention center. I have no doubt that all these intellectuals would affirm the innate human dignity of detained immigrants. They would honor the desire of those displaced individuals to live fully human lives. Moreover, these intellectuals also lend analytical clarity to the inner workings of liberating spiritualities. They help us better understand what is entailed in *doing* liberating spirituality, both in theory and in practice. In many ways, their intellectual musings help us better appreciate the profundity of the everyday "faith of the people."[1]

As we have seen throughout this book, all six thinkers take issue with colonial, or Constantinian, forms of Christianity. Each uniquely seeks to articulate a decolonial spirituality that privileges the experiences of those who, in the words of Enrique Dussel, find themselves on the "underside of modernity."[2]

These thinkers also approach spirituality as a quality, or dimension, of human experience at large, which goes beyond the question of one's particular religious affiliation (or nonaffiliation). Mariátegui and Anzaldúa advance liberating spiritualities from well outside the parameters of traditional religions, while others like Freire, Elizondo, Isasi-Díaz, and Gebara seek to reconstruct inherited traditions through critical engagement. In all cases, two organizing principles are clear: the goal is human liberation and the starting point is human experience, of which our innate spiritual strivings are an integral part.[3]

Lastly, each of these thinkers understands spirituality as a powerful tool for individual and social transformation. For them, spirituality is not simply something that we passively inherit and uncritically reproduce. Rather, spirituality is a form of critical intelligence that helps us reconstruct and transform experience in life-giving ways. As any good critical theory of spirituality would emphasize, the point is not simply to interpret what human spirituality is, but rather to mobilize it to help change the world.

There is still much to explore. In the space that remains, I sketch out three areas that deserve further consideration—namely, the ongoing need for decolonial approaches to spirituality, the value of nurturing a pragmatic "ethos," and the utility of reconceptualizing liberating spiritualities as critical forms of pedagogy.

## Decolonial Spiritualities

A central premise of *Liberating Spiritualities* has been that spirituality is an inherent dimension of human experience at large. However, to avoid abstracting spirituality into a kind of free-floating "generic trait of existence," I have grounded our discussion of spirituality within the context and history of the Americas. As we have seen, it is impossible to talk about spirituality in the Americas without acknowledging the historical legacy of colonial violence on this continent and the colonial logics that persist in its wake. In the Americas, race, class, and gender are shot through with what Aníbal Quijano aptly describes as a "coloniality of power."[4]

A growing body of literature in decolonial thought helps us to see just how imbricated we are, both historically and ideologically, with persistent logics of coloniality. Decolonial thinkers have helped to show that the underside of modernity (and Enlightenment "progress" in general) is, in fact, coloniality, which is premised on the creation—and subjugation—of the non-European "other." In this light, European modernity succeeds precisely because it stands, both materially and ideologically, on the backs of non-European and non-white populations throughout the globe.

Decolonial theory amplifies the important work of postcolonial criticism (as found in the work of Edward Said, Homi K. Bhabha, Gayatri Spivak, and others) by critiquing modern standards of rationality and Eurocentric conceptions of emancipation. However, whereas postcolonial criticism tends to lean on (European) postmodern theory, decolonial thought turns more to the wisdom of thinkers from the Global South. Furthermore, whereas postcolonial theory largely takes as its historical point of departure nation-states becoming independent from European powers in the twentieth century, decolonial thinkers tie their critique of modernity/coloniality to the so-called "discovery" of the New World and the logics of domination that emerged from it in the sixteenth century, which soon touched every corner of the globe.

The burning question that needs to be asked, of course, is: How, if at all, can we transcend—or at least minimize—the epistemic hegemony of modernity/coloniality? There is, of course, no single answer to this question. Decolonial thought puts forward a variety of responses, which, on my reading, could be grouped into three general areas: careful *historical analyses* that offer genealogies of coloniality and modern-day racism; courageous forms of *ideological deconstruction* that call into question embedded logics of modernity/coloniality; and the creation of *habits of "seeing" and "doing,"* of theory and practice, that open up new—and/or recover forgotten—life-giving ways of being in the world.[5]

Although some decolonial theorists have been allergic to issues of faith and spirituality, there is a growing awareness that religious faith and human spirituality can have an important role to play in decolonial projects. On the whole, decolonial theorists maintain a healthy hermeneutics of suspicion when it comes to matters of religion and spirituality. They wisely maintain that such concepts should not be imported unwittingly but, rather, must be framed within the larger context of modernity/coloniality.

All this said, some decolonial theorists engage this critical recovery of faith and spirituality better than others. While I am indebted to many aspects of Walter Mignolo's work, including his discussion of border gnosis and his articulation of a decolonial aesthetics, I find his treatment of religion and religious faith often flippant and dismissive.[6] In an important volume entitled *Decolonizing Epistemologies: Latina/o Theology and Philosophy*—which was one of the first volumes of its kind to bring together decolonial theorists, on the one hand, and scholars of religion and theologians, on the other—Mignolo, a key architect of decolonial thought, argues that "to extricate oneself (to de-link from modernity/rationality) means to de-link from the Right, the Left, and liberation theology."[7] The irony here is that in a volume aimed at creating space for a dialogue between decolonial philosophers and decolonially-minded theologians and religious studies scholars, Mignolo seems more intent on building walls than exploring shared pathways forward. He dismisses Marxism outright as the "modern liberating secular left," and he clearly has little regard for liberation theology as a decolonial option. In a very broad and generalizing stroke, he writes: "[d]ecolonizing epistemology means, in the long run, liberating thinking from sacralized texts, whether religious or secular."[8]

To be sure, part of Mignolo's critique is warranted: certain strands of Marxism and liberation theology can and should be critiqued for not going far enough. But, as we have seen, this critique is, in fact, shared by thinkers like Mariátegui (as regards Marxism) and Gebara (as regards liberation theology). Like Mignolo, Mariátegui and Gebara point out the limitations within these intellectual frameworks, but unlike Mignolo, they carefully tease out what is still worth retaining within these vast and varied traditions. They show that decolonizing epistemology can, in fact, be compatible with more critical and nuanced strands of Marxism and liberation theology alike.

Now more than ever, we need bridge-building between intellectual traditions. This is especially the case between decolonial thought, on the one hand, and the disciplines of theology and religious studies, on the other. Like Mariátegui and Gebara, scholars would be well served to carefully consider points of difference *and* connection. Fortunately, a number of thinkers are making promising forays in this direction. Within the field of decolonial thought, Nelson Maldonado-Torres, M. Jacqui Alexander, and Rafael Vizcaíno have offered thoughtful reflections on the ways in which spirituality may be refracted through a decolonial lens.[9] Likewise, within the fields of theology and religious studies, Joseph Drexler-Dries, Néstor Medina, Mayra Rivera, Teresa Delgado, An Yountae, and Santiago Slabodsky, among others, have begun to show how decolonial perspectives may be of great use to contemporary theology.[10] Within the study of African American religion, scholars like Carol Wayne White, Vincent Lloyd, J. Cameron Carter, and Willie James Jennings have offered penetrating studies that expose the racial logics of modern, Eurocentric Christian thought, all the while affirming the full humanity of people of African descent, whether they identify as Christians or not.[11]

## The Value of a Pragmatic Ethos

When thinking through the liberating dimensions of spirituality, we would be well served to build bridges with intellectual resources such as those mentioned above. Throughout *Liberating Spiritualities*, I have underscored the merits of philosophical pragmatism in this regard. Pragmatism can help us to theorize liberating spiritualities across a multiplicity of intellectual traditions. Rather than focus on spirituality and religion as institutionally rigid systems of belief, I have instead invited the reader to see them in a more pragmatic light. Accordingly, we have asked: How is spirituality manifested organically in and through experience? How does spirituality *function* in our ongoing search for value and meaning? Such questions invite us to think more deeply about what we mean by *experience* (a perennial question of metaphysics) and how we, as conscious and creative beings, actively generate meaning (a pivotal question of epistemology).

As I have suggested throughout this work, the philosophical tradition of US pragmatism (and its close cousin, process thought) has much to offer. To underscore this point, I turn to two major voices within the pragmatic tradition: Charlene Haddock Seigfried and Richard Bernstein. As both show, the value of pragmatism is found not mainly in its theory of truth (for which it commonly known) or even in its significance as a philosophical method, but rather, in the overall sensibility, or ethos, that it helps to engender. This ethos values all knowledge as provisional and testable, welcomes a diversity of disciplinary perspectives and worldviews, and strives to utilize inquiry as a tool for social and ecological betterment.

Seigfried, a leading pragmatist feminist, offers three successively expanding interpretations of pragmatism. First, she defines pragmatism in terms of the positions developed by those who are generally recognized as the historical founders of the movement, a group that most commonly includes Charles Sanders Peirce, William James, Josiah Royce, John Dewey, and George Herbert Mead, among others. Second, Seigfried observes that notably absent from this founding group are women and people of color. As a result, "systematic discussions of sexism or racism" are almost nonexistent among the classical pragmatists.[12] In light of such omissions, Seigfried intervenes by "extend[ing] the original group to include women who directly or indirectly influenced the historically recognized pragmatists, as well as women who were influenced by them."[13] In other words, Seigfried carefully analyzes the work of notable women who were adjacent to the classical pragmatists. She makes a case for the ways in which they may be considered pragmatist not only "according to the classical expressions of pragmatism" but also, and perhaps more importantly, to the extent to which they diverged from this group, especially as they "incorporated reflections on their own lives as women and developed feminist analyses."[14] As Seigfried makes clear, such analyses force a reconstruction of pragmatism that is both historical *and* conceptual—historical insofar as it offers an expanded genealogy of the tradition, and conceptual insofar as such a reinterpretation allows us to reenvision the potential of its theoretical reach.

Similar to what Seigfried does in her work, I have made occasional historical connections between the six central figures of this study and the traditions of pragmatism and process thought. It is worth recalling that Mariátegui was receptive to the "as if" philosophies of William James and Hans Vaihinger; Freire and Anzaldúa were sympathetic to the educational and aesthetic works of John Dewey; Elizondo's approach to mestizaje is indebted to the cosmic vision of Teilhard de Chardin; Isasi-Díaz was drawn to the pragmatic, everyday epistemologies of Agnes Heller and other leading Latin American feminists inspired by her (such as Teresita de Barbieri, Julieta Kirkwood, and Ana Sojo); and Gebara was intimately familiar with the pragmatic ecofeminism of Rosemary Radford Ruether and Sally McFague.

These various historical links notwithstanding, I have taken a second cue from Seigfried by placing an even greater emphasis on the *conceptual* links between these thinkers and pragmatic-style thinking. I have shown that, even in those cases where the central figures of this study do not draw explicitly on the intellectual tradition of US pragmatism, there are nevertheless striking similarities in the intellectual and methodological approaches taken, approaches that are very much reflective of a "pragmatic ethos."

Philosopher Richard Bernstein would concur with Seigfried that pragmatism is best understood not so much as a set of doctrines or even as a philosophical method, but rather as a general attitude or orientation toward living. As Bernstein puts it, pragmatism is best understood as a habitual posture or "*ēthos*" that helps us address pressing real-world problems. Bernstein describes the pragmatic *ēthos* in terms of five interlocking themes:

1.  It is *anti-foundational* insofar as it rejects the idea that knowledge rests on fixed and immutable foundations.
2.  In keeping with an experimental habit of mind, it espouses a thoroughgoing *fallibilism*, which holds that all knowledge is interpretive, tentative, and always subject to correction.
3.  It underscores the *social character of the self* and the need to nurture a *critical community of inquirers*.
4.  It accepts *radical contingency and chance* as pervasive features of the universe, our inquiries, and our lives. As Bernstein writes, pragmatists believe that human beings "can never hope to 'master' unforeseen and unexpected contingencies." Pragmatists fully acknowledge that "[w]e live in an 'open universe' which is always at once threatening and a source of tragedy and opportunity."[15] This dual focus on tragedy and opportunity marks the best of the pragmatic tradition, and, as Bernstein notes, it actually *conditions* the

way that pragmatists themselves understand experience and philosophy. For pragmatists, the proper existential and philosophical response to our "open universe" is the establishment of *critical habits of mind*, which Dewey refers to as "reflective intelligence" and Freire as "conscientization." In both cases, intelligence is less a mechanical means to solve or master problems, and more a disposition, an ethos, which allows us to respond to the precarity of the universe with care, courage, and foresight.

5.  Lastly, pragmatists acknowledge and uphold the value of *plurality*—a plurality of traditions, perspectives, and epistemic orientations, all of which add insight into an ever-changing and ever-fluid stream of experience. For pragmatists, there is always more to experience than meets the eye. As James once wrote, a pluralistic pragmatism holds that "there is no where extant a *complete* gathering up of the universe in *one* focus, either of knowledge, power, or purpose. *Something* escapes, even from God."[16] A major hallmark of the pragmatic ethos is therefore a radical openness to the inevitable excess of experience, or to what James at times refers to as "the more" of experience.

Weaving all of these aspects together, Bernstein summarizes the pragmatic tradition as a kind of "engaged fallibilistic pluralism." "Such a pluralistic *ēthos*," he writes, "places new responsibilities upon each of us. For it means taking our own fallibility seriously—resolving that however much we are committed to our own styles of thinking, we are willing to listen to others without denying or suppressing the otherness of the other."[17]

## Spirituality as Critical Pedagogy

Another consistent thread throughout this book has been what Paulo Freire refers to as conscientization, a process of developing a critical awareness of reality through reflection and action. As we have seen, Anzaldúa's concept of conocimiento is akin to Freire's understanding of conscientization, especially insofar that both point in the direction of what Anzaldúa calls "spiritual activism," an amalgamation of both reflective spiritual practices and political activism.

An important precursor to Freire's understanding of conscientization can be seen in Mariátegui's "new sense" of religion, which underscores the praxic dimensions of faith. It is worth recalling once again how pivotal Mariátegui's work was for Gustavo Gutiérrez's own understanding of the intimate relationship between theology and praxis. In a similar way, the work of Elizondo, Isasi-Díaz, and Gebara can be understood as historically subsequent articulations of conscientization. In large part, Elizondo is asking what conscientization looks like from the perspective of minoritized cultures. Isasi-Díaz is interested in how a "conscientized cotidiano" functions in the context of everyday life, particularly among women of color. Moreover, Gebara invites liberation thinkers to wrestle more boldly with embedded hierarchical logics that make it difficult, even within liberationist frameworks, to think and act in nondualistic and nonhierarchical ways. By centering relatedness and interconnectedness, Gebara helps liberation thinkers enter more deeply into processes of conscientization.

Concepts like conscientization and conocimiento are indispensable to socially transformative forms of education. Unlike more traditional forms of education that serve to maintain the status quo, critical education is fundamentally an education for social change: it seeks social transformation for individuals and communities alike.

While Freire's notion of conscientization has been central to this work, equally important is the educational work of John Dewey, whom Freire read.[18] Both thinkers approach education in ways that are learner-centered; both see education as a powerful tool for addressing real-world problems; and both believe that education contributes mightily to the full flourishing of individuals and communities.[19]

One pressing question that we could pose to both thinkers, however, is: In what ways can human spirituality itself function as a critical form of education? On the one hand, both Freire and Dewey write extensively about socially transformative forms of education. They make a strong case for showing how education extends well beyond the confines of classroom learning. Freire, for example, explicitly rejects a "banking model of education," and Dewey encourages us to think about education as the "reconstruction or reorganization of experience which adds to the meaning of experience, and which increases ability to direct the course of subsequent experience."[20] One striking feature of this definition is that it could apply to the process of reconstructing *any* experience (including those we deem religious or "spiritual"), as long as the process leads to increased meaning and growth.

On the other hand, however, both Freire and Dewey have surprisingly little to say about the educational function of human spirituality. This is especially ironic given Freire's many exchanges with early liberation theologians and given that his concept of conscientization was pivotal for liberation theology at large. Similarly, Dewey was himself no stranger to religious questions, having written a small but important treatise on religion, which I discuss further below.

All this said, there is no reason why those of us who find value in Freire's and Dewey's work cannot forge these links ourselves. Liberative and pragmatic approaches to education as informed by figures like Freire and Dewey, offer invaluable pathways for understanding spirituality. In this book, I have pursued this line of questioning largely along philosophical and theological lines. But one could draw on other approaches to probe further the connections between spirituality and education.

Constructive-developmental and psychosocial approaches to education, many of which have close ties to pragmatism, offer yet another way forward. Three recent studies that explore what it means to be "spiritual but not religious" help to underscore this point.[21] In her classic study, *Big Questions, Worthy Dreams: Mentoring Emerging Adults in Their Search for Meaning, Purpose, and Faith* (2010), Sharon Daloz Parks offers one of the most compelling accounts of how young adults in their twenties navigate meaning-making and questions of faith. As Parks suggests, "Faith is often linked exclusively to belief, particularly religious belief. But faith goes far beyond religious belief, narrowly understood. Faith is more adequately recognized as *the activity of seeking and discovering meaning in the most comprehensive dimensions of our experience*—that is, *faith* is as much a verb as a noun."[22] Parks borrows this idea of faith as a verb from the eminent historian of religion, Wilfred Cantwell Smith, whose own thinking is shaped by the work of John Dewey, as I discuss momentarily.[23]

Elizabeth Tisdell offers another insightful account of the role of spirituality in teaching and learning. In *Exploring Spirituality and Culture in Adult and Higher Education* (2003), Tisdell focuses on the potential role of spirituality in teaching for cultural relevance with multicultural populations in higher and adult education. As she makes clear, "*spirituality is* not *about pushing a religious agenda.*"[24] Instead, Tisdell articulates a set of assumptions that guide thinking about spirituality, which include the following: (a) spirituality and religion are not the same, but for many people they are interrelated; (b) spirituality is an awareness and honoring of wholeness and the interconnectedness of all things through the mystery of what many refer to as the Life-force, God, higher power, higher self, cosmic energy, Buddha nature, or Great Spirit; (c) spirituality is fundamentally about meaning-making; (d) spirituality is always present (although often unacknowledged) in the learning environment; (e) spiritual development constitutes moving toward greater authenticity or to a more authentic self; (f) spirituality is about how people construct knowledge through largely unconscious and symbolic processes, often made more concrete in art forms such as music, image, symbol, and ritual, all of which are manifested culturally; and (g) spiritual experiences most often happen by surprise.[25]

Writing around the same time as Parks and Tisdell, another group of re-searchers, led by Alexander Astin, Helen Astin, and Jennifer Lindholm, shared their findings of the first, national longitudinal study of spiritual growth among college-age students. One of their central research questions was: "What are institutions doing that aids or inhibits students in their spiritual quest?" The research team developed five measures connected to religious qualities and five measures connected to spiritual qualities. Whereas the religious qualities largely pertain to elements connected to organized religion, the research team describes spirituality in terms of the following measures:

> [Spirituality] involves an active quest for answers to life's "big questions" (<u>Spiritual Quest</u>), a global worldview that transcends ethnocentrism and egocentrism (<u>Ecumenical Worldview</u>), a sense of caring and compassion for others (<u>Ethic of Caring</u>) coupled with a lifestyle that includes service to others (<u>Charitable Involvement</u>), and a capacity to maintain one's sense of calm and centeredness, especially in times of stress (<u>Equanimity</u>).[26]

All three of these studies offered by Parks, Tisdell, and Astin et al. share a common assumption. They distinguish between organized religion and a more comprehensive sense of faith or spirituality. But one may ask: From where does this distinction arise? If we trace sources, it becomes clear that Parks and Tis-dell are drawing heavily on constructive-developmental approaches as found in the psychological work of Erik Erikson, Jean Piaget, Robert Kegan, Carol Gilligan, and others. In addition, James Fowler's groundbreaking work, which explores spirituality as a developmental process, is particularly central for both Parks and Tisdell.[27]

Significantly, all of these approaches, in turn, are indebted to the ground-breaking work of educator and philosopher John Dewey, who, notably, also made significant forays into psychology.[28] In 1934, Dewey published *A Common Faith*, a short and provocative book about the religious dimension of human experience. His central claim, which has proven generative for later thinkers, is that there is a fundamental difference between traditional conceptions of "religion" and a more pragmatic understanding of "the religious." Today, we may translate this distinction as the difference between religion and spirituality.

The first chapter of *A Common Faith*, titled "Religion Versus the Religious," elucidates the difference. Religion, Dewey explains, is often conceived of as a noun substantive.[29] It "signifies a special body of beliefs and practices having some kind of institutional organization, loose or tight."[30] In contrast, "the adjective 'religious' denotes nothing in the way of a specifiable entity, either institutional or as a system of beliefs."[31] Instead, "the religious" denotes attitudes that may be taken toward every object and every proposed end or ideal."[32] Thus, rather than focus on the question of what "a religion" is, Dewey urges his readers to consider how we may *enact* a sense of the religious in our everyday lives.

Dewey is able to shift the meaning of religion from a noun to an adjective and verb because he understands experience itself to be a constant, dynamic process of organisms interacting with their environment. In particular cases, this interaction involves the creation of powerful ideals that may stir and reorient us in deep-seated ways. For Dewey, such interactions need not be limited to the experiences of organized religion. If our transactions with our environment lead to a deep-seated reorientation or "adjustment" in life, then by virtue of this effect, the experience is a religious one.[33]

Dewey's attention to the "effect produced" is key to his argument. When we have what we deem to be a religious (or spiritual) experience, Dewey makes clear that "religious value" is not, strictly speaking, determined by the "manner and cause" of the experience, such as divine or supernatural intervention. Rather, "the way in which the experience operated, its function, determines its religious value."[34] Dewey thus flips the script on our traditional conception of religious faith. Religious studies scholar Eddie Glaude, Jr. aptly describes this as Dewey's "inversion strategy."[35] Rather than assume *a priori* that religious institutions are automatically and necessarily the source of deep-seated and enduring changes in attitude, Dewey turns the statement around, positing that "whenever this change takes place there is definitely a religious attitude. It is not a religion that brings it about, but when it occurs, from whatever cause and by whatever means, there is a religious outlook and function."[36]

Contemporary constructive-developmentalist approaches can help us understand better how, exactly, these deep-seated changes in attitude cognitively emerge. By situating spirituality in a more educative and developmentalist light, such approaches help fill a noticeable gap in the otherwise indispensable work of Freire and Dewey.

As *Liberating Spiritualities* has shown, human spirituality is a constitutive dimension of what it means to be human. As noted in the Introduction, spirituality emerges when human beings reconstruct and reorganize experience in ways that form a consistent pattern of habit and action that is measured by some ultimate concern. Spiritualities that are *liberating* take this definition one step further insofar as they also incorporate a *critical consciousness* that connects ultimate concern to acts of *redressing systems of oppression* and *promoting human flourishing*. To some, especially those with a more theistic and Abrahamic bent, this may sound like a very "secular" approach to spirituality that is best left to nontheistic "spiritual activists" like Anzaldúa or Mariátegui.

It is worth recalling, however, that within the Jewish tradition, the Torah urges the faithful to devote themselves to justice by aiding the wronged, upholding the rights of the orphan, and defending the cause of the widow (Isaiah 1:17). The Christian Scriptures make clear that Jesus came so that all may have life and have it abundantly (John 10:10), while the Islamic Qur'an is replete with themes of social justice, many of which are connected to Islam's institutional-ization of an alms tax (or *zakat*, one of the central Five Pillars of Islam), which is to be used toward the just treatment of debtors, widows, the poor, and orphans (90:13–16). But even far beyond traditional Abrahamic traditions, liberationist approaches have also been taken up in a variety of other religious frameworks, including Hinduism, Buddhism, Confucianism, Daoism, African traditional religions, Orisha traditions in the West, American Indian religious traditions, Minjung theology, and humanist traditions.[37]

I have chosen to focus this book around human spirituality rather than reli-gious faith because, in many ways, organic forms of spirituality precede formal articulations of faith. As theologian Roger Haight reminds us, "while individual spiritualities can exist without religion, religions cannot exist without spirituality but are precisely the institutionalization of spirituality. Spirituality is prior to religion, and religion has as its purpose to reflect and support spirituality."[38]

The preceding discussion about constructive-developmentalist approaches to spirituality corroborates this point, as does recent work in evolutionary an-thropology. The evolutionary record shows that human beings began having spiritual strivings well before the dawn of organized forms of religion. As an-thropologist Agustín Fuentes points out, "multiple lines of evidence suggest that having religious beliefs is much older than formal religious systems, struc-tures, and institutions."[39] Whereas formal religious institutions—such as Hin-duism, Buddhism, Judaism, Christianity, and Islam—have roots dating back 4,000 to 8,000 years ago, we know that humans were engaging in behaviors, such as burials, that "may have reflected collective transcendent experiences" as far back as 200,000 to 400,000 years ago.[40] Fuentes's insight lends further credibility to Dewey's distinction between organized religion and an innate and organic sense of the religious, which today we often refer to as spirituality.

Although spirituality predates formal modes of religious faith, *Liberating Spiritualities* has invited readers to consider how human spirituality—whether distinct from institutional religion or cultivated within it—can address some of the most pressing problems of our day. A necessary first step, of course, is recognizing that many prevailing forms of spirituality and religion in fact bol-ster the status quo and do little to address systems of inequality. Recall, for example, Anzaldúa's critique of certain forms of New Age thought that lean so heavily on the personal dimensions of spirituality that they overlook existing oppressive social structures. In a similar way, liberation theologians have denounced institutional structures of all stripes, including oppressive structures within churches themselves, that limit humanity's full flourishing.

Yet, even in light of such critiques, it would be shortsighted not to acknowledge that the cause of justice can be equally served by certain organic and activist expressions of spirituality as well as certain prophetic manifestations of religion. In this book, I have explored both sides of this coin: on the one hand, activist forms of spirituality that exist in their own right as intrinsic dimensions of human experience, and on the other, prophetic forms of religion that cultivate organic forms of spirituality. As we have seen, particularly in the case of Mariátegui and Anzaldúa, it is entirely possible to approach liberating forms of spirituality outside of the confines of organized religion. Mariátegui's new sense of religion and Anzaldúa's notions of spiritual activism and conocimiento allow for more humanist interpretations of spiritualities that liberate.

At the same time, we have seen how liberating spiritualities can also be cultivated through the grammar of organized religion. Contextual theologians like Elizondo, Isasi-Díaz, and Gebara take concrete human experience as their starting point, an approach that is indeed characteristic of the more "anthropological" point of departure that is part and parcel of many contextual and liberation theologies today.[41] Such an approach invites us to consider how theological interpretations of that which we may tentatively and imperfectly call "sacred" can be rendered more compelling by humanistic, anthropological, and naturalistic starting points. To put the matter another way, liberation theology invites us to problematize the old, inherited dualism between the sacred and the profane and, instead, reimagine how a sense of the sacred can emerge *in* and *through* our active engagement with everyday experience.[42]

Philosophical pragmatism lends further analytical clarity to such an approach. Pragmatism rejects any sharp separation between mind and body, subject and object, human and nature, spiritual and material. Instead, it champions continuity and connection by focusing on how we, as thinking and feeling creatures, actively transact with the environments in which we live. For pragmatists, this transaction *is* experience. Experience, therefore, is not simply something that we observe or passively undergo. Rather, it is also something that demands our input and guidance through the medium of human intelligence.

Liberating spiritualities are, at their best, intelligent modes of engaging the world that center those on the periphery of society and seek to redress unwarranted forms of human suffering. Of course, human beings suffer due to numerous causes, many of which are beyond human control. Contrary to what many critics of pragmatism argue, pragmatism squarely acknowledges the precarity and uncertainty of existence. A sense of the tragic undergirds the tradition. In a Darwinian "universe of chance," such a starting point is unavoidable. Pragmatists understand that human beings can never hope to master fully the unexpected and arbitrary contingencies that the universe puts in front of us. As Martin Heidegger would say, we are very much "thrown" into an existence that we have not actively chosen. Yet, for this reason, the animating question for pragmatists is precisely "What *can* we do, even in light of our very real limitations, to shape our experience in ways that promote individual, communal, and ecological flourishing?" This book has shown that liberating spiritualities are highly imaginative and socially engaged forms of intelligence that have been forged in the mighty kiln of human evolution. They are powerful tools to help us chart a yet uncertain future.

In closing, a case can be made that religion today remains very much in the shadow of Karl Marx, who is known for his terse observation that religion is "the opium of the people." For Marx, religion is a drug that anesthetizes people to their suffering. To drive this point home further, Marx adds: "The abolition of religion as the illusory happiness of the people is the demand for their real happiness." As these sentences seem to suggest, Marx sees no place for religion, which presumably refers here to institutional or organized religion.

But what is often overlooked is a second sense of religion that Marx entertains directly before his damning critique of organized religion. Here is the paragraph in its entirety:

> Religious suffering is, at one and the same time, the expression of real suffering and a protest against real suffering. Religion is the sigh of the oppressed creature, the heart of a heartless world, and the soul of soulless conditions. It is the opium of the people.[43]

The first two (largely sympathetic) sentences of this passage help to contextualize that famous (largely negative) third sentence. In so many words, Marx *begins* by saying that religion—which can be read as spirituality, in general—sustains people. He seems to acknowledge how very natural it is for human beings to use spiritual resources to confront their suffering. But this more general nod to human spirituality—religion with a small "r," let us call it—is quickly overtaken by Marx's critique of organized religion—or Religion with a capital "R."

Thus, when Marx writes that "[t]he abolition of religion as the illusory happiness of the people is the demand for their real happiness," the crucial question that needs to be asked is: The abolition of religion in what sense?

As we have seen throughout this work, certain mainstream manifestations of institutional religion can easily become the opium of the people, colonial forms of Christendom being a case in point. It is irrefutable that when aligned with the economic and ideological interests of those in power, organized religion can be an utterly destructive force. Yet, what Marx fails to consider in this passage are the ways in which more liberating approaches to religion and spirituality can serve to promote, instead of extinguish, the fullness of life.

At their best, both liberation theology and pragmatism help to chart new pathways forward. When put into dialogue with one another—and when aided by other critical discourses like decolonial thought, Third World feminism, and critical pedagogy—they show us how organic forms of spirituality and formal forms of religion alike may be approached in nondualistic, nonhierarchical, and nonhegemonic ways. Such interpretive tools equip us to better hear the "sigh of the oppressed creature" and to feel the "heart of a heartless world."

The pivotal next question, of course, is: What shall we *do* with these interpretations? As both Marx and liberation theology would note, it is one thing to interpret the world and another to change it.[44] Similarly, Dewey and pragmatism hold that once we recognize the power of humanity's implicit spirituality, we have "the responsibility of conserving, transmitting, rectifying and expanding the heritage of values we have received [so] that those who come after us may receive it more solid and secure. . . ."[45] Both stances urge us toward active forms of doing. They invite us to put our knowledge into practice.

Liberating spiritualities, as imaginative expressions of conscientization, can help us move humankind in this direction. Engaging them, however, is never easy. As Freire reminds us, conscientization is a painful birth; it "demands that we die to be reborn again."[46] Moreover, the process of dying and being reborn is never complete, never exhausted. Instead, it demands that we continually strive to cultivate habits of thought and action—an ethos of "engaged, fallibilistic pluralism," as Bernstein would say—if deep and lasting change is to come about.

For those on the underside of history, and for those in solidarity with them, one fact is clear: human spirituality can indeed be one vital resource for engaging this journey.

# Acknowledgments

This book has been in the works for close to a decade and has gone through numerous permutations. I am deeply grateful to colleagues and students alike for their feedback, support, and critique as the project evolved. I am delighted to be able to finally share it with a wider audience.

A number of institutions and related grants have helped to make this book possible, including the Louisville Institute (Sabbatical Grant for Researchers); DePaul University (Center for Latino/a Research Fellowship, Humanities Center Fellowship, University Research Council Research Grant, and a College Summer Research Grant) the University of San Diego (Portman Research Award); and Santa Clara University (Buckley Endowed Visiting Professorship).

One of the of the greatest joys of academic life has been forming friendships with individuals who are not only careful thinkers but also inspirational human beings. As such, I give thanks for the various scholarly communities in which I have participated, including the Society for the Advancement of American Philosophy (SAAP); the American Academy of Religion (AAR), particularly the "Religion in the Latina/o Americas" unit; the Academy of Catholic Hispanic Theologians of the U.S. (ACHTUS), the John Dewey Society; the Latin American Philosophy of Education Society (LAPES); and the Society of Christian Ethics (SCE). I am particularly indebted to a number of individuals both within and outside of these networks who have formally commented on my work and/or have offered helpful suggestions and critiques. They include Tom Alexander, Jerome Baggett, Victor Carmona, Davíd Carrasco, Jeremiah Coogan, MT Dávila, Theresa Delgadillo, Kim Díaz, Eddie Fernández, Marilyn Fischer, Nichole Flores, Sergio Gallegos, Jim Garrison, Ivone Gebara, Michelle

González Maldonado, Leo Guardado, Ed Hackett, Christopher Hadley, Roger Haight, Gina Hens-Piazza, Jaisy Joseph, AnaLouise Keating, David Lantigua, Bob Lassalle-Klein, Daisy Machado, Terrance MacMullan, Monica Marcelli-Chu, Elizabeth Martínez, Roberto Mata, Tim Matovina, James Nati, Denise Meda-Lambru, Alex Nava, José-Antonio Orosco, Gregory Fernando Pappas, Aaron Pratt, Devaka Premawardhana, Michael Raposa, Bobbie Rivera, Jorge Rodríguez, Julie Rubio, René Sánchez, John Phillip Santos, Eugene Schlesinger, Paul Schutz, Antonio Sison, Sabrina Starnaman, Alexander Stehn, Ken Stikkers, Lourdes Torres, Rafael Vizcaíno, Len Waks, and Raúl Zegarra. In addition, I would like to thank Richard Morrison at Fordham University Press for his engaging conversation and sage advice, as well as Gabriella Oldham and Lis Pearson for their excellent copyediting.

In addition to sharing this work with other scholars, I have had the opportunity to test-drive parts of the book with students at DePaul University, the Catholic Theological Union, the Hispanic Summer Program, and Santa Clara University. I have benefited immensely from their questions and feedback. As a teacher, I often think about a proverb that is commonly associated with Buddhism and theosophical traditions: "When the *student* is ready, the teacher appears." No doubt, my job as a teacher-scholar would be impossible without the readiness and hard work of my students. For their critical attentiveness to this text, and for the care and consideration they have shown me and each other, I am most grateful. I would also like to give special recognition to my fabulous research assistants over the years: Michelle Benavente, Araceli Llamas, Nick Noriega, Tony Perez Soto, Sadman Rahman, and Karla Velasco.

Finally, I want to express my deep thanks to my spouse, Allison, for her superb editorial suggestions and unwavering support. This text was written over a period of several major transitions in the life of our family, including our children's entrance into high schools and colleges, three extended stays in the Dominican Republic, COVID-19, moving across the country, and job transitions. I thank her for journeying with me and for helping, amid all our twists and turns, to make this book a reality.

# Notes

## Introduction. Toward a Liberating Spirituality

1. For ICDI's current ministries, visit http://icdichicago.org/.

2. Indeed, the term "religion" proves problematic when applied to Indigenous contexts given that it is by-and-large a colonial construction. See Philip P. Arnold, *The Urgency of Indigenous Values* (Syracuse: Syracuse University Press, 2023); and George E. Tinker, *American Indian Liberation: A Theology of Sovereignty* (Maryknoll, NY: Orbis Books, 2008).

3. As indicated here and in the book's subtitle, this work focuses on Spanish- and Portuguese-language authors of the "Américas," most of whom also speak English. As the reader will find, Latin American liberation theology and US Latine theology figure prominently in this work. That said, one should note that liberationist voices in the Americas represent a wide variety of languages, cultures, and subtraditions, which also include Black theology, Womanist theology, and Queer theology, as well as liberationist perspectives from Native American and Orisha traditions. See Miguel A. De La Torre, *Liberation Theology for Armchair Theologians* (Louisville, KY: Westminster John Knox, 2013); *The Hope of Liberation in World Religions*, ed. Miguel A. De La Torre (Waco, TX: Baylor University Press, 2008); and Lilian Calles Barger, *The World Come of Age: An Intellectual History of Liberation Theology* (New York: Oxford University Press, 2018).

4. David E. Stannard, *American Holocaust: Columbus, Christianity, and the Conquest of the Americas* (New York: Oxford University Press, 1992).

5. Aníbal Quijano, "Colonialidad del poder y clasificación social," *Journal of World-Systems Research* 6, no. 2 (2000): 342–86.

6. See, for example, David L. Dungan, *Constantine's Bible: Politics and the Making of the New Testament* (Minneapolis: Fortress, 2007).

7. Daniel Boyarin, *The Jewish Gospels: The Story of the Jewish Christ* (New York: The New Press, 2012).

8. Cornel West, *Democracy Matters: Winning the Fight Against Imperialism* (New York: Penguin, 2004), 148. West's largely Kierkegaardian critique of "Christendom" is also seen in the work of Willie James Jennings. See Jennings, *The Christian Imagination: Theology and the Origins of Race* (New Haven, CT: Yale University Press, 2010).

9. Sandra M. Schneiders, "Spirituality in the Academy," *Theological Studies* 50 (1989): 678.

10. Schneiders, "Spirituality in the Academy," 678, emphasis added. On this point, Schneiders cites the work of Heagle, who summarizes the difference between preconciliar and postconciliar spirituality. See John Heagle, "A New Public Piety: Reflections on Spirituality," *Church* 1 (1985): 53.

11. In addition to referring to this tradition as US *Latine* theology, scholars also frequently use the terms *Latina/o* and *Latinx*. As Nichole Flores points out, these two terms are used to interrogate gender essentialisms in the Spanish language and in Romance languages more generally. More specifically, *Latina/o* and *Latinx* help to call attention to "the complexity of gender identity, with each one foregrounding a marginalized group within the community: women-identified people in the former (both trans- and cis-) and trans-identified folx in the latter." With these concerns in mind, I use *Latine* here in much the same way that Flores and others do: as an encompassing (although always imperfect) attempt "to describe *la comunidad* in [*all*] our racial, cultural, linguistic, sexual, and gender diversity." Nichole M. Flores, *The Aesthetics of Solidarity: Our Lady of Guadalupe and American Democracy* (Washington, D.C.: Georgetown University Press, 2021), 16.

12. Anita De Luna, *Faith Formation and Popular Religion: Lessons from Tejano Experience* (Lanham, MD: Rowman & Littlefield, 2002), 14.

13. Edwin Aponte, *¡Santo!: Varieties of Latina/o Spirituality* (Maryknoll, NY: Orbis, 2012), 55.

14. See Christopher Tirres, *The Aesthetics and Ethics of Faith: A Dialogue Between Liberationist and Pragmatic Thought* (New York: Oxford University Press, 2014), 88–98.

15. As Schneiders shows, the dogmatic approach is typified by the work of C.-A. Bernard, and the anthropological approach is reflected in the work of J.-C. Breton. Schneiders, "Spirituality in the Academy," 682.

16. Schneiders, "Spirituality in the Academy," 682.

17. Roger Haight, *Spiritual and Religious: Explorations for Seekers* (Maryknoll, NY: Orbis, 2016), xi, emphasis added.

18. Haight takes a cue here from Paul Tillich, who speaks of faith as being grasped by an ultimate concern. Along these lines, I also find helpful Charles Long's understanding of religion as a deep form of "orientation." See Charles Long, *Significations: Signs, Symbols, and Images in the Interpretation of Religion* (Aurora, CO: Davies Group, 1995).

19. Schneiders, "Spirituality in the Academy," 678; Haight, *Spiritual and Religious*, 2; Aponte, *¡Santo!*, 55.

20. De Luna, *Faith Formation and Popular Religion*, 14, emphasis added.

21. Ronald Rolheiser, *The Holy Longing: The Search for a Christian Spirituality* (New York: Doubleday, 1999), 7.

22. John E. Smith, *Experience and God* (New York: Fordham University Press), 25. I am indebted to Smith's discussion of "reflection" and "refraction," which he discusses in terms of experience in general.

23. I explore some of the fundamental convergences between these two traditions in *The Aesthetics and Ethics of Faith.*

24. Such is articulated in Charles Sanders Peirce's foundational "pragmatic maxim," which holds that meaning is best acquired not through *a priori* appeal to self-evidence (as Descartes presumed) or through abstract definition (as Leibniz argued), but, rather, by remaining ever attentive to the conceivably practical *effects* that any given idea may have. For Peirce, our conception of the effects of any given idea, in fact, constitutes the whole of its meaning. Charles S. Peirce, "How to Make Our Ideas Clear" in *Selected Writings (Values in a Universe of Chance)*, ed. Philip P. Wiener (New York: Dover, 1958), 124.

25. It is worth noting, however, that the more time we spend inquiring further about either, the more we are likely to see overlap between the two. A video, after all, is a series of sequential photos that tell a story, such as seen in time-lapse photography and flipbooks. Similarly, when we view a photo, our imagination may lead us to explore multiple layers of meaning beyond simply the "things" that are depicted. We may, for instance, inquire further into the photo's context, creating our own story of what the things in the photo are actively "doing." Thus, the more we imagine and inquire, the more the boundaries dissolve between photo and video, object and action, stasis and movement. Alejandro Nava makes a similar observation in his perceptive study of the religious dimensions of hip-hop. Hip-hop reminds us, writes Nava, that "most scriptures, before becoming frozen on paper, were originally recited, chanted, rhapsodized, incanted, declaimed, and sung in ways that set them apart from ordinary speech." Alejandro Nava, *Street Scriptures: Between God and Hip-Hop* (Chicago: University of Chicago Press, 2022), 6.

26. I am grateful to Antonio Sison for our conversations on this topic. See Antonio D. Sison, *World Cinema, Theology, and the Human: Humanity in Deep Focus* (New York: Routledge, 2012).

27. As I will show in Chapter 2, Freire proves to be a helpful bridge figure for the present study, as his work straddles all three questions. In Chapter 4, I will explore Anzaldúa's rich concept of "spiritual activism."

28. David Hildebrand, *Dewey: A Beginner's Guide* (Oxford: Oneworld, 2008), 41.

29. In his excellent study of human understanding, Mark Johnson underscores this point by drawing liberally on the work of Antonio Damasio. As Johnson puts it, "Before there is abstract thinking, before there is reasoning, before there is speech, there is emotion." Furthermore, Johnson convincingly shows that adult human

intelligence is not so far removed from the meaning-making processes of babies. In this sense, "[a]dults are big babies," Johnson writes. He explains: the "many bodily ways by which infants and children find and make meaning are not transcended and left behind when children eventually grow into adulthood. On the contrary, these very same sources of meaning are carried forward into, and thus underlie and make possible, our mature acts of understanding, conceptualization, and reasoning." Mark Johnson, *The Meaning of the Body: Aesthetics of Human Understanding* (Chicago: University of Chicago Press, 2008), 52, 33.

30. The pragmatic tradition resonates with Ellacuría and Zubiri's understanding of sentient intelligence. John Dewey, for instance, sees a close connection between immediate experience and related forms of sense apprehension, on the one hand, and more reflective and deliberative forms of inquiry that speak to higher-order forms of reason and understanding, on the other. Similarly, Peirce's categories of Firstness, Secondness, and Thirdness bear a striking resemblance to a Zubirian understanding of intelligence.

31. Thomas B. Fowler, "Informal Introduction to the Philosophy of Xavier Zubiri," http://www.zubiri.org/works/informalintro.htm.

32. Fowler, "Informal Introduction."

33. For Ellacuría, the proper starting point of faith is God's saving action *in* and *through* historical reality, which is much different from a more traditional and extrinsic conception of God who "breaks into" reality. See Michael E. Lee, *Bearing the Weight of Salvation: The Soteriology of Ignacio Ellacuría* (New York: Crossroad, 2008); Kevin F. Burke and Robert A. Lassalle-Klein, eds., *Love That Produces Hope: The Thought of Ignacio Ellacuría* (Collegeville, MN: Liturgical Press, 2006); and Mayra Rivera, *The Touch of Transcendence: A Postcolonial Theology of God* (Louisville, KY: Westminster John Knox, 2007), 41–47.

34. Although the focus of each chapter will be on the author's intellectual contributions, I would like to take a moment to acknowledge Virgilio Elizondo's surprising and tragic passing, which still reverberates among those who knew and loved him. In 2016, Elizondo took his own life. In 2015, he had been named as a secondary defendant in a civil case against the young priest Jesús Armando Domínguez for sexual abuse of a minor that allegedly occurred over a period of several years in the early 1980s. The plaintiff claimed that he reported his abuse at Domínguez's hands to Elizondo, but that Elizondo failed to help him, and instead, kissed and fondled him. Elizondo fervently denied the charges against him and consistently maintained his innocence. While Dominguez was found guilty of multiple counts of sexual abuse, in both civil and criminal suits in Texas and later in California, no evidence was found to support the charges against Elizondo, no other accuser ever stepped forward, and the case was eventually closed. Upon being charged, and as a matter of common practice, Elizondo was removed from his ministerial and teaching duties while the case was pending. The proceedings were delayed, and his suspension continued for ten months. (Even after Elizondo's death, the case dragged on for an additional seven years until it was finally closed.) While

we cannot ever fully know the reasons why Elizondo chose to end his life, those who were close to him know that in this period of isolation he was in ill health and low spirits. As one of his many friends, I struggle to understand his untimely death but, at the same time, I celebrate his remarkable contributions as a pastor, scholar, teacher, colleague, and friend. As such, I resonate deeply with the comments offered by Fr. Daniel Groody at Elizondo's memorial mass at the University of Notre Dame: "[T]he final question about Virgil can never be, 'Why did he take his own life?'" Rather, the "central question must always be, 'How did he give us life?'" Catherine Owens, "Mass Remembers Theology Professor Fr. Elizondo," *The Observer,* April 8, 2016, https://ndsmcobserver.com/2016/04/mass-remembers-fr -elizondo/, accessed Dec 30, 2023. See also Victor Carmona's touching tribute, "Virgilio Elizondo, A Man of the Marginalized," *America: The Jesuit Review,* April 18, 2016, https://www.americamagazine.org/content/all-things/virgilio-elizondo-man -marginalized.

35. John Dewey, *Democracy and Education* MW9: 82. This and all subsequent citations of Dewey's works are taken from the thirty-seven-volume critical edition, *The Collected Works of John Dewey,* 1882–1953, ed. Jo Ann Boydston (Carbondale: Southern Illinois University Press, 1967–1990). Citations give the name of the text, series abbreviation (EW-Early Works, MW-Middle Words, LW-Later Works), volume number, and page number.

36. Freire read Dewey's work and was clearly influenced by it, thanks in large part to Anísio Teixeira, one of Brazil's foremost translators and interpreters of Dewey. See Darcísio Natal Muraro, "Relações entre a filosofia e a educação de John Dewey e de Paulo Freire," *Educação & Realidade* 38, no. 3, (2013): 813–29; and Marcus Vinicius Da Cunha and Débora Cristina Garcia, "Pragmatism in Brazil: John Dewey and Education," in *Pragmatism in the Americas,* ed. Gregory Fernando Pappas (New York: Fordham University Press, 2011), esp. 41–43.

37. Freire hints at a phenomenological expansion of experience when he writes: "Whereas banking education anesthetizes and inhibits creative power, problem-posing education involves a constant unveiling of reality." Paulo Freire, *Pedagogy of the Oppressed* (New York: Continuum, 1992), 68. In a similar vein, Dewey notes: "In a certain sense every experience should do something to prepare a person for later experiences of a deeper and more expansive quality. That is the very meaning of growth, continuity, reconstruction of experience." Dewey, *Experience and Education,* LW13:28.

38. Along these lines, Dewey notes that "[t]he things in civilization we most prize" are, indeed, "not of ourselves." Rather, they "exist by grace of the doings and sufferings of the continuous human community of which we are a link." Dewey, *A Common Faith,* LW9:57. In another passage that may surprise many, Dewey writes sympathetically of the mystical qualities of experience: "There is no reason for denying the existence of experiences that are called mystical. On the contrary, there is every reason to suppose that, in some degree of intensity, they occur so frequently that they may be regarded as normal manifestations that take place at certain

rhythmic points in the movement of experience." Dewey, *A Common Faith*, LW9:26. I would argue that such insights are as relevant for committed naturalists, like Dewey, as for empirically grounded theists, like Elizondo, Isasi-Díaz, or Gebara.

### Chapter 1. A "New Sense" of Religion:
### José Carlos Mariátegui's Pragmatic Sensibility

1. Daniel Franklin Pilario, "Mapping Postcolonial Theory: Appropriations in Contemporary Theology," *Hapag* 3, no. 1–2 (2006): 9–10.

2. Pilario, "Mapping Postcolonial Theory." See also Ofelia Schutte's comprehensive chapter, "The Philosophy of Liberation in Critical Perspective" in *Cultural Identity and Social Liberation in Latin American Thought* (Albany: SUNY Press, 1993), 175–205.

3. Enrique Dussel, "Philosophy in Latin America in the Twentieth Century: Problems and Currents," in *Latin American Philosophy: Currents, Issues, Debates*, ed. Eduardo Mendieta (Bloomington: Indiana University Press, 2003), 33.

4. Dussel is drawn to the pragmatic communicative ethics of Jürgen Habermas and Karl-Otto Apel, both of whom draw heavily on Peirce for inspiration. Yet, invoking the work of Emmanuel Levinas, Dussel moves beyond the "formal" discourse ethics of both Habermas and Apel to an understanding of ethics that remains materially and historically attentive to Levinas's face of the "Other." Among other places, these insights are captured in a chapter entitled "Hermeneutics and Liberation," wherein Dussel describes pragmatic "instrumentality" as something that is always presupposed within community. Dussel explains:

> [W]e always presuppose a world where we *speak* (we are educated in culture, by the Other, in and through a particular language), and where *tools are used* (we live in a cultural world as a system of instruments, tools). "Pragmatics" subsumes mere linguisticality in a communicative relation with the Other, in the communication community (the overcoming of solipsism by Apel and Habermas). "Signs" (as Peirce or Charles Morris would say) have a syntactic, semantic, and *pragmatic* dimension. As such, the sign is a material reality produced by human, cultural, signifying (producing) work (*le travail du texte*), we could say with Ricoeur.

Enrique Dussel, *The Underside of Modernity: Apel, Ricoeur, Rorty, Taylor, and the Philosophy of Liberation*, trans. Eduardo Mendieta (Atlantic Highlands, NJ: Humanities Press, 1996), 85. For an excellent overview of Dussel's thought, which includes a useful discussion of Dussel's interest in Apel and Habermas, see Eduardo Mendieta's "Introduction" in Dussel's *Beyond Philosophy: Ethics, History, Marxism, and Liberation Theology*, ed. Eduardo Mendieta (Lanham, MD: Rowman & Littlefield, 2003), 1–18.

5. See Eduardo Mendieta, *The Adventures of Transcendental Philosophy: Karl-Otto Apel's Semiotics and Discourse Ethics* (Lanham, MD: Rowman & Littlefield,

2002), *Global Fragments: Globalizations, Latinamericanisms, and Critical Theory* (Albany: SUNY Press, 2007), and "Three Pragmatist Lectures," in *Poligrafi* 49, no. 13 (2008): 11–94; Gregory Fernando Pappas, ed., *Pragmatism in the Americas* (New York: Fordham University Press, 2011); José-Antonio Orosco, "Pragmatism, Interculturalism, and the Transformation of American Democracy," in *Pragmatism in the Americas*; Alexander Stehn, "Toward an Inter-American Philosophy: Pragmatism and the Philosophy of Liberation," *Inter-American Journal of Philosophy* 2, no. 2 (2011): 20–36, and "Religiously Binding the Imperial Self: Classical Pragmatism's Call and Liberation Philosophy's Response," in *Pragmatism in the Americas*; Christopher Tirres, *The Aesthetics and Ethics of Faith: A Dialogue Between Liberationist and Pragmatic Thought* (New York: Oxford University Press, 2014); Lilian Calles Barger, *The World Come of Age: An Intellectual History of Liberation Theology* (New York: Oxford University Press, 2018); Michael L. Raposa, *Theosemiotic: Religion, Reading, and the Gift of Meaning* (New York: Fordham University Press, 2020); and Terrance MacMullan, *From American Empire to América Cósmica through Philosophy: Prospero's Reflection* (Lanham, MD: Lexington Books, 2023).

Barger's comprehensive *The World Come of Age: An Intellectual History of Liberation Theology* is especially important here because it illuminates shared approaches and common origins between Latin American and North American liberation theologies. In Barger's estimation, liberation theology represents a kind of secularization of theology, whose intellectual roots are characteristic of American pragmatism. Although the book overplays at times the meaning of "secularization" within liberation theology, it is nevertheless significant in offering one of the widest lenses yet in demonstrating the philosophical connections between pragmatism's method of empiricism and liberationist thought. As for Barger's debatable claim that liberation theologians proposed a "full secularization of religion," see Raúl Zegarra, *A Revolutionary Faith: Liberation Theology Between Public Religion and Public Reason* (Stanford, CA: Stanford University Press, 2023), 24–30; and J. Matthew Ashley, "To Change the World: An Intellectual History of Liberation Theology," *Commonweal*, January 31, 2019, https://www.commonwealmagazine.org/change-world.

In addition to those mentioned above, a number of scholars in the area of US Latine theology draw on pragmatism. Alejandro García-Rivera was especially influential in introducing a younger generation to the work of C. S. Peirce and Josiah Royce. See Nichole M. Flores, *The Aesthetics of Solidarity: Our Lady of Guadalupe and American Democracy* (Washington, D.C.: Georgetown University Press, 2021); Nathan García, "Creating A Soulful Anthropology: Extending Thomas Moore's Spirituality Using Charles S. Peirce's Categories and Modes of Inference," PhD diss. (Oblate School of Theology, 2022); Alejandro García-Rivera, *The Community of the Beautiful: A Theological Aesthetics* (Collegeville, MN: Liturgical Press, 1999), and *The Garden of God: A Theological Cosmology* (Minneapolis: Fortress Press, 2009); Cecilia González-Andrieu, *Bridge to Wonder: Art as Gospel of Beauty* (Waco, TX: Baylor University Press, 2012); Robert Lassalle-Klein, "The

Potential Contribution of C. S. Peirce to Interpretation Theory in US Hispanic/ Latino Theology and Other Culturally Contextualized Theologies," *Journal of Hispanic/Latino Theology* 6, no. 3 (1999): 5–34; and Nancy Pineda-Madrid, *Suffering and Salvation in Ciudad Juárez* (Minneapolis: Fortress Press, 2011). For a more Deweyan and Jamesian interpretation of García-Rivera's work, see Christopher Tirres, "Theological Aesthetics and the Many Pragmatisms of Alejandro García-Rivera," *Diálogo: An Interdisciplinary Studies Journal* 16, no. 2 (2013): 59–64.

6. Michael Löwy, quoted in Schutte, *Cultural Identity and Social Liberation*, 19. Michael Löwy, ed., *El marxismo en América Latina* (Mexico: Ediciones Era, 1982), 19.

7. John M. Baines, *Revolution in Peru: Mariátegui and the Myth* (Tuscaloosa: University of Alabama Press, 1972), 20.

8. Curt Cadorette, *From the Heart of the People: The Theology of Gustavo Gutiérrez* (Oak Park, IL: Meyer Stone Books, 1988), 77.

9. This term, which may be roughly translated as "bossism," is derived from gamonal, which means "large landowner."

10. José Carlos Mariátegui, "The Problem of the Indian," in *Latin American Philosophy for the 21st Century*, ed. Jorge J. E. Gracia and Elizabeth Millán-Zaibert (Amherst, NY: Prometheus, 2004), 259.

11. Mariátegui, "The Problem of the Indian," 261–62.

12. Mariátegui, "The Problem of the Indian," 261.

13. Mariátegui, "The Problem of the Indian."

14. Mariátegui, "The Problem of the Indian."

15. Baines, *Revolution in Peru*, 14.

16. José Carlos Mariátegui, *Siete ensayos de interpretación de la realidad peruana* (Lima, Peru: Amauta, 1928), 263–64.

17. Michael Löwy, "Communism and Religion: José Carlos Mariátegui's Revolutionary Mysticism," *Latin American Perspectives* 35, no. 2 (2008): 77.

18. Ofelia Schutte, *Cultural Identity and Social Liberation in Latin American Thought* (Albany: SUNY Press, 1993), 33.

19. Omar Rivera, *Delimitations of Latin American Philosophy: Beyond Redemption* (Bloomington: Indiana University Press), 142.

20. Rivera, *Delimitations of Latin American Philosophy*, 142.

21. Rivera, *Delimitations of Latin American Philosophy*, 142–43.

22. José Carlos Mariátegui, "Man and Myth," in *José Carlos Mariátegui: An Anthology*, ed. Harry E. Vanden and Marc Becker (New York: Monthly Review Press, 2011), 387.

23. Rudolf Otto, *The Idea of the Holy: An Inquiry into the Non-Rational Factor in the Idea of the Divine and its Relation to the Rational* (New York: Oxford University Press), 1923.

24. Schutte, *Cultural Identity and Social Liberation*, 48.

25. Schutte, *Cultural Identity and Social Liberation*.

26. Ivone Gebara, *Longing for Running Water: Ecofeminism and Liberation* (Minneapolis: Fortress Press, 1999), 88.

27. Mariátegui, "Man and Myth," 383.

28. Mariátegui, "Man and Myth."

29. Mariátegui, "Man and Myth," 383–84.

30. Mariátegui, "Man and Myth," 384.

31. José Carlos Mariátegui, "Pessimism of Reality, Optimism of the Idea," in *José Carlos Mariátegui: An Anthology*, 397.

32. Mariátegui, "Pessimism of Reality, Optimism of the Idea."

33. John Shook, "F.C.S. Schiller and European Pragmatism," in *A Companion to Pragmatism*, ed. John R. Shook and Joseph Margolis (Malden, MA: Blackwell, 2006), 52.

34. William James, *The Varieties of Religious Experience* in *Writings: 1902–1910* (New York: Library of America, 1987), 56.

35. Mariátegui also approvingly quotes the following summary of Vaihinger's philosophy by Italian philosopher Giuseppe Rensi: "Moral principles, just like aesthetic ones, legal criteria, just like those upon which science operates, the very foundations of logic, have no objective existence. They are our fictitious constructions that serve only as regulatory precepts for our actions, which are conducted as if they were true." Mariátegui, "Pessimism of Reality, Optimism of the Idea," 397.

36. Mariátegui, "Man and Myth," 385.

37. Gaspar Martínez, *Confronting the Mystery of God: Political, Liberation, and Public Theologies* (New York: Continuum, 2001), 125.

38. For good discussions on the meaning and history of Gutiérrez's understanding of integral liberation, see Raúl Zegarra, *A Revolutionary Faith: Liberation Theology Between Public Religion and Public Reason* (Stanford, CA: Stanford University Press, 2023), 31–41; and Daniel P. Castillo, *An Ecological Theology of Liberation: Salvation and Political Ecology* (Maryknoll, NY: Orbis Books, 2019), 38–52.

39. Martínez, *Confronting the Mystery of God*, 98.

40. Cadorette, *From the Heart of the People*, 67.

41. Gutiérrez, quoted in Cadorette, *From the Heart of the People*, 76.

42. Mariátegui, quoted in Gustavo Gutiérrez, *A Theology of Liberation: History, Politics, and Salvation* (Maryknoll, NY: Orbis Books, 1973), 90.

43. Mariátegui, quoted in Gutiérrez, *A Theology of Liberation.*

44. Mariátegui, "The Problem of the Indian," 264.

45. Kim Díaz, "Mariátegui's Myth," *APA Newsletter. Hispanic/Latino Issues in Philosophy* 13, no. 1 (2013): 21–22.

46. Mariátegui, "Man and Myth," 387.

47. See Kim Díaz, *Radical Democracy in the Thought and Work of Paulo Freire and Luis Villoro*, PhD diss. (Texas A&M University, 2012), esp. 44–50.

48. Gutiérrez, *A Theology of Liberation*, 91.

**Chapter 2. Conscientization as a Spiritual Praxis:**
**Paulo Freire's Implicit Spirituality**

1. Important earlier anthologies include Gregory Pappas, *Pragmatism in the Americas*, ed. Gregory Fernando Pappas (New York: Fordham University Press, 2011); Susana Nuccetelli, Ofelia Schutte, and Otávio Bueno, eds., *A Companion to Latin American Philosophy* (Malden, MA: Wiley-Blackwell, 2010); Iván Márquez, *Contemporary Latin American Social and Political Thought: An Anthology* (Lanham, MD: Rowman & Littlefield, 2008); Jorge Gracia and Elizabeth Millán-Zaibert, *Latin American Philosophy for the 21st Century* (Amherst, NY: Prometheus, 2004); Susana Nuccetelli and Gary Seay, *Latin American Philosophy: An Introduction with Readings* (Upper Saddle River, NJ: Pearson, 2004); and Eduardo Mendieta, *Latin American Philosophy: Currents, Issues, Debates* (Bloomington: Indiana University Press, 2003).

2. See, for example, David Ignatius Gandolfo's 2010 essay, "Liberation Philosophy," in *A Companion to Latin American Philosophy*, 185–98; Eduardo Mendieta's 2016 entry, "The Philosophy of Liberation," in the *Stanford Encyclopedia of Philosophy*; and Grant Silva's 2018 essay "'The Americas Seek Not Enlightenment but Liberation': On the Philosophical Significance of Liberation for Philosophy in the Americas," *The Pluralist* 13 (2018): 1–21.

3. See Nicolás Panotto's "A Critique of the Coloniality of Theological Knowledge: Rereading Latin American Liberation Theology as Thinking Otherwise," in *Decolonial Christianities: Latinx and Latin American Perspectives*, ed. Raimundo Barreto and Roberto Sirvent (Cham, Switzerland: Palgrave MacMillan, 2019), 217–37; Alexander Stehn, "El Pueblo and Its Problems: Democracy of, by, and for Whom?," *The Pluralist* 6, no. 3 (2011): 103–16, "Religiously Binding the Imperial Self: Classical Pragmatism's Call and Liberation, Philosophy's Response," in *Pragmatism in the Americas*, ed. Gregory Fernando Pappas (New York: Fordham University Press, 2011), and "Toward an Inter-American Philosophy," *Inter-American Journal of Philosophy* 2, no. 2: 14–36; Márquez, *Contemporary Latin American Social and Political Thought*; Antonio González, "Assessing the Philosophical Achievement of Ignacio Ellacuría," in *Love that Produces Hope: The Thought of Ignacio Ellacuría*, ed. Kevin Burke and Robert Lassalle-Klein (Collegeville, MN: Liturgical Press, 2006).

4. Paulo Freire, *Pedagogy of the Oppressed* (New York: Continuum, 1992), 19, fn1.

5. Barger also notes Freire's influence on independent Black education movements in the United States and feminist theology. Lilian Calles Barger, *The World Come of Age: An Intellectual History of Liberation Theology* (New York: Oxford University Press, 2018), 76. See also James D. Kirylo's biography of Freire, *Paulo: The Man from Recife* (New York: Peter Lang, 2011); James D. Kirylo and Drick Boyd, *Paulo Freire: His Faith, Spirituality, and Theology* (Rotterdam: Sense Publishers, 2017), esp. 87–104; John Elias, *Paulo Freire: Pedagogue of Liberation* (Malabar, FL: Krieger, 1994); and Irwin Leopando, *A Pedagogy of Faith: The Theological Vision of Paulo Freire* (London: Bloomsbury, 2017).

6. Leopando, *A Pedagogy of Faith*, 6. See Paulo Freire, *Pedagogy of the Heart* (New York: Continuum, 1997), 104.

7. Daniel S. Schipani, *Religious Education Encounters Liberation Theology* (Birmingham, AL: Religious Education Press, 1988), 30.

8. Kirylo and Boyd, *Paulo Freire*, 83.

9. Kirylo and Boyd, *Paulo Freire*, 85.

10. In a provocative and insightful article, Jacob W. Neumann makes a similar argument about critical pedagogy at large, underscoring "the essential nature of critical pedagogy as a practice of faith." Jacob W. Neumann, "Critical Pedagogy and Faith," *Educational Theory* 61, no. 5 (2011): 601–19. Although Kirylo and Boyd do not exactly frame conscientization in this way, I find helpful their discussion of the "thought" and "behavioral" dimensions of conscientization, which I believe naturally lend themselves to the direction in which Neumann and I are pointing. Kirylo and Boyd, *Paulo Freire*, 16.

11. Stanley Aronowitz, "Paulo Freire's Radical Democratic Humanism: The Fetish of Method," *Counterpoints* 422 (2012): 263. See also Freire's own assessment of Fromm in "Conversation with Paulo Freire," *Religious Education* 79, no. 4 (1984): 521.

12. Irwin Leopando follows a similar approach in *A Pedagogy of Faith*.

13. As stated at the outset of this book, I resonate with theologian Roger Haight's largely Tillichian understanding of spirituality, which "refers to the logic, or character, or consistent quality of a person's or a group's pattern of living insofar as it measured before some ultimate reality." Significantly, Haight points out that spirituality occurs prior to both religion, which may be understood as the institutionalization of spirituality, and theology, insofar that it helps to supply theology with its the source and subject matter. Roger Haight, *Spiritual and Religious: Explorations for Seekers* (Maryknoll, NY: Orbis Books, 2016), 2, 7.

14. Kirylo and Boyd, *Paulo Freire*, 30.

15. Freire, *Pedagogy of the Oppressed*, 27. The reader may notice my insertion of [sic] after Freire's use of gendered language when referring to human beings in general. I will address this point further toward the end of this chapter.

16. Freire, *Pedagogy of the Oppressed*, 80.

17. Paulo Freire, "Conscientizing as a Way of Liberating," in *Liberation Theology: A Documentary History*, ed. Alfred T. Hennelly (Maryknoll, NY: Orbis Books, 1990), 5.

18. Freire, *Pedagogy of the Oppressed*, 89.

19. Freire, *Pedagogy of the Oppressed*, 89, fn15. Freire is citing here Vieira Pinto's work *Consciência Realidade Nacional* (Rio de Janeiro: Ministerio da Educação e Cultura, Instituto Superior de Estudos Brasileiros, 1960), 284.

20. Freire, *Pedagogy of the Oppressed*, 89.

21. Freire, *Pedagogy of the Oppressed*, 93.

22. Freire, "Letter to a Young Theology Student," *LADOC Keyhole Series* 2, no. 29b (1972): 11–12.

23. Freire, "Letter to a Young Theology Student," 12.

24. Paulo Freire, "Know, Practice, and Teach the Gospels," *Religious Education* 79, no. 4 (1984): 547.

25. Freire, "Know, Practice, and Teach the Gospels," 548. Freire discusses the differences between traditionalist, modernizing, and prophetic forms of Christianity in his 1972 essay, "Education, Liberation and the Church." This essay, along with Freire's two letters to theology students, helps to provide a more nuanced picture of Freire's approach to Christianity than the one offered by Ofelia Schutte (1993), who tends to read Freire's Christianity along more traditionalist lines.

26. Freire, "Know, Practice, and Teach the Gospels," 547.

27. As Kirylo puts it, for Freire, "to teach the Gospel is to not only have experienced the message, but also to live and personify it." Kirylo, *Paulo*, 123.

28. Freire, *Pedagogy of the Oppressed*, 80.

29. Freire, *Pedagogy of the Oppressed*, 33.

30. Freire, *Pedagogy of the Oppressed*, 58.

31. Freire, *Pedagogy of the Oppressed*, 59. For a good discussion on Freire's use of the Hegelian dialectic, see Eduardo Duarte, "Conscientizacion y Comunidad: A Dialectical Description of Education as the Struggle for Freedom," *Studies in Philosophy and Education* 18 (1999): 389–403.

32. Freire, *Pedagogy of the Oppressed*, 56.

33. Duarte, "Conscientizacion y Comunidad," 401. Freire, *Pedagogy of the Oppressed*, 73. Along these lines, Kirylo and Boyd underscore the intersubjective character of Freire's personalism, owing, again, to his interest in Mounier. Kirylo and Boyd, *Paulo Freire*, 29–30.

34. Freire, "Conscientizing as a Way of Liberating," 11.

35. Freire, "Letter to a Young Theology Student," 12. Here, Freire seems to be anticipating the idea of a God who "lures" us to our better possibilities, as seen, for example, in the process theology of Marjorie Suchocki.

36. Freire, "Letter to a Young Theology Student," 12.

37. Ofelia Schutte, *Cultural Identity and Social Liberation in Latin American Thought* (Albany: SUNY Press, 1993), 149.

38. Michael L. Raposa, *Theosemiotic: Religion, Reading, and the Gift of Meaning* (New York: Fordham University Press, 2020), 155–56. In the last chapter of this magnificent work, entitled "On Prayer and the Spirit of Pragmatism," Raposa creatively reads Gutiérrez's liberation theology through the lens of C. S. Peirce's semiotics. See also Alejandro García-Rivera's groundbreaking *The Community of the Beautiful: A Theological Aesthetics* (Collegeville, MN: Liturgical Press, 1999), and my assessment of García-Rivera's use of pragmatism in Christopher Tirres, "Theological Aesthetics and the Many Pragmatisms of Alejandro García-Rivera," *Diálogo: An Interdisciplinary Studies Journal* 16, no. 2 (2013): 59–64. Of note, this special issue of *Diálogo* also includes incisive interpretations of other aspects of García-Rivera's thought by Peter J. Casarella ("Beauty and the Little Stories of Holiness: What Alejandro García-Rivera Taught Me"); Eduardo C. Fernández ("A

Litany for Alex: Remembering his Contributions to Pastoral Theology"); Michelle A. González ("Alejandro García-Rivera: A Legacy in Theological Aesthetics"); Roberto S. Goizueta ("The Theologian as Wounded Innocent"); Robert J. Schreiter ("Spaces Engaged and Transfigured: Alejandro García-Rivera's Journey from Little Stories to Cosmic Reconciliation"); Timothy Matovina ("Little Stories of Christmas and the Big Story of God's Love"); and Daniel P. Castillo ("Agony in the Garden?: Evaluating the Cosmology of Alejandro García-Rivera in View of the 'Little Story' and the 'Principle of Foregrounding'").

39. Freire, "Conscientizing as a Way of Liberating," 12.

40. Freire, "Conscientizing as a Way of Liberating," 12–13, emphasis added.

41. Freire, "Conscientizing as a Way of Liberating," 13.

42. Paulo Freire, "Education, Liberation and the Church," in *The Politics of Education: Culture, Power and Liberation*, ed. Henry Giroux (South Hadley, MA: Bergin & Garvey, 1985), 123.

43. Freire, *Pedagogy of the Oppressed*, 33, emphasis added.

44. Freire, "Conversation with Paulo Freire," 514–15.

45. Freire, "Conscientizing as a Way of Liberating," 13, emphasis added.

## Chapter 3. A Cosmic Vision from the Borderlands: Virgilio Elizondo's Evolutionary Cosmology

1. Virgilio Elizondo, *The Future Is Mestizo: Life Where Cultures Meet*, rev. ed. (Boulder: University Press of Colorado, 2000), 5.

2. Elizondo, *The Future Is Mestizo*, 6.

3. Elizondo, *The Future Is Mestizo*, 7.

4. Elizondo also describes his earliest experience of church as a "great circus of God's people." Elizondo, *The Future Is Mestizo*, 11.

5. Elizondo, *The Future Is Mestizo*.

6. Elizondo, *The Future Is Mestizo*, 15.

7. Elizondo, *The Future Is Mestizo*.

8. Elizondo, *The Future Is Mestizo*, 16.

9. Elizondo, *The Future Is Mestizo*, 23.

10. Elizondo, *The Future Is Mestizo*.

11. Elizondo, *The Future Is Mestizo*, 24.

12. Elizondo, *The Future Is Mestizo*, 25.

13. Elizondo, *The Future Is Mestizo*.

14. Elizondo, *The Future Is Mestizo*, 72.

15. Elizondo, *The Future Is Mestizo*.

16. Robert Schreiter, *Constructing Local Theologies* (Maryknoll, NY: Orbis Books, 1997), 1–16. See also Steven Bevans, *Models of Contextual Theology* (Maryknoll, NY: Orbis Books, 1992).

17. Virgilio Elizondo, *Virgilio Elizondo: Spiritual Writings* (Maryknoll, NY: Orbis Books, 2010), 83.

18. Virgilio Elizondo, *San Fernando Cathedral: Soul of the City* (Maryknoll, NY: Orbis Books, 1998), 12.

19. In recent years, there has been a vigorous debate over Teilhard's legacy. On one hand, John Slattery has argued that Teilhard was somewhat hostile to the Catholic affirmation of human dignity, racial justice, and concern for the disadvantaged. On the other hand, John Haught has critiqued Slattery for cherry-picking comments from Teilhard's personal letters and other scattered writings and the comments in question are "provocative and interrogatory, not declarative." In Haught's estimation, "Exactly what Teilhard really meant by them is, in every single case, highly debatable." See John P. Slattery, "Pierre Teilhard de Chardin's Legacy of Eugenics and Racism Can't be Ignored," May 21, 2018, *Religion Dispatches*, https://religiondispatches.org/pierre-teilhard-de-chardins-legacy-of-eugenics-and -racism-cant-be-ignored/; and John F. Haught, "Trashing Teilhard: How Not to Read a Great Religious Thinker," *Commonweal*, February 12, 2019, https://www.common wealmagazine.org/trashing-teilhard.

The issues raised in these debates do not, in my estimation, fundamentally impact Elizondo's use of Teilhard. One observation that may be more germane to this chapter, however, is Robert Shedinger's suggestion that although there is always a good degree of contingency in Teilhard's thought, his cosmos also has a certain teleological thrust, wherein evolution exists "for the purpose of creating beings with the ability of reflective thought so that they could commune with their Creator." The same could likely be said of Elizondo. For those philosophical emergentists who argue against any and all forms of teleology, such a position might seem incompatible within a truly open and indeterminate universe. However, following the thought of C. S. Peirce and other process theists, I believe that there is a place for more speculative forms of teleological thinking within an evolutionary framework. As the reader will see momentarily, it is within this framework that I place Elizondo's work. Shedinger, "Teilhard de Chardin and the Incomplete Nature of Evolutionary Theory," *Evolution News and Science Today*, February 13, 2020, https://evolutionnews.org/2020/02/teilhard-de-chardin-and-the-incomplete-nature -of-evolutionary-theory/.

20. Ursula King, "Teilhard De Chardin, Pierre," in *Encyclopedia of Religion* (sec. ed.), ed. Lindsay Jones (Detroit, MI: Macmillan, 2005), 9033.

21. Virgilio Elizondo, *The Human Quest: The Search for Meaning Through Life and Death* (Huntington, IN: Our Sunday Visitor, 1978), 37.

22. Teilhard, as cited in Elizondo, *The Human Quest*, 142. See Pierre Teilhard de Chardin, *The Divine Milieu* (New York: Harper, 1960), 91.

23. Elizondo, *The Human Quest*, 143.

24. Elizondo, *The Human Quest*.

25. Elizondo, *Spiritual Writings*, 19. In the book's introductory chapter, Matovina cites the work of García-Rivera and Oropeza, *Mestizaje e Intellectus Fidei: Acercamiento Teológico Fundamental* (Rome: Pontificiae Universitatis Gregorianae, 2007).

26. Alejandro García-Rivera, "Crossing Theological Borders: Virgilio Elizondo's Place Among Theologians of Culture," in *Beyond Borders: Writings of Virgilio Elizondo and Friends*, ed. Timothy Matovina (Maryknoll, NY: Orbis Books, 2000), 249.

27. García-Rivera, "Crossing Theological Borders."

28. Elizondo, *The Future Is Mestizo*, 101.

29. Elizondo, *The Future Is Mestizo*, 87.

30. Elizondo, *The Future Is Mestizo*, 88.

31. In a similar way, Ignacio Ellacuría's understanding of "historical reality" and John Dewey's understanding of "experience" can be read as theologically rich categories that point to a sense of "fulfillment" and "consummation" within an evolutionary framework.

32. As John Haught, a leading interpreter of Teilhard explains, "Concern for the cosmic future and for what is going on in the physical universe has not yet become a major theme in Western theology. Classical Christianity and its theologies first came to expression at a time when people took for granted that the universe is fundamentally fixed and unchanging. Today, however, especially because of developments in the natural sciences, theologians can no longer plausibly ignore the fact that the whole universe, not just life and human history, is still in the process of becoming" (xiv). John F. Haught, *The Cosmic Vision of Teilhard de Chardin* (Maryknoll, NY: Orbis Books, 2021).

33. Elizondo, *The Future Is Mestizo*, 103.

34. Elizondo, *The Future Is Mestizo*, 105.

35. Elizondo, *The Future Is Mestizo*, 107.

36. Elizondo, *The Future Is Mestizo*, 109.

37. Elizondo, *The Future Is Mestizo*, 108.

38. See Rubén Rosario Rodríguez, *Racism and God-Talk: A Latino/a Perspective* (New York: NYU Press, 2008); and Néstor Medina, *Mestizaje: (Re)mapping Race, Culture, and Faith in Latina/o Catholicism* (Maryknoll, NY: Orbis Books, 2009).

39. José Vasconcelos, *The Cosmic Race/La raza cósmica*, trans. Didier T. Jaén (Baltimore, MD: Johns Hopkins University Press, 1997), 3.

40. On this point, see Roberto S. Goizueta, *Caminemos con Jesús: Toward a Hispanic/Latino Theology of Accompaniment* (Maryknoll, NY: Orbis Books, 1995), 120–22.

41. Aside from Teilhard, interpreters of Elizondo may be better served to look at Mexican thinkers who were invoking the term mestizaje *prior* to Vasconcelos, particularly those who wrote about mestizaje in relation to devotions around Nuestra Señora de Guadalupe in Mexico. To be clear, Vasconcelos did not coin the term *mestizaje*. Rather, he inherited it from others, including novelist and journalist Ignacio Manuel Altamirano (1834–1893), who was frequently cited in the editorials of the San Antonio periodical *La Prensa* during the time in which Elizondo was a child. Altamirano was no stranger to the social fissures that existed in Mexican society, but he also acknowledged that ritual and devotional practices honoring

Guadalupe, especially on her feast day (December 12), served to bring together disparate sectors of the Mexican nation. Altamirano marveled at the way that Mexicans from all economic classes and political persuasions gathered "in equality before the Virgin." As Altamirano famously writes: "The day that the cult of the Indian Virgin [of Guadalupe] disappears, the Mexican nationality will also disappear." In his 1977 essay "Our Lady as a Cultural Symbol," Elizondo riffs on this idea when he writes: "If Our Lady of Guadalupe had not appeared, the collective struggles of the Mexican people to find meaning in their chaotic existence would have created her" (Elizondo, "Our Lady of Guadalupe as a Cultural Symbol," in *Beyond Borders*, 118). Readers should note, however, that whereas the thrust of Altamirano's comment has to do with Mexican nationalism, Elizondo is more interested in the capacity of Guadalupe, as a religious and cultural symbol, to help redress situations of existential chaos. Stated otherwise, Elizondo's understanding of mestizaje speaks more to the symbolic power of Guadalupe to generate a new cosmology than to Altamirano's more limited and nationalistic conception of mestizaje or to Vasconcelos's more racialized conception of a biological "new race." For a good discussion on the "Catholic" stream of reflection on Guadalupe and mestizaje that likely influenced Elizondo, see chapter 4 of Timothy Matovina's excellent study, *Theologies of Guadalupe: From the Era of Conquest to Pope Francis* (New York: Oxford University Press, 2019), 117–54.

42. Ed Conroy, "Mestiso Identity is the Heart of Virgil Elizondo's Life and Work," *National Catholic Reporter*, October 8, 2004, https://natcath.org/NCR_Online /archives2/2004d/100804/100804n.php.

43. As Fernando Ortiz, Mary Louise Pratt, and Robert Carlsen make clear, transculturation is a process in which "subordinated or marginal groups select and invent from materials transmitted to them by a dominant or metropolitan culture." As Pratt (as quoted in Carlsen) notes, "while subjugated peoples cannot readily control what emanates from the dominant culture, they do determine to varying extents what they absorb into their own and what they use it for." Elizondo, on my reading, is highly sensitive to the ways in which colonized peoples selectively absorb elements from the dominant culture. See Robert Carlsen, "Transculturation," in *The Oxford Encyclopedia of Mesoamerican Cultures: The Civilizations of Mexico and Central America*, ed. Davíd Carrasco (New York: Oxford University Press, 2001), https://www.oxfordreference.com/display/10.1093/acref/9780195108156.001.0001/acref -9780195108156.

44. Gary B. Nash, "The Hidden History of Mestizo America," *The Journal of American History* 82, no. 3 (1995): 958.

45. In this respect, I agree with Andrew Prevot's assessment of Elizondo when he writes: "Although [Elizondo] mentions the idea of a 'cosmic race,' he shifts the focus of *mestizaje* from racial mixture to an open-ended intercultural dialogue. Instead of a universal fusion of identities, he argues for a loving communion that maintains respect for local differences. In place of an antinomian philosophy of aesthetic oneness, he proposes a Christian theological aesthetics and liberative praxis normed

by popular Catholic devotions to Our Lady of Guadalupe and the life, death, and resurrection of Jesus." See his detailed study, *The Mysticism of Ordinary Life: Theology, Philosophy, and Feminism* (New York: Oxford University Press, 2023), 188.

46. I resonate with Devaka Premawardhana's reading of Elizondo as a "loco-centric" (and not primarily "logocentric") thinker. See his insightful "Between Logocentrism and *Lococentrism: Alambrista* Challenges to Traditional Theology," *Harvard Theological Review* 101, no. 3–4 (2008), 399–416.

## Chapter 4. Spiritual Activism as Conocimiento:
## Gloria Anzaldúa's Mature Spirituality

1. Gloria Anzaldúa, *Interviews/Entrevistas*, ed. AnaLouise Keating (New York: Routledge, 2000), 7.

2. Gloria Anzaldúa, *Light in the Dark/Luz en lo oscuro: Rewriting Identity, Spirituality, Reality*, ed. AnaLouise Keating (Durham, NC: Duke University Press, 2015), 19.

3. William James, *The Varieties of Religious Experience in Writings: 1902–1910* (New York: Library of America, 1987), 39.

4. Anzaldúa, *Interviews/Entrevistas*, 23.

5. Frances Ann Day, *Latina and Latino Voices in Literature: Lives and Works* (Westport, CT: Greenwood Press, 2003), 78.

6. Anzaldúa, *Interviews/Entrevistas*, 22.

7. Anzaldúa, *Interviews/Entrevistas*, 23.

8. Anzaldúa, *Interviews/Entrevistas*, 29.

9. Anzaldúa, *Interviews/Entrevistas*, 25.

10. Anzaldúa, *Interviews/Entrevistas*.

11. Anzaldúa, *Interviews/Entrevistas*.

12. Anzaldúa, *Interviews/Entrevistas*, 29–30.

13. Anzaldúa, *Interviews/Entrevistas*, 45.

14. Day, *Latina and Latino Voices in Literature*, 78.

15. AnaLouise Keating, "Anzaldúa, Gloria E.," *American National Biography* (New York: Oxford University Press, 2018), www.anb.org/articles/16/16-03593.html.

16. Anzaldúa, *Interviews/Entrevistas*, 57.

17. Keating, "Anzaldúa, Gloria E."

18. Anzaldúa, *Light in the Dark/Luz en lo oscuro*, 119.

19. Anzaldúa, *Light in the Dark/Luz en lo oscuro*.

20. Anzaldúa, *Light in the Dark/Luz en lo oscuro*, 119.

21. In her notes, Anzaldúa adds, "*Conocimiento* is a politics of embodied spirituality, el legado spiritual." Anzaldúa, *Light in the Dark/Luz en lo oscuro*, 224, fn 3.

22. Anzaldúa, *Light in the Dark/Luz en lo oscuro*, 119.

23. Anzaldúa, *Light in the Dark/Luz en lo oscuro*, 72.

24. Anzaldúa, *Light in the Dark/Luz en lo oscuro*, 25.

25. Anzaldúa, *Light in the Dark/Luz en lo oscuro*, 36, 37–38, 104.

26. Anzaldúa, *Light in the Dark/Luz en lo oscuro*, 17.

27. Anzaldúa, *Light in the Dark/Luz en lo oscuro*, 18. Aside from such professional ramifications, Anzaldúa's writing has also led to several personal hardships, such as seen in the following: "My mother says I'm shameless because to me, nothing is private. Maybe that's why I became a writer." Anzaldúa, *Interviews/Entrevistas*, 81.

28. Anzaldúa, *Interviews/Entrevistas*, 18.

29. See Ann Taves, "2010 Presidential Address: 'Religion' in the Humanities and the Humanities in the University," *Journal of the American Academy of Religion* 79, no. 2 (2011): 287–314; and Jeffrey J. Kripal, *Authors of the Impossible: The Paranormal and the Sacred* (Chicago: University of Chicago Press, 2010).

30. Taves, "2010 Presidential Address," 298.

31. Anzaldúa, *Interviews/Entrevistas*, 26.

32. Anzaldúa, *Interviews/Entrevistas*, 73.

33. Anzaldúa, *Light in the Dark/Luz en lo oscuro*, 23.

34. Anzaldúa, *Light in the Dark/Luz en lo oscuro*.

35. Anzaldúa, *Light in the Dark/Luz en lo oscuro*, 25.

36. Anzaldúa, *Light in the Dark/Luz en lo oscuro*, 25–26.

37. Anzaldúa, *Light in the Dark/Luz en lo oscuro*, 31.

38. Anzaldúa, *Light in the Dark/Luz en lo oscuro*, 25.

39. Anzaldúa, *Light in the Dark/Luz en lo oscuro*, 29.

40. Anzaldúa, *Light in the Dark/Luz en lo oscuro*, 30.

41. Anzaldúa, *Light in the Dark/Luz en lo oscuro*.

42. Anzaldúa, *Light in the Dark/Luz en lo oscuro*, 31.

43. Anzaldúa, *Light in the Dark/Luz en lo oscuro*, 37.

44. Anzaldúa, *Light in the Dark/Luz en lo oscuro*.

45. Anzaldúa, *Light in the Dark/Luz en lo oscuro*.

46. An earlier footnote in the chapter, however, suggests that Anzaldúa may be thinking of this other type of reality as a "mundis imaginalis," or world of images, which serves as a "a median and mediating place." On this point, Anzaldúa is indebted to the work of Henry Corbin, a scholar of Islamic mysticism, and James Hillman, author of *The Myth of Analysis: Three Essays in Archetypal Psychology*. Anzaldúa, *Light in the Dark/Luz en lo oscuro*, 225, fn 12.

47. Anzaldúa, *Light in the Dark/Luz en lo oscuro*, 38; Mary Watkins, *Waking Dreams* (New York: Harper and Row, 1976).

48. Anzaldúa, *Light in the Dark/Luz en lo oscuro*, 37.

49. Anzaldúa, *Light in the Dark/Luz en lo oscuro*.

50. Anzaldúa, *Light in the Dark/Luz en lo oscuro*, 38.

51 Along these lines, Anzaldúa also writes: "A source reality exists, and both physical and nonphysical worlds emanate from it, forming a secondary reality." Anzaldúa, *Light in the Dark/Luz en lo oscuro*, 38.

52. Anzaldúa, *Light in the Dark/Luz en lo oscuro*, 226.

53. Anzaldúa, *Light in the Dark/Luz en lo oscuro*, 19.

54. Anzaldúa, *Light in the Dark/Luz en lo oscuro*, 39.

55. Anzaldúa, *Light in the Dark / Luz en lo oscuro*, 227, fn. 34.

56. AnaLouise Keating, "'I'm a citizen of the universe': Gloria Anzaldúa's Spiritual Activism as Catalyst for Social Change," *Feminist Studies* 34, no. 1–2 (2008): 53–69. See also AnaLouise Keating, "Risking the Personal: An Introduction," in *Interviews/Entrevistas*, 8.

57. Anzaldúa, *Light in the Dark / Luz en lo oscuro*, 39.

58. Anzaldúa, *Light in the Dark / Luz en lo oscuro*, 19.

59. As Laura E. Pérez puts it, "Anzaldúa dedicated herself to thinking about consciousness as a very real, spiritual, and productive site which, if invisible, is visible in its effects." Pérez brilliantly adds the following: "And so I want to argue that if Frantz Fanon has been invaluable in helping us to think about the internalization of colonial thought in, for example, discussing how self-loathing colonized peoples have been force-fed by racist regimes of power, and if Foucault has helped us to think better about the way in which we internalize power in general and at large in policing ourselves for the state by wanting to be good citizens, party to hegemony in whatever measure possible, Anzaldúa goes even further. For discourse and ideology are not just powerful intellectual phenomena with effects that are materialized on the social, cultural, economic, and political planes. Discourse and ideology are themselves the effects of spiritual awareness or ignorance, of conocimiento and desconocimiento. . . . At our core, within Anzalduan thought, we are all by nature powerful beings, and 'being-becoming' is the reclamation of the right use of that power." As I read her, Pérez is picking up here on the profundity of the pragmatic and process-oriented aspects of Anzaldúa's thought, and I resonate deeply with her insights. Indeed, the present chapter is my attempt to make these aspects even more explicit. See Laura E. Pérez, *Eros Ideologies: Writings on Art, Spirituality, and the Decolonial* (Durham, NC: Duke University Press, 2019), 142–43.

60. Larry A. Hickman, *John Dewey's Pragmatic Technology* (Bloomington: Indiana University Press, 1992), 37.

61. Anzaldúa, *Interviews/Entrevistas*, 72–73.

62. Anzaldúa, *Interviews/Entrevistas*, 24.

63. Yasuo Yuasa, *The Body: Toward an Eastern Mind-Body Theory*, ed. Thomas P. Kasulis (Albany: SUNY Press, 1987). See also Ruth Frankenberg, *Living Spirit, Living Practice: Poetics, Politics, Epistemology* (Durham, NC: Duke University Press, 2004), especially the book's second chapter.

64. Anzaldúa, *Light in the Dark / Luz en lo oscuro*, 10.

65. Anzaldúa, *Light in the Dark / Luz en lo oscuro*, 155–56.

66. Anzaldúa, *Light in the Dark / Luz en lo oscuro*, 41.

67. James, *The Varieties of Religious Experience*, 56.

68. James, *The Varieties of Religious Experience*.

69. See Theresa Delgadillo, *Spiritual Mestizaje: Religion, Gender, Race, and Nation in Contemporary Chicana Narrative* (Durham, NC: Duke University Press, 2011); Tace Hedrick, "Queering the Cosmic Race: Esotericism, Mestizaje, and Sexuality in the Work of Gabriela Mistral and Gloria Anzaldúa," *Aztlán: A Journal*

*of Chicano Studies* 34, no. 2 (2009): 67–98; AnaLouise Keating, "I'm a citizen of the universe," and "Re-envisioning Coyolxauhqui, Decolonizing Reality: Anzaldúa's Twenty-First-Century Imperative," in *Light in the Dark / Luz en lo oscuro*, ix–xxxvii; and Pérez, *Eros Ideologies*. See also Andrea J. Pitts, *Nos/Otras: Gloria E. Anzaldúa, Multiplicitous Agency, and Resistance* (Albany: SUNY Press, 2021). While Pitts's book is more philosophically focused than the other studies mentioned here, it nevertheless implicitly addresses core elements of Anzaldúa's spirituality, including her relational ontology, existential phenomenology, and coalitional politics.

70. Gloria Anzaldúa, *The Gloria Anzaldúa Reader* (Durham, NC: Duke University Press, 2009), 49.

71. Anzaldúa, *Light in the Dark / Luz en lo oscuro*, 44.

72. As Delgadillo persuasively argues in *Spiritual Mestizaje*, "[s]pirituality informs every aspect of the work that *Borderlands* performs with respect to subjectivity, epistemology, and transformation" (6).

73. Delgadillo, *Spiritual Mestizaje*, 1.

74. Gloria Anzaldúa, *Borderlands/La Frontera: The New Mestiza* (San Francisco: Aunt Lute Books, 2007), 103.

75. Gregory Fernando Pappas, *John Dewey's Ethics: Democracy as Experience* (Bloomington: Indiana University Press, 2008), 155.

76. Anzaldúa, *Light in the Dark / Luz en lo oscuro*, 20.

77. Jim Garrison, *Dewey and Eros: Wisdom and Desire in the Art of Teaching.* (New York: Teachers College Press, 1997), 6.

78. In *Light in the Dark*, Anzaldúa notes that this translation is usually offered by the Catholic Church (220, fn 2). Similarly, in an earlier interview from 1983, Anzaldúa speculates that it was "probably during the time of the witchburnings" that "society made 'daemon' synonymous with 'demon,' possession, like *The Exorcist* and other popularized, trivialized motion pictures" (*Interviews/Entrevistas*, 102).

79. Anzaldúa, *Interviews/Entrevistas*, 25.

## Chapter 5. Subversive Everyday Knowledge: Ada María Isasi-Díaz's "Conscientized Cotidiano"

1. See Christopher Tirres, *The Aesthetics and Ethics of Faith: A Dialogue Between Liberationist and Pragmatic Thought* (New York: Oxford University Press, 2014), especially chapter 3.

2. Lisa Isherwood, "An Interview with Ada María Isasi-Díaz," *Feminist Theology* 20, no. 1 (2011): 10.

3. Orlando Espín, "The State of US Latino/a Theology: An Understanding," *Perspectivas: Occasional Papers* (Fall 2000): 29.

4. Mará Pilar Aquino, "Theological Method in US Latino/a Theology: Toward an Intercultural Theology for the Third Millennium," in *From the Heart of Our People*, ed. Orlando Espín and Miguel Díaz (Maryknoll, NY: Orbis Books), 38.

5. Another important work in this regard, which was published the same year, is Daphne Patai's *Brazilian Women Speak: Contemporary Life Stories* (New Brunswick, NJ: Rutgers University Press, 1988).

6. Ada María Isasi-Díaz, "*Lo Cotidiano*: Everyday Struggles in Hispanas/Latinas' Lives," in *La Lucha Continues: Mujerista Theology* (Maryknoll, NY: Orbis Books), 95.

7. Isasi-Díaz, "*Lo Cotidiano*," 94.

8. Isasi-Díaz, "*Lo Cotidiano*, 95.

9. Isasi-Díaz, "*Lo Cotidiano*, 95; Ada María Isasi-Díaz, "Mujerista Discourse: A Platform for Latinas' Subjugated Knowledge," in *Decolonizing Epistemologies*, ed. Ada María Isasi-Díaz and Eduardo Mendieta (New York: Fordham University Press, 2011), 49, and "Burlando al Opresor: Mocking/Tricking the Oppressor: Hispanas/Latinas' Dreams and Hopes," in *La Lucha Continues: Mujerista Theology*, 100.

10. Agnes Heller, *Everyday Life* (London: Routledge & Kegan Paul, 1984), 195.

11. Heller, *Everyday Life*.

12. Heller, *Everyday Life*, 196–97.

13. Heller, *Everyday Life*, 196.

14. Isasi-Díaz, "Burlando al Opresor," 166. María Pilar Aquino also underscores the significance of desire in *Our Cry for Life: Feminist Theology from Latin America* (Maryknoll, NY: Orbis Books), 1993.

15. Isasi-Díaz, "Burlando al Opresor," 167.

16. Tim Shallice, *The Organisation of Mind* (Oxford: Oxford University Press, 2011); Mark Johnson, *The Meaning of the Body: Aesthetics of Human Understanding* (Chicago: University of Chicago Press, 2008).

17. Heller, *Everyday Life*, 197.

18. Orlando Espín, *The Faith of the People: Theological Reflections on Popular Catholicism* (Maryknoll, NY: Orbis Books, 1997).

19. Isasi-Díaz, "*Lo Cotidiano*," 95.

20. Isasi-Díaz, "Mujerista Discourse," 48.

21. Heller, *Everyday Life*, 208.

22. Heller, *Everyday Life*.

23. C. S. Peirce, "The Fixation of Belief," in *Selected Writings (Values in a Universe of Chance)*, ed. Philip P. Wiener (New York: Dover, 1958), 99.

24. Isasi-Díaz, "*Lo Cotidiano*," 95.

25. Isasi-Díaz, "*Lo Cotidiano*," 97.

26. Isasi-Díaz, "*Lo Cotidiano*," 95.

27. Isasi-Díaz, "*Lo Cotidiano*."

28. Isasi-Díaz, "*Lo Cotidiano*," 97.

29. See, for example, Thomas E. Alexander, *John Dewey's Theory of Art, Experience, and Nature* (Albany: SUNY Press, 1987), and *The Human Eros: Eco-ontology and the Aesthetics of Existence* (New York: Fordham University Press, 2013); Steven Fesmire, *John Dewey and Moral Imagination: Pragmatism in Ethics*

(Bloomington: Indiana University Press, 2003); Stephen Fishman and Lucille McCarthy, *John Dewey and the Philosophy and the Practice of Hope* (Urbana: University of Illinois Press, 2007); Jim Garrison, *Dewey and Eros: Wisdom and Desire in the Art of Teaching* (New York: Teachers College Press, 1997); Mark Johnson, *Moral Imagination: Implications of Cognitive Science for Ethics* (Chicago: University of Chicago Press, 1993); Melvin L. Rogers, *The Undiscovered Dewey: Religion, Morality, and the Ethos of Democracy* (New York: Columbia University Press, 2009); and Tirres, *The Aesthetics and Ethics of Faith.*

30. Seen from another angle, Afrika Bambaataa's understanding of "knowledge" is akin to these more intuitive, aesthetic, and passionate interpretations of Dewey's theory of inquiry. As Alejandro Nava explains, Bambaataa holds that knowledge— the "fifth element" of hip-hop (in addition to deejaying, emceeing, breaking, and graffiti)—is "[l]ess cerebral than existential, less about dry information or rote learning than experiential . . ." Rather, Bambaataa's understanding of knowledge is "rich and multidimensional, involving traces of self-awareness, social consciousness, and spiritual wakefulness," all the while remaining tethered to the rich history and artistry of hip-hop. Alejandro Nava, *Street Scriptures: Between God and Hip-Hop* (Chicago: University of Chicago Press, 2022), 10–11.

31. Heller, *Everyday Life*, 198.

32. Heller, *Everyday Life*, 188.

33. Heller, *Everyday Life*, 188–89.

34. Andrew Prevot, *The Mysticism of Ordinary Life: Theology, Philosophy, and Feminism* (New York: Oxford University Press, 2023), 193.

35. Michelle A. González highlights the centrality of Isasi-Díaz's narrative style when she writes, "The autobiographical voice Isasi-Díaz embraces within many of her writings is an example of the significance of daily life in her work." Michelle A. González, "Keeping It Real: The Theological Contribution of Ada María Isasi-Díaz," *Feminist Theology* (2011): 30. Also significant are the many contributions that Gonzalez herself has made to the field of US Latina feminist theology. See, for example, her *Created in God's Image: An Introduction to Feminist Theological Anthropology* (Maryknoll, NY: Orbis Books, 2007), *Sor Juana: Beauty and Justice in the Americas* (Maryknoll, NY: Orbis Books, 2003), and *Embracing Latina Spirituality: A Woman's Perspective* (Cincinnati, OH: St. Anthony Messenger Press, 2009).

36. Ada María Isasi-Díaz, "La Lucha: My Story," in *La Lucha Continues: Mujerista Theology*, 17.

37. Isasi-Díaz, "La Lucha: My Story," 17–18.

## Chapter 6. Ecofeminism and Relatedness: Ivone Gebara's Pragmatic Inheritance

1. Mev Puleo, *The Struggle Is One: Voices and Visions of Liberation* (Albany: SUNY Press, 1994), 206.

2. Ivone Gebara, *Out of the Depths: Women's Experience of Evil and Salvation* (Minneapolis: Fortress Press, 2002), 48. In two interviews, Gebara gives similar

accounts of why she became a woman religious. In a 1994 interview, Gebara explains that she entered the convent "not so much because I was in love with God, but because I wanted to change the world." She adds, "In fact, I experienced a strong crisis of atheism while studying philosophy. To this day, I have much sympathy for certain types of atheism." Likewise, in a 2012 interview with Mariana Carbajal, Gebara notes that when she began studying philosophy in 1960, she met some Catholic nuns at the university "who were very political and extremely involved with the struggle for liberation and against poverty. I began seeing that as an alternative lifestyle for me. It was not very clear, but it seemed a better life, with more freedom than having a husband and a traditional family life." See Puleo, *The Struggle Is One*, 206, and Elaine Nogueira-Godsey, "A History of Resistance: Ivone Gebara's Transformative Feminist Liberation Theology," *Journal for the Study of Religion* 26, no. 2 (2013): 91.

3. ITER was especially inspired by the work of Archbishop Dom Hélder Câmara, who is famously known for saying, "When I give food to the poor, they call me a saint. When I ask why they are poor, they call me a communist." Gebara began teaching at ITER to replace Jospeh Comblin, a liberation theologian who drew ire from Brazil's military regime and was exiled from the country in 1971. Gebara was the only female theologian at ITER and soon became its vice-director.

4. Puleo, *The Struggle Is One*, 206.

5. Virginia Fabella and Mercy A. Oduyoye, eds., *With Passion and Compassion: Third World Women Doing Theology: Reflections from the Women's Commission of the Ecumenical Association of Third World Theologians* (Maryknoll, NY: Orbis Books, 1988), 26. Decades later, Gebara similarly acknowledged that the "wounds inflicted on my own life are minimal compared to what other women have suffered" in different parts of Brazil and the world. Gebara, *Out of the Depths*, 46.

6. Quoted in Nogueira-Godsey, "A History of Resistance," 96.

7. Nogueira-Godsey, "A History of Resistance," 100.

8. Anne Patrick Ware, "Translator's Note," in *Out of the Depths*, vii.

9. Leslie Wirpsa, "Before Silencing, Gebara Speaks Her Mind," *National Catholic Reporter* 31, no. 37 (1995): 13.

10. Ivone Gebara, *Longing for Running Water: Ecofeminism and Liberation* (Minneapolis: Fortress Press, 1999), 45.

11. Gebara, *Longing for Running Water*, 9.

12. As Gebara notes in a 1995 interview, one of the greatest challenges for Christianity is whether it will be "flexible enough to change the foundations of its anthropology and cosmology to respond to holistic ecofeminism." Mary Judith Ress, "Interview with Brazilian Feminist Theologian Ivone Gebara, *Feminist Theology*. This interview was first published in Spanish in *Con-Spirando* 4 (June 1993).

13. Gebara, *Longing for Running Water*, 83.

14. Gebara, *Longing for Running Water*, 92.

15. Gebara, *Longing for Running Water*, 83

16. Gebara, *Longing for Running Water*, 8.

17. An excellent article that explores the implicit connection between feminist theology and pragmatism is Rebecca Chopp, "Feminism's Theological Pragmatics: A Social Naturalism of Women's Experience," *The Journal of Religion* 67, no. 2 (1987): 239–56. Chopp shows that feminist theology "combines pragmatics, a theory of purposive intent, with hermeneutics, a theory of interpretation. The implications are obvious but must nonetheless be underscored: *feminist theology is explicitly oriented toward the concrete transformation of meanings and structures, of consciousness and of roles.*" One example may be found in the work of Elisabeth Schüssler Fiorenza. Chopp explains:

> Fiorenza's own model of the hermeneutical moment—suspicion, proclamation, remembrance, creative actualization—follows a distinctly pragmatic pattern. First, the situation of oppression causes suspicion and the need to investigate; second, the moments of proclamation and remembrance occur, wherein proclamation assesses the Bible's significance for the contemporary situation, and remembrance reclaims all of women's history; and, third, creative actualization provides new possibilities for transformation. In each moment, the horizon of the present must be rendered explicit, for it is the present that makes possible the reading, the evaluating, and the retrieving of the past. The combination of inquiry into a situation, interpretation of text in relation to that inquiry, and the creative imagination of new possibilities for the text and the situation illustrates the intrinsic relation between pragmatics and hermeneutics in feminist theology; only by her implicit feminist pragmatics can Fiorenza provide a hermeneutics that "does not permit a mere repetition or application of biblical texts, but demands a translation of their meaning and context into our own situation." (250–51)

18. Gebara's relationship to McFague is long-standing and significant. Gebara pays tribute to her longtime friend in "Ecofeminism: A Latin American Perspective," *Crosscurrents* (Spring 2003), which is based off a paper that was first presented at a conference honoring the work of Ruether at Garrett-Evangelical Theological Seminary in Evanston, IL. Also worth noting is Ruether's 1985 article "Feminist Interpretation: A Method of Correlation," which argues that, of the three traditional sources of religious faith—scripture, tradition, and experience—theological method must necessarily privilege of human experience. Although detractors may assume that any form of human experience, including "women's experience," is subjectively culture-bound and cannot compete with the objectivity of scripture or the weight of accumulated tradition, such a response, says Ruether, misunderstands the role of human experience in the formation of scripture and theological tradition. "Human experience," she writes, "is both the starting point and the ending point of the circle of interpretation." Furthermore, Ruether adds that "[c]odified tradition both reaches back to its roots in experience and is constantly renewed through the test of experience." Rosemary Radford Ruether, "Feminist

Interpretation: A Method of Correlation," in *Feminist Interpretation of the Bible*, ed. Letty M. Russell (Philadelphia: Westminster Press, 1985), 111. Gebara's interpretation of religion follows this basic anthropological insight. In fact, Ruether, who has become a great admirer of and spokesperson for Gebara's work, commented in 2008 that in some ways, Gebara seems to follow the Feuerbachian view that theology is anthropology and theology is a human construct. While all true, Ruether also notes that for Gebara these relations go well beyond the human to include our relations with nature and the cosmos at large.

19. Although Richard Grigg is writing here about McFague, the same language may be applied to Gebara. Richard Grigg, *Gods after God: An Introduction to Contemporary Radical Theologies* (Albany: SUNY Press, 2006), 53.

20. More specifically, *The Body of God* argues that ecology fundamentally has to do with "bodies," because ecology involves the interrelationship between an organism and its environment. The nature of this relationship, however, can either be understood mechanistically (such as seen in Newtonian causality) or organically, wherein there is a dynamic continuum between matter and energy (as seen in more postmodern approaches to sciences). McFague locates her project within the second approach and makes a special case for the value of "deep ecology," which insists that we are "not merely connected to nature but that all its parts, including ourselves, intermingle and interpenetrate." Sallie McFague, *The Body of God: An Ecological Theology* (Minneapolis: Fortress Press, 1993), 125. On the topic of deep ecology, McFague cites, among others, the work of Aldo Leopold, Bill Devall, George Sessions, Gary Snyder, and Warwick Fox.

21. For a rich and detailed analysis of a Deweyan understanding of "transaction," see Jim Garrison, "An Introduction to Dewey's Theory of Functional 'Trans-Action': An Alternative Paradigm for Activity Theory," *Mind, Culture, and Activity* 8, no. 4 (2001): 275–96.

22. See William T. Myers, "Dewey, Whitehead, and Process Metaphysics," in *The Oxford Handbook of Dewey*, ed. Steven Fesmire (New York: Oxford University Press, 2019), 53–72; and Samuel Enoch Stumpf and James Fieser, "Pragmatism and Process Philosophy," in *Socrates to Sartre and Beyond: A History of Philosophy*, 8th edition (Boston: McGraw Hill, 2008), 371–97.

23. Garrison, "An Introduction to Dewey's Theory of Functional 'Trans-Action.'"

24. As John Dewey so eloquently puts it at the end of *A Common Faith*:

> The things in civilization we most prize are not of ourselves. They exist by grace of the doings and sufferings of the continuous human community in which we are a link. Ours is the responsibility of conserving, transmitting, rectifying and expanding the heritage of values we have received that those who come after us may receive it more solid and secure, more widely accessible and more generously shared than we have received it. Here are all the elements for a religious faith that shall not be confined to sect, class, or race. Such a faith has always been implicitly the common faith of

mankind. It remains to make it explicit and militant. (Dewey, *A Common Faith*, LW9: 58–59)

25. To be clear, Gebara does in fact make some important gestures in the direction of evolutionary science through her references to the work of Brian Swimme and Thomas Barry. This is certainly a welcome move. My point, however, is that this line of thinking could be extended further in the direction of process thought and pragmatic theology to make the philosophical and theological implications of evolutionary thought even more explicit.

26. More than anyone else, Gregory Fernando Pappas has made the case in various articles and books that pragmatism has not only been "imported" to Latin America in some obvious ways, but more importantly, that certain strains of Latin American thought are independently and autochthonously pragmatic in their own right. See, for example, his *Pragmatism in Americas* (New York: Fordham University Press, 2011), especially chapters 11 and 16; also, Pappas, "Zapatismo, Luis Villoro, and American Pragmatism on Democracy, Power, and Injustice," *The Pluralist* 12, no. 1 (2017): 85–100. In a similar vein, Scott Pratt has challenged pragmatists to rethink how philosophical pragmatism mirrors—if not outright borrows—key insights from Indigenous ways of knowing. For example, it is generally accepted that pragmatism's genealogy should begin with Peirce, but why not couple this origin myth with Kicking Bear, a contemporary of Peirce's who was also theorizing the importance of relationality (and place), but who did so explicitly within the context of settler colonialism? For that matter, what can pragmatists learn from pre-Columbian cosmologies of the Americas, such as found in the Andean and Nahua traditions? As James Maffie writes, such cosmologies can help to lay the groundwork for an "ethics of reciprocity" wherein human beings are "obliged to perform reciprocating actions that maintain the equilibrium and continuing existence of the cosmos and humankind." See Scott L. Pratt, *Native Pragmatism: Rethinking the Roots of American Philosophy* (Bloomington: Indiana University Press, 2002); James Maffie, "Pre-Columbian Philosophies," in *A Companion to Latin American Philosophy*, ed. Susan Nuccetelli, Ofelia Schutte, and Otavio Bueno (Hoboken, NJ: Wiley-Blackwell, 2013), 9–22; and Bruce Wilshire, *The Primal Roots of American Philosophy: Pragmatism, Phenomenology, and Native American Thought* (University Park: Pennsylvania State University Press, 2000).

27. Gebara's Latin American feminist interlocutors include Maria Clara Bingemer, Beatriz Melano Couth, Nelly Ritchie, and Elsa Tamez, and the ecofeminist network of *Con-Spirando*. Nogueira-Godsey, "A History of Resistance," 93.

28. Gebara names here Rosemary Radford Ruether, Delores Williams, Dorothee Soelle, Sallie McFague, and Thomas Berry. Gebara, *Longing for Running Water*, vii.

29. Gebara, *Longing for Running Water*.

30. Gebara, "Ecofeminism," 95.

## Conclusion. Spiritual Praxis and the Fullness of Life

1. I borrow this phrase from theologian Orlando Espín, who writes extensively on Latine popular religion. See, for example, *The Faith of the People: Theological Reflections on Popular Catholicism* (Maryknoll, NY: Orbis Books, 1997).

2. Enrique Dussel, *The Underside of Modernity: Apel, Ricoeur, Rorty, Taylor and the Philosophy of Liberation* (Atlantic Highlands, NJ: Humanities Press, 1996).

3. W. E. B. Du Bois invokes this phrase, "spiritual strivings," in his classic study, *The Souls of Black Folk* (New York: Penguin, 1989).

4. Aníbal Quijano, "Colonialidad del poder y clasificación social," *Journal of World-Systems Research* 6, no. 2 (2000): 342–86.

5. Regarding attempts in decolonial theory to create new habits of "seeing" and "doing," see for example Mireille Fanon Mendès Franc and Nelson Maldonado-Torres, "For a Combative Decoloniality Sixty Years after Fanon's Death: An Invitation from the Frantz Fanon Foundation," https://fondation-frantzfanon.com/for-a-combative-decoloniality-sixty-years-after-fanons-death-an-invitation-from-the-frantz-fanon-foundation/. The title of this thoughtful statement may mislead some readers. In pointing toward a "combative" decoloniality, the authors are invoking Fanon's sense of *le combat colectif*, which may be alternatively translated as "the collective struggle," an idea with which Ada María Isasi-Díaz, among others in this book, would surely resonate. Fanon Mendès Franc and Maldonado-Torres explain:

> Different from critique, combativity emerges when racialized subjects start to address other racialized subjects in the effort to generate the sense of a collective struggle. While critique draws its power from crisis, decolonial combativity addresses the catastrophe of modernity/coloniality. Combativity goes beyond cries of protests, laments, and appeals, even as these may be necessary moments of the struggle. Combativity is about the path from individual to collective responsibility, and it requires the will and ability to connect with others and to engage in collective movement against coloniality.

6. Like Mignolo, Ramón Grosfugel, another important decolonial thinker, is similarly dismissive. See Joseph Drexler-Dreis, *Decolonial Theology in the North Atlantic World* (Leiden: Brill, 2019), 27–28.

7. Walter Mignolo, "Decolonizing Western Epistemology: Building Decolonial Epistemologies," in *Decolonizing Epistemologies: Latina/o Theology and Philosophy*, ed. Ada María Isasi-Díaz and Eduardo Mendieta (New York: Fordham University Press, 2012), 25. Another important early volume that puts postcolonial and decolonial theory in conversation with religious studies is Purushottama Bilimoria and Andrew B. Irvine, eds., *Postcolonial Philosophy of Religion* (London: Springer, 2009).

8. Mignolo, "Decolonizing Western Epistemology," 25–26.

9. Nelson Maldonado-Torres, "AAR Centennial Roundtable: Religion, Conquest, and Race in the Foundations of the Modern/Colonial World," *Journal of the American Academy of Religion* 82, no. 3 (2014): 636–65, and "Race, Religion,

and Ethics in the Modern/Colonial World," *Journal of Religious Ethics* 42, no. 4 (2014): 691–711; M. Jacqui Alexander, *Pedagogies of Crossing: Meditations on Feminism, Sexual Politics, Memory, and the Sacred* (Durham, NC: Duke University Press, 2005); Rafael Vizcaíno, "Secular Decolonial Woes," *Journal of Speculative Philosophy* 35, no. 1 (2021): 71–92, and "Introduction to Special Issue: Decolonizing Spiritualities," *CLR James Journal* 27, no. 1–2 (2021): 17–24.

10. Joseph Drexler-Dries, *Decolonial Love: Salvation in Colonial Modernity* (New York: Fordham University Press, 2019); Néstor Medina, Becca Whitla, and Ary Fernández-Albán, "Liberation Theologies, Decolonial Thinking, and Practical Theologies: Odd Combinations?," *International Journal of Practical Theology* 25, no. 1 (2021): 110–31; Néstor Medina, "A Decolonial Primer," *Toronto Journal of Theology* 33, no. 2 (2017): 279–87; Mayra Rivera, *Poetics of the Flesh* (Durham, NC: Duke University Press, 2015); Teresa Delgado, *A Puerto Rican Decolonial Theology: Prophesy Freedom* (Cham, Switzerland: Palgrave Macmillan/Springer Nature, 2017); An Yountae, *The Decolonial Abyss: Mysticism and Cosmopolitics from the Ruins* (Durham, NC: Duke University Press, 2017); and Santiago Slabodsky, *Decolonial Judaism: Triumphal Failures of Barbaric Thinking* (New York: Palgrave Macmillan, 2014).

11. Carol Wayne White, *Black Lives and Sacred Humanity* (New York: Fordham University Press, 2016); Vincent Lloyd, *Religion of the Field Negro* (New York: Fordham University Press, 2017); J. Cameron Carter, *Race: A Theological Account* (New York: Oxford University Press, 2008); and Willie James Jennings. *The Christian Imagination: Theology and the Origins of Race* (New Haven, CT: Yale University Press, 2010).

12. Charlene Haddock Seigfried, *Pragmatism and Feminism: Reweaving the Social Fabric* (Chicago: University of Chicago Press, 1996), 6.

13. Seigfried, *Pragmatism and Feminism.* On this question, see also the important work of Marilyn Fischer, including *On Addams* (Australia: Thomson Wadsworth, 2004) and *Jane Addams's Evolutionary Theorizing: Constructing "Democracy and Social Ethics"* (Chicago: University of Chicago Press, 2019).

14. Seigfried, *Pragmatism and Feminism*, 6.

15. Richard Bernstein, "Pragmatism, Pluralism, and the Healing of Wounds," in *Pragmatism: A Reader*, ed. Louis Menand (New York: Vintage, 1997), 382–401.

16. William James, *Correspondence of William James, vol.* 12, ed. Ignas Skrupskelis and Elizabeth Berkeley (Charlottesville: University Press of Virginia, 2005), 407.

17. Bernstein, "Pragmatism, Pluralism, and the Healing of Wounds," 397.

18. Darcísio Natal Muraro, "Relações entre a filosofia e a educação de John Dewey e de Paulo Freire," *Educação & Realidade* 38, no. 3 (2013); and Marcus Vinicius Da Cunha and Débora Cristina Garcia, "Pragmatism in Brazil: John Dewey and Education," in *Pragmatism in the Americas*, ed. Gregory Fernando Pappas (New York: Fordham University Press, 2011), 40–52.

19. See Joseph Betz, "John Dewey and Paulo Freire," *Transactions of the Charles S. Peirce Society* 28 (1992), 107–26; Daniel S. Schipani, *Religious Faith Encounters Liberation Theology* (Birmingham, AL: Religious Education Press, 1988).

20. Dewey, *Democracy and Education*, MW9: 82.

21. As recent data from the Pew Research Center suggests, over 25 percent of the US population now identifies as "spiritual but not religious." See Michael Lipka and Claire Gecewicz, "More Americans Now Say They're Spiritual but not Religious," 2017, https://www.pewresearch.org/short-reads/2017/09/06/more-americans-now-say -theyre-spiritual-but-not-religious/.

22. Sharon Daloz Parks, *Big Questions, Worthy Dreams: Mentoring Emerging Adults in Their Search for Meaning, Purpose, and Faith* (San Francisco: Jossey-Bass, 2000), 10.

23. Wilfred Cantwell Smith, *The Meaning and End of Religion* (Minneapolis: Fortress Press, 1962). In this watershed book, Smith notes that "the notion of religion can become an enemy to piety" and "it is probably easier to be religious without the concept" (19). Smith does not want readers to stop thinking critically about religion altogether, but he invites them to approach the subject from a different vantage point than is normally taken—namely, religion as an adjective (i.e., a quality of experience) rather than a noun. For Smith, the act of "living religiously is an attribute of persons," and this attribute arises "not because those persons participate in some entity called *religion*" but, rather, because they actively *live out* their faith in ways that are directed toward some form of transcendence (195, 178–85). Smith thus encourages us to think about faith and spirituality in terms of their active and operational qualities.

24. Elizabeth Tisdell, *Exploring Spirituality and Culture in Adult and Higher Education* (San Francisco: Jossey-Bass, 2003), xi.

25. Tisdell, *Exploring Spirituality and Culture*, 28–35.

26. Alexander W. Astin, Helen S. Astin, and Jennifer A. Lindholm, *Cultivating the Spirit: How College Can Enhance Students' Inner Lives* (San Francisco: Jossey-Bass, 2011), https://spirituality.ucla.edu/background/, underlining in original.

27. See especially James W. Fowler's *Stages of Faith: The Psychology of Human Development and the Quest for Meaning* (San Francisco: Jossey Bass, 1981), and *Faithful Change: The Personal and Public Challenges of Postmodern Life* (Nashville, TN: Abingdon Press, 1996).

28. See Donald J. Morse, *Faith in Life: John Dewey's Early Philosophy* (New York: Fordham University Press, 2011).

29. Dewey, *A Common Faith*, LW9:8.

30. Dewey, *A Common Faith*, LW9:8.

31. Dewey, *A Common Faith*, LW9:8.

32. Dewey, *A Common Faith*, LW9:8.

33. For a discussion of Dewey's somewhat technical understanding of "adjustment," see Thomas E. Alexander, *The Human Eros: Eco-ontology and the Aesthetics of Existence* (New York: Fordham University Press, 2013), 362–68; Hans Joas, *The Genesis of Values* (Chicago: University of Chicago Press, 2000), 113–19; and Christopher Tirres, *The Aesthetics and Ethics of Faith: A Dialogue Between Liberationist and Pragmatic Thought* (New York: Oxford University Press, 2014), 95–96.

34. Dewey, *A Common Faith*, LW9:11.

35. Eddie Glaude Jr., *An Uncommon Faith: A Pragmatic Approach to the Study of African American Religion* (Athens: The University of Georgia Press, 2018), 8. See also his elegant *In a Shade of Blue: Pragmatism and the Politics of Black America* (Chicago: University of Chicago Press, 2007).

36. Dewey, *A Common Faith*, LW9:13.

37. A good overview of liberationist strains within all of these traditions is presented in Miguel A. De La Torre, ed., *The Hope of Liberation in World Religions* (Waco, TX: Baylor University Press, 2008).

38. Roger Haight, *Spiritual and Religious: Explorations for Seekers* (Maryknoll, NY: Orbis Books, 2016), 6–7.

39. Agustín Fuentes, *Why We Believe: Evolution and the Human Way of Being* (New Haven, CT: Yale University Press, 2019), 123.

40. Fuentes, *Why We Believe*, 121, 136.

41. Sandra M. Schneiders, "Spirituality in the Academy," *Theological Studies* 50 (1989): 683.

42. Writing more broadly about the division between spirituality and theology, J. Matthew Ashley makes a similar point: this division, he says, "cannot be overcome by theory alone but by a new praxis, both of doing theology and of practicing spirituality, an ecclesial praxis that is at the same time individual and social-political" (xiii). See his insightful *Renewing Theology: Ignatian Spirituality and Karl Rahner, Ignacio Ellacuría, and Pope Francis* (Notre Dame, IN: University of Notre Dame Press, 2022).

43. David McLellan, ed., *Karl Marx: Selected Writings* (New York: Oxford University Press, 1990), 64.

44. Robert C. Tucker, ed., *The Marx-Engels Reader*, second ed. (New York: W.W. Norton, 1978), 145.

45. Dewey, *A Common Faith*, LW9:57–58.

46. Paulo Freire, "Conscientizing as a Way of Liberating," in *Liberation Theology: A Documentary History*, ed. Alfred T. Hennelly (Maryknoll, NY: Orbis Books, 1990), 12–13.

# Bibliography

Alexander, M. Jacqui. *Pedagogies of Crossing: Meditations on Feminism, Sexual Politics, Memory, and the Sacred.* Durham, NC: Duke University Press, 2005.

Alexander, Thomas E. *John Dewey's Theory of Art, Experience, and Nature.* Albany: SUNY Press, 1987.

———. *The Human Eros: Eco-ontology and the Aesthetics of Existence.* New York: Fordham University Press, 2013.

Anzaldúa, Gloria. *Borderlands/La Frontera: The New Mestiza.* San Francisco: Aunt Lute Books, 2007.

———. *Interviews/Entrevistas.* Edited by AnaLouise Keating. New York: Routledge, 2000.

———. *Light in the Dark / Luz en lo oscuro: Rewriting Identity, Spirituality, Reality.* Edited by AnaLouise Keating. Durham, NC: Duke University Press, 2015.

———. *The Gloria Anzaldúa Reader.* Durham, NC: Duke University Press, 2009.

Aponte, Edwin. *¡Santo!: Varieties of Latina/o Spirituality.* Maryknoll, NY: Orbis Books, 2012.

Aquino, María Pilar. *Our Cry for Life: Feminist Theology from Latin America.* Maryknoll, NY: Orbis Books, 1993.

———. "Theological Method in U.S. Latino/a Theology: Toward an Intercultural Theology for the Third Millennium." In *From the Heart of Our People: Latino/a Explorations in Catholic Systematic Theology.* Edited by Orlando Espín and Miguel Díaz. Maryknoll, NY: Orbis Books, 1999.

Arnold, Philip P. *The Urgency of Indigenous Values.* Syracuse, NY: Syracuse University Press, 2023.

Aronowitz, Stanley. "Paulo Freire's Radical Democratic Humanism: The Fetish of Method." *Counterpoints* 422 (2012): 257–74.

Ashley, J. Matthew. *Renewing Theology: Ignatian Spirituality and Karl Rahner, Ignacio Ellacuría, and Pope Francis.* Notre Dame, IN: University of Notre Dame Press, 2022.

———. "To Change the World: An Intellectual History of Liberation Theology." *Commonweal,* January 31, 2019. https://www.commonwealmagazine.org/change -world.

Astin, Alexander W., Helen S. Astin, and Jennifer A. Lindholm. *Cultivating the Spirit: How College Can Enhance Students' Inner Lives.* San Francisco: Jossey-Bass, 2011. https://spirituality.ucla.edu/background/.

Baines, John M. *Revolution in Peru: Mariátegui and the Myth.* Tuscaloosa: University of Alabama Press, 1972.

Barger, Lilian Calles. *The World Come of Age: An Intellectual History of Liberation Theology.* New York: Oxford University Press, 2018.

Bernstein, Richard. "Pragmatism, Pluralism, and the Healing of Wounds." In *Pragmatism: A Reader,* edited by Louis Menand, 382–401. New York: Vintage, 1997.

Betz, Joseph. "John Dewey and Paulo Freire." *Transactions of the Charles S. Peirce Society* 28 (1992): 107–26.

Bevans, Steven. *Models of Contextual Theology.* Maryknoll, NY: Orbis Books, 1992.

Bilimoria, Purushottama, and Andrew B. Irvine, eds. *Postcolonial Philosophy of Religion.* London: Springer, 2009.

Boyarin, Daniel. *The Jewish Gospels: The Story of the Jewish Christ.* New York: The New Press, 2012.

Burke, Kevin F., and Robert A. Lassalle-Klein, eds. *Love That Produces Hope: The Thought of Ignacio Ellacuría.* Collegeville, MN: Liturgical Press, 2006.

Cadorette, Curt. *From the Heart of the People: The Theology of Gustavo Gutiérrez.* Oak Park, IL: Meyer Stone Books, 1988.

Carlsen, Robert. "Transculturation." In *The Oxford Encyclopedia of Mesoamerican Cultures: The Civilizations of Mexico and Central America,* edited by Davíd Carrasco. New York: Oxford University Press, 2001. https://www.oxfordreference .com/display/10.1093/acref/9780195108156.001.0001/acref-9780195108156-e-671 ?rskey=C9GzAA&result=670.

Carter, J. Cameron. *Race: A Theological Account.* New York: Oxford University Press, 2008.

Casarella, Peter J. "Beauty and the Little Stories of Holiness: What Alejandro García-Rivera Taught Me." *Diálogo: An Interdisciplinary Studies Journal* 16, no. 2 (2013): 53–58

Castillo, Daniel P. "Agony in the Garden?: Evaluating the Cosmology of Alejandro García-Rivera in View of the 'Little Story' and the 'Principle of Foregrounding.'" *Diálogo: An Interdisciplinary Studies Journal* 16, no. 2 (2013): 65–68.

———. *An Ecological Theology of Liberation: Salvation and Political Ecology.* Maryknoll, NY: Orbis Books, 2019.

Chopp, Rebecca. "Feminism's Theological Pragmatics: A Social Naturalism of Women's Experience." *The Journal of Religion* 67, no. 2 (1987): 239–56.

Conroy, Ed. "Mestiso Identity is the Heart of Virgil Elizondo's Life and Work." *National Catholic Reporter*, October 8, 2004. https://natcath.org/NCR_Online/archives2/2004d/100804/100804n.php.

Da Cunha, Marcus Vinicius, and Débora Cristina Garcia. "Pragmatism in Brazil: John Dewey and Education." In *Pragmatism in the Americas*, edited by Gregory Fernando Pappas, 40–52. New York: Fordham University Press, 2011.

Day, Frances Ann. *Latina and Latino Voices in Literature: Lives and Works.* Westport, CT: Greenwood Press, 2003.

De La Torre, Miguel A. *Liberation Theology for Armchair Theologians.* Louisville, KY: Westminster John Knox, 2013.

De La Torre, Miguel A., ed. *The Hope of Liberation in World Religions.* Waco, TX: Baylor University Press, 2008.

De Luna, Anita. *Faith Formation and Popular Religion: Lessons from Tejano Experience.* Lanham, MD: Rowman & Littlefield, 2002.

Delgadillo, Theresa. *Spiritual Mestizaje: Religion, Gender, Race, and Nation in Contemporary Chicana Narrative.* Durham, NC: Duke University Press, 2011.

Delgado, Teresa. *A Puerto Rican Decolonial Theology: Prophesy Freedom.* Cham, Switzerland: Palgrave Macmillan/Springer Nature, 2017.

Dewey, John. *The Collected Works of John Dewey, 1882–1953*, 37 vols. Edited by Jo Ann Boydston. Carbondale: Southern Illinois University Press, 1967–1990.

Díaz, Kim. "Mariátegui's Myth." *APA Newsletter. Hispanic/Latino Issues in Philosophy* 13, no. 1 (2013): 21–22.

———. *Radical Democracy in the Thought and Work of Paulo Freire and Luis Villoro.* PhD dissertation, Texas A&M University, 2012.

Drexler-Dries, Joseph. *Decolonial Love: Salvation in Colonial Modernity.* New York: Fordham University Press, 2019.

———. *Decolonial Theology in the North Atlantic World.* Leiden: Brill, 2019.

Du Bois, W. E. B. *The Souls of Black Folk.* New York: Penguin, 1989.

Duarte, Eduardo. "Conscientizacion y Comunidad: A Dialectical Description of Education as the Struggle for Freedom." *Studies in Philosophy and Education* 18 (1999): 389–403.

Dungan, David L. *Constantine's Bible: Politics and the Making of the New Testament.* Minneapolis: Fortress, 2007.

Dussel, Enrique. *Beyond Philosophy: Ethics, History, Marxism, and Liberation Theology*, edited by Eduardo Mendieta. Lanham, MD: Rowman & Littlefield, 2003.

Dussel, Enrique. "Philosophy in Latin America in the Twentieth Century: Problems and Currents." In *Latin American Philosophy: Currents, Issues, Debates*, edited by Eduardo Mendieta, 11–56. Bloomington: Indiana University Press, 2003.

———. *The Underside of Modernity: Apel, Ricoeur, Rorty, Taylor, and the Philosophy of Liberation.* Translated by Eduardo Mendieta. Atlantic Highlands, NJ: Humanities Press, 1996.

Elias, John. *Paulo Freire: Pedagogue of Liberation*. Malabar, FL: Krieger, 1994.

Elizondo, Virgilio. *The Future Is Mestizo: Life Where Cultures Meet*, revised edition. Boulder: University Press of Colorado, 2000.

———. *The Human Quest: The Search for Meaning through Life and Death*. Huntington, IN: Our Sunday Visitor, 1978.

———. "Our Lady of Guadalupe as a Cultural Symbol." In *Beyond Borders: Writings of Virgilio Elizondo and Friends*, edited by Timothy Matovina, 118–25. Maryknoll, NY: Orbis Books, 2000.

———. *San Fernando Cathedral: Soul of the City*. Maryknoll, NY: Orbis Books, 1998.

———. *Virgilio Elizondo: Spiritual Writings*. Maryknoll, NY: Orbis Books, 2010.

Espín, Orlando. *The Faith of the People: Theological Reflections on Popular Catholicism*. Maryknoll, NY: Orbis Books, 1997.

———. "The State of U.S. Latino/a Theology: An Understanding." *Perspectivas: Occasional Papers* (Fall 2000): 19–55.

Fabella, Virginia, and Mercy A. Oduyoye, eds. *With Passion and Compassion: Third World Women Doing Theology: Reflections from the Women's Commission of the Ecumenical Association of Third World Theologians*. Maryknoll, NY: Orbis Books: 1988.

Fanon Mendès Franc, Mireille and Nelson Maldonado-Torres. "For a Combative Decoloniality Sixty Years after Fanon's Death: An Invitation from the Frantz Fanon Foundation." https://fondation-frantzfanon.com/for-a-combative -decoloniality-sixty-years-after-fanons-death-an-invitation-from-the-frantz-fanon -foundation/.

Fernández, Eduardo C. "A Litany for Alex: Remembering his Contributions to Pastoral Theology." *Diálogo: An Interdisciplinary Studies Journal* 16, no. 2 (2013): 28–32

Fesmire, Steven. *John Dewey and Moral Imagination: Pragmatism in Ethics*. Bloomington: Indiana University Press, 2003.

Fischer, Marilyn. *Jane Addams's Evolutionary Theorizing: Constructing "Democracy and Social Ethics."* Chicago: University of Chicago Press, 2019.

———. *On Addams*. Australia: Thomson Wadsworth, 2004.

Fishman, Stephen, and Lucille McCarthy. *John Dewey and the Philosophy and the Practice of Hope*. Urbana: University of Illinois Press, 2007.

Flores, Nichole M. *The Aesthetics of Solidarity: Our Lady of Guadalupe and American Democracy*. Washington, D.C.: Georgetown University Press, 2021.

Fowler, James W. *Faithful Change: The Personal and Public Challenges of Postmodern Life*. Nashville, TN: Abingdon Press, 1996.

———. *Stages of Faith: The Psychology of Human Development and the Quest for Meaning*. San Francisco: Jossey-Bass, 1981.

Fowler, Thomas B. "Informal Introduction to the Philosophy of Xavier Zubiri." http://www.zubiri.org/works/informalintro.htm.

Frankenberg, Ruth. *Living Spirit, Living Practice: Poetics, Politics, Epistemology.* Durham, NC: Duke University Press, 2004.

Freire, Paulo. "Conscientizing as a Way of Liberating." In *Liberation Theology: A Documentary History*, edited by Alfred T. Hennelly. Maryknoll, NY: Orbis Books, 1990.

———. "Education, Liberation and the Church." In *The Politics of Education: Culture, Power and Liberation*, edited by Henry Giroux. South Hadley, MA: Bergin & Garvey Publishers, 1985.

———. "Know, Practice, and Teach the Gospels." *Religious Education* 79, no. 4 (1984): 547–48.

———. "Letter to a Young Theology Student." *LADOC Keyhole Series* 2.29b (1972): 11–12.

———. *Pedagogy of the Oppressed.* New York: Continuum, 1992.

Fuentes, Agustín. *Why We Believe: Evolution and the Human Way of Being.* New Haven, CT: Yale University Press, 2019.

Gandolfo, David Ignatius. "Liberation Philosophy." In *A Companion to Latin American Philosophy*, edited by Susana Nuccetelli, Ofelia Schutte, and Otávio Bueno, 185–98. Malden, MA: Wiley-Blackwell, 2010.

García, Nathan. "Creating a Soulful Anthropology: Extending Thomas Moore's Spirituality Using Charles S. Peirce's Categories and Modes of Inference." PhD dissertation, Oblate School of Theology, 2022.

García-Rivera, Alejandro. "Crossing Theological Borders: Virgilio Elizondo's Place Among Theologians of Culture." In *Beyond Borders: Writings of Virgilio Elizondo and Friends*, edited by Timothy Matovina, 246–56. Maryknoll, NY: Orbis Books, 2000.

———. *The Community of the Beautiful: A Theological Aesthetics.* Collegeville, MN: Liturgical Press, 1999.

———. *The Garden of God: A Theological Cosmology.* Minneapolis: Fortress Press, 2009.

Garrison, Jim. "An Introduction to Dewey's Theory of Functional 'Trans-Action': An Alternative Paradigm for Activity Theory." *Mind, Culture, and Activity* 8, no. 4 (2001): 275–96.

———. *Dewey and Eros: Wisdom and Desire in the Art of Teaching.* New York: Teachers College Press, 1997.

Gebara, Ivone. "Ecofeminism: A Latin American Perspective." *Crosscurrents* 53, no. 1 (Spring 2003): 93–103.

———. *Longing for Running Water: Ecofeminism and Liberation.* Minneapolis: Fortress Press, 1999.

———. *Out of the Depths: Women's Experience of Evil and Salvation.* Minneapolis: Fortress Press, 2002.

Glaude, Jr., Eddie. *An Uncommon Faith: A Pragmatic Approach to the Study of African American Religion.* Athens: The University of Georgia Press, 2018.

———. *In a Shade of Blue: Pragmatism and the Politics of Black America.* Chicago: University of Chicago Press, 2007.

Goizueta, Roberto S. *Caminemos con Jesús: Toward a Hispanic/Latino Theology of Accompaniment.* Maryknoll, NY: Orbis Books, 1995.

———. "The Theologian as Wounded Innocent." *Diálogo: An Interdisciplinary Studies Journal* 16, no. 2 (2013): 37–42

González, Antonio. "Assessing the Philosophical Achievement of Ignacio Ellacuría." In *Love that Produces Hope: The Thought of Ignacio Ellacuría,* edited by Kevin Burke and Robert Lassalle-Klein, 73–87. Collegeville, MN: Liturgical Press, 2006.

González, Michelle A. "Alejandro García-Rivera: A Legacy in Theological Aesthetics." *Diálogo: An Interdisciplinary Studies Journal* 16, no. 2 (2013): 33–36

———. *Created in God's Image: An Introduction to Feminist Theological Anthropology.* Maryknoll, NY: Orbis Books, 2007.

———. *Embracing Latina Spirituality: A Woman's Perspective.* Cincinnati, OH: St. Anthony Messenger Press, 2009.

———. "Keeping It Real: The Theological Contribution of Ada María Isasi-Díaz." *Feminist Theology* 20, no. 1 (2011).

———. *Sor Juana: Beauty and Justice in the Americas.* Maryknoll, NY: Orbis Books, 2003.

González-Andrieu, Cecilia. *Bridge to Wonder: Art as Gospel of Beauty.* Waco, TX: Baylor University Press, 2012.

Gracia, Jorge J. E., and Elizabeth Millán-Zaibert. *Latin American Philosophy for the 21st Century.* New York: Prometheus, 2004.

Grigg, Richard. *Gods after God: An Introduction to Contemporary Radical Theologies.* Albany: SUNY Press, 2006.

Gutiérrez, Gustavo. *A Theology of Liberation: History, Politics, and Salvation.* Maryknoll, NY: Orbis Books, 1973.

Haight, Roger. *Spiritual and Religious: Explorations for Seekers.* Maryknoll, NY: Orbis Books, 2016.

Haught, John F. *The Cosmic Vision of Teilhard de Chardin.* Maryknoll, NY: Orbis Books, 2021.

———. "Trashing Teilhard: How Not to Read a Great Religious Thinker." *Commonweal,* February 12, 2019. https://www.commonwealmagazine.org /trashing-teilhard.

Heagle, John. "A New Public Piety: Reflections on Spirituality." *Church* 1 (1985): 52–55.

Hedrick, Tace. "Queering the Cosmic Race: Esotericism, Mestizaje, and Sexuality in the Work of Gabriela Mistral and Gloria Anzaldúa." *Aztlán: A Journal of Chicano Studies* 34, no. 2 (2009): 67–98.

Heller, Agnes. *Everyday Life.* London: Routledge & Kegan Paul, 1984.

Hickman, Larry A. *John Dewey's Pragmatic Technology.* Bloomington: Indiana University Press, 1992.

Hildebrand, David. *Dewey: A Beginner's Guide*. Oxford, UK: Oneworld, 2008.

Hillman, James. *The Myth of Analysis: Three Essays in Archetypal Psychology*. Evanston, IL. Northwestern University Press, 1998.

Isasi-Díaz, Ada María. "Burlando al Opresor: Mocking/Tricking the Oppressor: Hispanas/Latinas' Dreams and Hopes." In *La Lucha Continues: Mujerista Theology*, edited by Ada María Isasi-Díaz, 157–86. Maryknoll, NY: Orbis Books, 2004.

———. "La Lucha: My Story." In *La Lucha Continues: Mujerista Theology*, edited by Ada María Isasi-Díaz, 11–23. Maryknoll, NY: Orbis Books, 2004.

———. "*Lo Cotidiano*: Everyday Struggles in Hispanas/Latinas' Lives." In *La Lucha Continues: Mujerista Theology*, edited by Ada María Isasi-Díaz, 92–106. Maryknoll, NY: Orbis Books, 2004.

———. "Mujerista Discourse: A Platform for Latinas' Subjugated Knowledge." In *Decolonizing Epistemologies*, edited by Ada María Isasi-Díaz and Eduardo Mendieta, 44–67. New York: Fordham University Press, 2011.

Isherwood, Lisa. "An Interview with Ada María Isasi-Díaz." *Feminist Theology* 20, no. 1 (2011): 8–17.

James, William. *Correspondence of William James, vol. 12*, edited by Ignas Skrupskelis and Elizabeth Berkeley, 407. Charlottesville: University Press of Virginia, 2005.

———. *The Varieties of Religious Experience* in *Writings: 1902–1910*. New York: Library of America, 1987.

Jennings, Willie James. *The Christian Imagination: Theology and the Origins of Race*. New Haven, CT: Yale University Press, 2010.

Joas, Hans. *The Genesis of Values*. Chicago: University of Chicago Press, 2000.

Johnson, Mark. *Moral Imagination: Implications of Cognitive Science for Ethics*. Chicago: University of Chicago Press, 1993.

———. *The Meaning of the Body: Aesthetics of Human Understanding*. Chicago: University of Chicago Press, 2008.

Keating, AnaLouise. "Anzaldúa, Gloria E." In *American National Biography*. New York: Oxford University Press, 2018. www.anb.org/articles/16/16-03593.html.

———. "'I'm a citizen of the universe': Gloria Anzaldúa's Spiritual Activism as Catalyst for Social Change." *Feminist Studies* 34, no. 1–2 (2008): 53–69.

———. "Risking the Personal: An Introduction." In *Interviews/Entrevistas*, edited by AnaLouise Keating, 1–15. New York: Routledge, 2000.

Kennedy, William B. "Conversation with Paulo Freire." *Religious Education* 79, no. 4 (1984): 511–22.

King, Ursula. "Teilhard De Chardin, Pierre." In *Encyclopedia of Religion, second edition*, edited by Lindsay Jones, 13; 9032–35. Detroit, MI: Macmillan, 2005.

Kirylo, James D. *Paulo: The Man from Recife*. New York: Peter Lang, 2011.

Kirylo, James D., and Drick Boyd. *Paulo Freire: His Faith, Spirituality, and Theology*. Rotterdam: Sense Publishers, 2017.

Kripal, Jeffrey J. *Authors of the Impossible: The Paranormal and the Sacred*. Chicago: University of Chicago Press, 2010.

Lassalle-Klein, Robert. "The Potential Contribution of C. S. Peirce to Interpretation Theory in U.S. Hispanic/Latino Theology and Other Culturally Contextualized Theologies." *Journal of Hispanic/Latino Theology* 6, no. 3 (1999): 5–34.

Lee, Michael E. *Bearing the Weight of Salvation: The Soteriology of Ignacio Ellacuría.* New York: Crossroad, 2008.

Leopando, Irwin. *A Pedagogy of Faith: The Theological Vision of Paulo Freire.* London: Bloomsbury, 2017.

Lipka, Michael, and Claire Gecewicz. "More Americans Now Say They're Spiritual but not Religious." Pew Research Center, 2017. https://www.pewresearch.org /short-reads/2017/09/06/more-americans-now-say-theyre-spiritual-but-not -religious/.

Lloyd, Vincent. *Religion of the Field Negro.* New York: Fordham University Press, 2017.

Long, Charles. *Significations: Signs, Symbols, and Images in the Interpretation of Religion.* Aurora, CO: Davies Group, 1995.

Löwy, Michael. "Communism and Religion: José Carlos Mariátegui's Revolutionary Mysticism." *Latin American Perspectives* 35, no. 2 (2008): 77.

Löwy, Michael, ed. *El marxismo en América Latina.* Mexico: Ediciones Era, 1982.

MacMullan, Terrance. *From American Empire to América Cósmica Through Philosophy: Prospero's Reflection.* Lanham, MD: Lexington Books, 2023.

Maffie, James. "Pre-Columbian Philosophies." In *A Companion to Latin American Philosophy*, edited by Susan Nuccetelli, Ofelia Schutte, and Otavio Bueno, 9–22. Hoboken, NJ: Wiley-Blackwell, 2013.

Maldonado-Torres, Nelson. "AAR Centennial Roundtable: Religion, Conquest, and Race in the Foundations of the Modern/Colonial World." *Journal of the American Academy of Religion* 82, no. 3 (2014): 636–65.

———. "Race, Religion, and Ethics in the Modern/Colonial World." *Journal of Religious Ethics* 42, no. 4 (2014): 691–711.

Mariátegui, José Carlos. "Man and Myth." In *José Carlos Mariátegui: An Anthology*, edited by Harry E. Vanden and Marc Becker, 383–88. New York: Monthly Review Press, 2011.

———. "Pessimism of Reality, Optimism of the Idea." In *José Carlos Mariátegui: An Anthology*, edited by Harry E. Vanden and Marc Becker, 395–98. New York: Monthly Review Press, 2011.

———. *Siete ensayos de interpretación de la realidad peruana.* Lima, Peru: Amauta, 1928.

———. "The Problem of the Indian." In *Latin American Philosophy for the 21st Century*, edited by Jorge J. E. Gracia and Elizabeth Millán-Zaibert, 259–65. Amherst, NY: Prometheus, 2004.

Márquez, Ivan. *Contemporary Latin American Social and Political Thought: An Anthology.* New York: Rowman & Littlefield, 2008.

Martínez, Gaspar. *Confronting the Mystery of God: Political, Liberation, and Public Theologies.* New York: Continuum, 2001.

Matovina, Timothy. "Little Stories of Christmas and the Big Story of God's Love."
    *Diálogo: An Interdisciplinary Studies Journal* 16, no. 2 (2013): 49–52
————. *Theologies of Guadalupe: From the Era of Conquest to Pope Francis.* New
    York: Oxford University Press, 2019.
McFague, Sallie. *The Body of God: An Ecological Theology.* Minneapolis: Fortress
    Press, 1993.
McLellan, David, ed. *Karl Marx: Selected Writings.* New York: Oxford University
    Press, 1990.
Medina, Néstor. "A Decolonial Primer." *Toronto Journal of Theology* 33, no. 2 (2017):
    279–87.
————. *Mestizaje: (Re)mapping Race, Culture, and Faith in Latina/o Catholicism.*
    Maryknoll, NY: Orbis Books, 2009.
Medina, Néstor, Becca Whitla, and Ary Fernández-Albán. "Liberation Theologies,
    Decolonial Thinking, and Practical Theologies: Odd Combinations?"
    *International Journal of Practical Theology* 25, no. 1 (2021): 110–31.
Mendieta, Eduardo. *Global Fragments: Globalizations, Latinamericanisms, and
    Critical Theory.* Albany: SUNY Press, 2007.
————. *Latin American Philosophy: Currents, Issues, Debates.* Bloomington:
    Indiana University Press, 2003.
————. *The Adventures of Transcendental Philosophy: Karl-Otto Apel's Semiotics
    and Discourse Ethics.* Lanham, MD: Rowman & Littlefield, 2002.
————. "Philosophy of Liberation." In *Stanford Encyclopedia of Philosophy* (Winter
    2020 edition), edited by Edward N. Zalta and Uri Nodelman. Stanford, CA:
    Stanford University Press. https://plato.stanford.edu/archives/win2020/entries
    /liberation/.
————. "Three Pragmatist Lectures." *Poligrafi* 49, no. 13 (2008): 11–94.
Mignolo, Walter. "Decolonizing Western Epistemology: Building Decolonial
    Epistemologies." In *Decolonizing Epistemologies: Latina/o Theology and
    Philosophy*, edited by Ada María Isasi-Díaz and Eduardo Mendieta, 19–43. New
    York: Fordham University Press, 2012.
Morse, Donald J. *Faith in Life: John Dewey's Early Philosophy.* New York: Fordham
    University Press, 2011.
Muraro, Darcísio Natal. "Relações entre a filosofia e a educação de John Dewey e
    de Paulo Freire." *Educação & Realidade* 38, no. 3 (2013): 813–29.
Myers, William T. "Dewey, Whitehead, and Process Metaphysics." In *The Oxford
    Handbook of Dewey*, edited by Steven Fesmire, 53–72. New York: Oxford
    University Press, 2019.
Nash, Gary B. "The Hidden History of Mestizo America." *The Journal of American
    History* 82, no. 3 (1995): 941–64.
Nava, Alejandro. *Street Scriptures: Between God and Hip-Hop.* Chicago: University
    of Chicago Press, 2022.
Neumann, Jacob W. "Critical Pedagogy and Faith." *Educational Theory* 61, no. 5
    (2011): 601–19.

Nogueira-Godsey, Elaine. "A History of Resistance: Ivone Gebara's Transformative Feminist Liberation Theology." *Journal for the Study of Religion* 26, no. 2 (2013): 91.

Nuccetelli, Susana, and Gary Seay. *Latin American Philosophy: An Introduction with Readings.* London: Pearson, 2004.

Nuccetelli, Susana, Ofelia Schutte, and Otávio Bueno, eds. *A Companion to Latin American Philosophy.* Malden, MA: Wiley-Blackwell, 2010.

Oropeza, Eduardo. *Mestizaje e Intellectus Fidei: Acercamiento Teológico Fundamental.* Rome: Pontificiae Universitatis Gregorianae, 2007.

Orosco, José-Antonio. "Pragmatism, Interculturalism, and the Transformation of American Democracy." In *Pragmatism in the Americas,* edited by Gregory Fernando Pappas. New York: Fordham University Press, 2011.

Otto, Rudolf. *The Idea of the Holy: An Inquiry into the Non-Rational Factor in the Idea of the Divine and Its Relation to the Rational.* New York: Oxford University Press, 1923.

Owens, Catherine. "Mass Remembers Theology Professor Fr. Elizondo." *The Observer,* April 8, 2016. https://ndsmcobserver.com/2016/04/mass-remembers -fr-elizondo/.

Panotto, Nicolás. "A Critique of the Coloniality of Theological Knowledge: Rereading Latin American Liberation Theology as Thinking Otherwise." In *Decolonial Christianities: Latinx and Latin American Perspectives,* edited by Raimundo Barreto and Roberto Sirvent, 217–37. Cham, Switzerland: Palgrave MacMillan, 2019.

Pappas, Gregory Fernando. *John Dewey's Ethics: Democracy as Experience.* Bloomington: Indiana University Press, 2008.

———. "Zapatismo, Luis Villoro, and American Pragmatism on Democracy, Power, and Injustice." *The Pluralist* 12, no. 1 (2017): 85–100.

Pappas, Gregory Fernando, ed. *Pragmatism in the Americas.* New York: Fordham University Press, 2011.

Parks, Sharon Daloz. *Big Questions, Worthy Dreams: Mentoring Emerging Adults in Their Search for Meaning, Purpose, and Faith.* San Francisco: Jossey-Bass, 2000.

Patai, Daphne. *Brazilian Women Speak: Contemporary Life Stories.* New Brunswick, NJ: Rutgers University Press, 1988.

Peirce, C. S. "How to Make Our Ideas Clear." In *Selected Writings (Values in a Universe of Chance),* edited by Philip P. Wiener, 113–36. New York: Dover, 1958.

———. "The Fixation of Belief." In *Selected Writings (Values in a Universe of Chance),* edited by Philip P. Wiener, 91–112. New York: Dover, 1958.

Pérez, Laura E. *Eros Ideologies: Writings on Art, Spirituality, and the Decolonial.* Durham, NC: Duke University Press, 2019.

Pilario, Daniel Franklin. "Mapping Postcolonial Theory: Appropriations in Contemporary Theology." *Hapag* 3, no. 1–2 (2006): 9–51.

Pineda-Madrid, Nancy. *Suffering and Salvation in Ciudad Juárez.* Minneapolis: Fortress Press, 2011.

Pitts, Andrea J. *Nos/Otras: Gloria E. Anzaldúa, Multiplicitous Agency, and Resistance.* Albany: SUNY Press, 2021.

Pratt, Scott L. *Native Pragmatism: Rethinking the Roots of American Philosophy.* Bloomington: Indiana University Press, 2002.

Premawardhana, Devaka. "Between Logocentrism and Lococentrism: *Alambrista* Challenges to Traditional Theology." *Harvard Theological Review* 101, no. 3–4 (2008): 399–416.

Prevot, Andrew. *The Mysticism of Ordinary Life: Theology, Philosophy, and Feminism.* New York: Oxford University Press, 2023.

Puleo, Mev. *The Struggle Is One: Voices and Visions of Liberation.* Albany: SUNY Press, 1994.

Quijano, Aníbal. "Colonialidad del poder y clasificación social." *Journal of World-Systems Research* 6, no. 2 (2000): 342–86.

Raposa, Michael L. *Theosemiotic: Religion, Reading, and the Gift of Meaning.* New York: Fordham University Press, 2020.

Ress, Mary Judith. "Interview with Brazilian Feminist Theologian Ivone Gebara." *Feminist Theology* 3, no. 8 (1995).

Rivera, Mayra. *Poetics of the Flesh.* Durham, NC: Duke University Press, 2015.

———. *The Touch of Transcendence: A Postcolonial Theology of God.* Louisville, KY: Westminster John Knox, 2007.

Rivera, Omar. *Delimitations of Latin American Philosophy: Beyond Redemption.* Bloomington: Indiana University Press, 2019.

Rodríguez, Rubén Rosario. *Racism and God-Talk: A Latino/a Perspective.* New York: NYU Press, 2008.

Rogers, Melvin L. *The Undiscovered Dewey: Religion, Morality, and the Ethos of Democracy.* New York: Columbia University Press, 2009.

Rolheiser, Ronald. *The Holy Longing: The Search for a Christian Spirituality.* New York: Doubleday, 1999.

Ruether, Rosemary Radford. "Feminist Interpretation: A Method of Correlation." In *Feminist Interpretation of the Bible*, edited by Letty M. Russell, 111–24. Philadelphia: Westminster Press, 1985.

Schipani, Daniel S. *Religious Faith Encounters Liberation Theology.* Birmingham, AL: Religious Education Press, 1988.

Schneiders, Sandra M. "Spirituality in the Academy." *Theological Studies* 50 (1989): 676–97.

Schreiter, Robert. *Constructing Local Theologies.* Maryknoll, NY: Orbis Books, 1997.

———. "Spaces Engaged and Transfigured: Alejandro García-Rivera's Journey from Little Stories to Cosmic Reconciliation." *Diálogo: An Interdisciplinary Studies Journal* 16, no. 2 (2013): 43–47

Schutte, Ofelia. *Cultural Identity and Social Liberation in Latin American Thought.* Albany: SUNY Press, 1993.

———. "The Philosophy of Liberation in Critical Perspective." In *Cultural Identity and Social Liberation in Latin American Thought.* Albany: SUNY Press, 1993.

Seigfried, Charlene Haddock. *Pragmatism and Feminism: Reweaving the Social Fabric.* Chicago: University of Chicago Press, 1996.

Shallice, Tim. *The Organisation of Mind.* Oxford: Oxford University Press, 2011.

Shedinger, Robert F. "Teilhard de Chardin and the Incomplete Nature of Evolutionary Theory." *Evolution News and Science Today,* February 13, 2020. https://evolutionnews.org/ 2020/02/teilhard-de-chardin-and-the-incomplete -nature-of-evolutionary-theory/.

Shook, John. "F. C. S. Schiller and European Pragmatism." In *A Companion to Pragmatism*, edited by John R. Shook and Joseph Margolis, 44–53. Malden, MA: Wiley-Blackwell, 2006.

Silva, Grant. "'The Americas Seek Not Enlightenment but Liberation': On the Philosophical Significance of Liberation for Philosophy in the Americas." *The Pluralist* 13 (2018): 1–21.

Sison, Antonio D. *World Cinema, Theology, and the Human: Humanity in Deep Focus.* New York: Routledge, 2012.

Slabodsky, Santiago. *Decolonial Judaism: Triumphal Failures of Barbaric Thinking.* New York: Palgrave Macmillan, 2014.

Slattery, John P. "Pierre Teilhard de Chardin's Legacy of Eugenics and Racism Can't Be Ignored." *Religious Dispatches,* May 21, 2018. https://religiondispatches .org/pierre-teilhard-de-chardins-legacy-of-eugenics-and-racism-cant-be-ignored/.

Smith, John E. *Experience and God.* New York: Fordham University Press, 1999.

Smith, Wilfred Cantwell. *The Meaning and End of Religion.* Minneapolis: Fortress Press, 1962.

Stannard, David E. *American Holocaust: Columbus, Christianity, and the Conquest of the Americas.* New York: Oxford University Press, 1992.

Stehn, Alexander. "El Pueblo and Its Problems: Democracy of, by, and for Whom?" *The Pluralist* 6, no. 3 (2011): 103–16.

———. "Religiously Binding the Imperial Self: Classical Pragmatism's Call and Liberation Philosophy's Response." In *Pragmatism in the Americas*, edited by Gregory Fernando Pappas, 297–314. New York: Fordham University Press, 2011.

———. "Toward an Inter-American Philosophy: Pragmatism and the Philosophy of Liberation." *Inter-American Journal of Philosophy* 2, no. 2 (2011): 20–36.

Stumpf, Samuel Enoch, and James Fieser. "Pragmatism and Process Philosophy." In *Socrates to Sartre and Beyond: A History of Philosophy*, 8th edition, edited by Samuel Enoch Stumpf and James Fieser, 371–97. Boston: McGraw Hill, 2008.

Taves, Ann. "2010 Presidential Address: 'Religion' in the Humanities and the Humanities in the University." *Journal of the American Academy of Religion* 79, no. 2 (2011): 287–314.

Teilhard de Chardin, Pierre. *The Divine Milieu.* New York: Harper, 1960.

Tinker, George E. *American Indian Liberation: A Theology of Sovereignty.* Maryknoll, NY: Orbis Books, 2008.

Tirres, Christopher. *The Aesthetics and Ethics of Faith: A Dialogue Between Liberationist and Pragmatic Thought.* New York: Oxford University Press, 2014.

———. "Spiritual Healing at the Border: Lessons in Art, Culture, and Education." *Education & Culture* 38, no. 2 (2022): 91–126.

———. "Theological Aesthetics and the Many Pragmatisms of Alejandro García-Rivera." *Diálogo: An Interdisciplinary Studies Journal* 16, no. 2 (2013): 59–64.

Tisdell, Elizabeth. *Exploring Spirituality and Culture in Adult and Higher Education.* San Francisco: Jossey-Bass, 2003.

Tucker, Robert C., ed. *The Marx-Engels Reader*, second edition. New York: W.W. Norton, 1978.

Vasconcelos, José. *The Cosmic Race/La raza cósmica.* Translated by Didier T. Jaén. Baltimore, MD: Johns Hopkins University Press, 1997.

Victor Carmona, "Virgilio Elizondo, A Man of the Marginalized." *America: The Jesuit Review*, April 18, 2016. https://www.americamagazine.org/content/all-things/virgilio-elizondo-man-marginalized.

Vieira Pinto, Rede Álvaro. *Consciência Realidade Nacional.* Rio de Janeiro: Ministerio da Educação e Cultura, Instituto Superior de Estudos Brasileiros, 1960.

Vizcaíno, Rafael. "Introduction to Special Issue: Decolonizing Spiritualities." *CLR James Journal* 27, no. 1–2 (2021): 17–24.

———. "Secular Decolonial Woes." *Journal of Speculative Philosophy* 35, no. 1 (2021): 71–92.

Ware, Anne Patrick. "Translator's Note." In *Out of the Depths: Women's Experience of Evil and Salvation*, edited by Ivone Gebara and Ann Patrick Ware. Minneapolis: Fortress Press, 2002.

Watkins, Mary. *Waking Dreams.* New York: Harper and Row, 1976.

West, Cornel. *Democracy Matters: Winning the Fight Against Imperialism.* New York: Penguin, 2004.

White, Carol Wayne. *Black Lives and Sacred Humanity.* New York: Fordham University Press, 2016.

Wilshire, Bruce. *The Primal Roots of American Philosophy: Pragmatism, Phenomenology, and Native American Thought.* University Park: Pennsylvania State University Press, 2000.

Wirpsa, Leslie. "Before Silencing, Gebara Speaks Her Mind." *National Catholic Reporter* 31, no. 37 (1995): 13.

Yountae, An. *The Decolonial Abyss: Mysticism and Cosmopolitics from the Ruins.* Durham, NC: Duke University Press, 2017.

Yuasa, Yasuo. *The Body: Toward an Eastern Mind-Body Theory.* Edited by Thomas P. Kasulis. Albany: SUNY Press, 1987.

Zegarra, Raúl. *A Revolutionary Faith: Liberation Theology Between Public Religion and Public Reason.* Stanford, CA: Stanford University Press, 2023.

# Index

action, 66; conscientization and, 46; creative, 73–74, 82–86; dehumanization and, 48–50; experience and, 10–12; faith and, 23, 30, 58–59, 63–64; Freire and, 38–39, 41; habit and, 4, 16–17, 92, 94, 111, 114–15, 123; liberation and, 109; salvation and, 45; social change and, 37–39, 57–59; spirituality and, 9–10, 38, 80–81

activism, 12; in Christianity, 38–39; immigrants and, 71. *See also* spiritual activism

Addams, Jane, 107

Alexander, M. Jacqui, 112, 154n9

Alexander, Thomas, 147n29, 155n33

Altamirano, Ignacio Manuel, 141n41

Americas, 7; colonialism and, 6, 110; liberationist voices in, 61, 127n3

anthropology, 28, 75–86, 103; religion and, 45, 150n18; spirituality and, 8–9, 120–21, 128n15

Anzaldúa, Gloria, 12, 15–16, 69–71, 115, 120–21, 146n78; conocimiento and, 72–74, 81–82, 85, 121; imaginal realities of, 68, 75–76, 79–80, 144n46; *Light in the Dark*, 67–68, 72, 77–81, 84–86, 144n51; mature spirituality of, 73–74; pragmatism and, 68, 82, 114, 145n59; spirit and, 67–68, 74–75, 78–79; spiritual activism and, 67–68, 76, 80–86; storytelling and, 69, 75, 144n27

Aponte, Edwin, 8

Aquino, María Pilar, 5, 88, 146n4, 147n14

Arnold, Philip, 127n2

Aronowitz, Stanley, 137n11

Ashley, J. Matthew, 133n5, 156n42

Astin, Alexander, 118

authentic dialogue. *See* communion

Bambaataa, Afrika, 148n30

Barger, Lilian Calles, 132n5; Freire and, 37, 136n5

Bernstein, Richard, 114–15, 123

binaries. *See* dualisms

Bourdieu, Pierre, 21

Boyd, Drick, 37–40, 137n10, 138n33

Brazil, 41, 44–45, 100–102, 149n3

Cadorette, Kurt, 32

Câmara, Hélder, 149n3

Carlsen, Robert, 142n43

Carmona, Victor, 131n34

Carmelites, 23, 54

Carter, J. Cameron, 112, 154n11

Casarella, Peter, 138n38

Castañeda, Carlos, 80

Castillo, Daniel, 135n38, 139n38

Catholic Church, 3; Carmelites of, 23, 54; conscientization and, 37; criticism of, 24–25, 101–2, 120–21; education and, 52–53; Freire and, 39–40, 46–48; injustice and, 53; power and, 24–26; religious pluralism and, 56, 59, 61–62; spirituality and, 66; women religious of, 100, 148n2

Chopp, Rebecca, 150n17

Christ, as teacher, 42–43

Christianity, 3, 149n12; activism in, 38–39; colonialism and, 6–7; criticism of, 33;

Christianity (continued)
    prophetic, 6–7, 43, 138n25; revolution
        and, 46–47; witness in, 42–43
collective struggle, 141n41, 153n5
colonialism, 11, 84, 127n2, 152n26; Americas
    and, 6, 110; Christianity and, 6–7; decolo-
    nialism and, 15, 109–12, 123; land owners
    and, 24, 33, 134n9
colonization, 64–65, 141n41, 142n43, 145n59
A Common Faith (Dewey), 118–19
communion, 38; Freire and, 43–45; with God,
    44–45, 138n35
community, 103, 114; semiotics and, 45;
    Mexican-American, 52–54, 66
conocimiento: Anzaldúa and, 72–74, 81–82,
    85, 121; conscientization and, 115; spiritual
    activism and, 15–16, 81–82, 85, 116; vio-
    lence and, 67–68
conscientization, 22, 116, 137n10; action and,
    46; Catholic Church and, 37; cono-
    cimiento and, 115; Freire and, 12, 15,
    37–50, 115, 123; hope and, 38–41, 47;
    praxis and, 40, 42, 47–48, 50; revolution
    and, 34–35
conscientized cotidiano, 88, 90–92, 96, 116;
    the poor and, 93–94
contextualism, 33–35, 66, 87
conversion, 23, 38; Freire and, 46–48
cosmology, 103, 105–6, 141n41, 152n26; evolu-
    tionary, 52, 60–66; God and, 104, 151n20
lo cotidiano: conscientized, 88, 90–94, 96,
    116; Isasi-Díaz and, 88–90, 98–99;
    knowledge and, 94–96; religion and,
    96–97
creative action, 73–74, 84–86; praxis and,
    82–83
creativity, 58, 95; truth and, 30–31
critical awareness. See conscientization
critical pedagogy, 47–48, 90, 137n10; spiritual-
    ity and, 115–22
criticism: of Catholic Church, 24–25, 101–2,
    120–21; of Christianity, 33; of liberation
    theology, 102–3, 111–12
cultural context, 33–35, 51, 87, 101–2, 111, 121;
    Elizondo and, 54–55, 61, 66
culture: Elizondo and, 51, 61, 127n3; liberation
    and, 51–56, 60; religion and, 53; transcul-
    turation, 65, 142n43
curanderismo, 76–79

daily life. See lo cotidiano
daimons, 85–86, 146n78
decolonialism, 5–7; spirituality and, 109–12,
    123

dehumanization, 40–44, 107; action and,
    48–50
De La Torre, Miguel, 127n3, 156n37
Delgadillo, Theresa, 84–85, 145n69, 146n72
Delgado, Teresa, 112, 154n10
De Luna, Anita, 7–9
detention, of immigrants, 1–4, 16–18, 109
deviance, 70, 85–86
Dewey, John, 10, 115, 123, 130n30, 131n41,
    151n24; A Common Faith, 118–19; on edu-
    cation, 17, 116–17; on experience,
    131nn37–38; Freire and, 114, 131n36;
    knowledge and, 94–95, 97, 148n30
dialectic, action and, 38–39, 41
Díaz, Kim, 34
domination, 46, 106, 111; liberation and, 42
dreams, 79–80; social change and, 60–61
Drexler-Dries, Joseph, 112, 153n6, 154n10
dualisms, 11, 28, 103, 105, 129n25
Du Bois, W.E.B., 153n3
Dussel, Enrique, 21–22, 37, 132nn3–4, 110, 132n4
dynamism, 12, 105, 119; of spirituality, 11, 66,
    83–85

ecofeminism, 104, 114, 149n12; relatedness
    and, 102–3
ecology, liberation and, 104, 150n18, 151n20
education: Catholic Church and, 52–53;
    Dewey on, 17, 116–17; experience and,
    17–18; Freire on, 17, 37, 43–44, 47–48,
    116; liberation theology and, 100; racism
    and, 69–70; spirituality and, 116–17
Elizondo, Virgilio, 15, 52–53, 121, 130n34; cul-
    tural context and, 54–55, 61, 66; evolu-
    tionary cosmology and, 60–66; The
    Future is Mestizo, 59–66; The Human
    Quest, 58–59; Latine theology and, 51;
    liberation theology and, 51, 55–56; Teil-
    hard de Chardin and, 51, 58–66, 114,
    140n19; universal mestizaje of, 60–64, 66,
    141n41, 142n45
Ellacuría, Ignacio, 13–14, 94, 130n30, 131n41
emotions, knowledge and, 28–29, 91–92
esotericism, 71, 75–76, 81
Espín, Orlando, 87–89, 92, 153n1
ethics, 11–12, 19, 85, 132n4; Freire and, 41–42
ethnographic theology, 55, 87, 89
Everyday Life (Heller), 91–93
evolution, 120, 141n31; Gebara and, 152n25;
    God and, 57–58; intelligence and, 57, 61;
    philosophy and, 106; teleology and,
    140n19; theology and, 51
evolutionary cosmology, 52; Elizondo and,
    60–66

experience, 66, 73, 104, 108, 115; action and, 10–12; Dewey on, 131nn37–38; education and, 17–18; feminism and, 107; liberation and, 110; pragmatism and, 89, 121–22; of religion, 27–31; spirituality and, 5–9, 110, 113, 128n10; tradition and, 150n18; transcendence and, 19, 45, 77–78

faith, 3, 16–17, 78–79, 128n18; action and, 23, 30, 58–59, 63–64; Freire and, 37–38, 42–45, 50, 138n25; imagination and, 30–31; intelligence and, 13–14, 130n33; Isasi-Díaz and, 97–99; love and, 43, 45, 50; Mariátegui and, 27–28; meaning and, 4, 14, 27; spirituality and, 120
fallibilism, 106, 114–15, 123
Fanon, Frantz, 145n59
Fanon Mendés Franc, Mirielle, 153n5
feminism, 71–72, 123; ecofeminism, 102–4, 114, 149n12; experience and, 107; in Latin America, 88–90; liberation theology and, 102; philosophy and, 28, 88–89, 91, 113
feminist theology, 87, 89–90; pragmatism and, 103–4, 150n17
Fernández, Eduardo, 138n38
Fischer, Marilyn, 154n13
Flores, Nichole, 128n11, 133n5
Fowler, James, 118
Franck, Henri, 30
Freire, Paolo, 16, 90, 131n37; Barger and, 37, 136n5; Catholic Church and, 39–40, 46–48; communion and, 43–45; conscientization and, 12, 15, 37–50, 115, 123; conversion and, 46–48; Dewey and, 114, 131n36; on education, 17, 37, 43–44, 47–48, 116; ethics and, 41–42; faith and, 37–38, 42–45, 50, 138n25; gendered language and, 48–50, 137n15; Gutiérrez and, 34–35; implicit spirituality of, 37–40; liberation theology and, 36–37, 42–43, 46–47; Marxism of, 38–39; *Pedagogy of the Oppressed*, 40–41, 48
Fuentes, Agustín, 120
functionalism, 12–13, 38, 68, 80, 82, 85. *See also* pragmatism
*The Future is Mestizo* (Elizondo), 59–66

gamonalismo, in Peru, 24, 33, 134n9
Gandolfo, David, 136n2
García, Nathan, 134n5
García-Rivera, Alejandro, 59, 65, 133n5, 138n38
Garrison, Jim, 85–86
Gebara, Ivone, 16, 28, 148n2, 149n3; ecofeminism of, 102–4, 114, 149n12; evolution and, 152n25; liberation and, 112, 116;

liberation theology and, 100–102, 106–7; McFague and, 104–7, 150n18, 151n20; pragmatism and, 103–8, 114; Ruether and, 104, 150n18
gender, 128n11; faith and, 97–99; knowledge and, 100–101; liberation theology and, 89; religion and, 88; struggle and, 101–2, 107, 149n5
gendered language, 48–50, 101, 128n11, 137n15
Glaude, Eddie, Jr., 119
God, 3; communion with, 44–45, 138n35; cosmology and, 104, 151n20; evolution and, 57–58; love and, 63–64; philosophy and, 57; Word of, 42–43
Goizueta, Roberto, 139n38, 141n40
González, Antonio, 37, 136n3
González, Michelle A., 139n38, 148n35
González-Andrieu, Cecilia, 133n5
González Prada, Manuel, 25–26
Groody, Daniel, 130n34
Grosfugel, Ramón, 153n6
Guadalupe, Our Lady of, 55, 77, 141n41
Gutiérrez, Gustavo: Freire and, 34–35; liberation theology and, 21, 25, 138n38; Mariátegui and, 25, 31–35, 115–16; *A Theology of Liberation*, 31–35

habit and action, 4, 16–17, 92, 94, 111, 114–15, 123
Haight, Roger, 8–9, 120, 137n13
Haught, John, 140n19, 141n32
Heagle, John, 128n10
Hedrick, Tace, 84, 145n69
Heidegger, Martin, 21, 122
Heller, Agnes, 96–97, 114; *Everyday Life*, 91–93
Hickman, Larry, 82
Hildebrand, David, 12
hope, 18, 54, 61; conscientization and, 38–41, 47; spirituality and, 109
humanism, 24–25, 38
humanization, 38, 40–43; conscientization and, 47–48; education and, 44
*The Human Phenomenon* (Teilhard de Chardin), 57–59
*The Human Quest* (Elizondo), 58–59

ICDI. *See* Interfaith Community for Detained Immigrants
imaginal realities, 68, 75–76, 79–80, 144n46
imagination, 18, 76–81, 129n25; faith and, 30–31
immigrants, 52–53; activism and, 71; detention of, 1–4, 16–18, 109

implicit spirituality, of Freire, 37–40
Indigenous people, 6, 32–34, 104–5; of Peru, 23–26; pragmatism and, 152n26; religion and, 4, 127n2
injustice: Catholic Church and, 53; liberation theology and, 55, 107, 120–21
instrumentalism, 9–14, 115–16, Anzaldúa and, 78–79, 82–85; Freire and, 38–39, 47–48; Mariátegui and, 29–31. *See also* functionalism
intelligence, 110, 115, 121–22, 129n39; dynamism of, 12; evolution and, 57, 61; faith and, 13–14, 130n33
Interfaith Community for Detained Immigrants (ICDI), 1–4, 17–18, 109
interiority, 23, 40, 42, 57–58, 75–76
intersectionality, 5–6, 15, 101
intuition, 72–73, 94–96
Isasi-Díaz, Ada María, 16, 121; conscientized cotidiano of, 88, 90–94, 96, 116; lo cotidiano and, 88–90, 98–99; faith and gender and, 97–99; Heller and, 91–93, 96–97, 114
ITER. *See* Theology Institute of Recife

James, William, 29–30, 68, 84, 115
Jasper, Karl, 41
Jennings, Willie James, 112, 128n8, 154n11
Jesus, 10, 55; love and, 7; praxis and, 63
Joas, Hans, 155n33
Johnson, Mark, 129n29

Keating, AnaLouise, 74–75, 81
King, Ursula, 57
Kirylo, James, 37–40, 137n10, 138n27, 138n33
knowledge, 75, 83, 114; lo cotidiano and, 94–96; Dewey and, 94–95, 97, 148n30; emotions and, 28–29, 91–92; gender and, 100–101; problems and, 12, 92–93, 115–16; religious, 28–31, 82, 96–97; social change and, 72; subversive, 90–91, 93–96, 107–8. *See also* conocimiento
Kripal, Jeffrey, 75–76

land owners, colonialism and, 24, 33, 134n9
language, 34, 127n3; gendered, 48–50, 101, 128n11, 137n15; Spanish, 1–2, 71–72
Lassalle-Klein, Robert, 133n5
Latin America, 31–32, 36, 132n5; feminism in, 88–90; the poor in, 102; pragmatism in, 152n26; US and, 51; violence in, 2
Latine theology, 7–8, 97, 128n11; Elizondo and, 51; feminist, 87–88
Lee, Michael, 130n33

Leopando, Irwin, 37
lesbianism, 70–71
liberation, 21, 50, 119–20; action and, 109; lo cotidiano and, 90; culture and, 51–56, 60; domination and, 42; ecology and, 104, 150n18, 151n20; experience and, 110; Gebara and, 112, 116; oppression and, 34–35, 44, 71, 81–82, 89–90; the poor and, 31; pragmatism and, 112–15; revolution and, 22, 32; salvation and, 43
liberation philosophy, liberation theology and, 36–37
liberation theology, 5, 10, 14–15, 87, 123, 127n3, 132n5; criticism of, 102–3, 111–12; Elizondo and, 51, 55–56; Freire and, 36–37, 42–43, 46–47; Gebara and, 100–102, 106–7; Gutiérrez and, 21, 25, 138n38; injustice and, 55, 107, 120–21; Isasi-Díaz and, 89; liberation philosophy and, 36–37; Mariátegui and, 21–22, 31, 112
*Light in the Dark/Luz en lo oscuro* (Anzaldúa), 67–68, 72, 77–81, 84–86, 144n51
limit-situations, limit-acts and, 41–43
Lloyd, Vincent, 112, 154n11
Long, Charles, 128n18
*Longing for Running Water* (Gebara), 102–5
love: faith and, 43, 45, 50; God and, 63–64; Jesus and, 7
Löwy, Michel, 26

MacMullan, Terrance, 22, 36
Maffie, James, 152n26
Maldonado-Torres, Nelson, 112, 153n5, 153n9
Mariátegui, José Carlos, 15, 121; faith and, 27–28; Gutiérrez and, 25, 31–35, 115–16; liberation theology and, 21–22, 31, 112; Marxism of, 23–24, 26, 32–33; new sense of religion and, 24–31, 115–16; pragmatism and, 29–30, 35, 114; religious knowledge and, 28–31; *Seven Interpretive Essays on Peruvian Reality*, 23–26
Márquez, Iván, 37, 136n3
Martínez, Gaspar, 32
Marx, Karl, 21–22, 31–32, 45, 122–23
Marxism, 112; of Freire, 38–39; of Mariátegui, 23–24, 26, 32–33
Matovina, Timothy, 59, 139n38, 142n41
mature spirituality, of Anzaldúa, 73–74
McFague, Sally, 104–7, 114, 150n18, 151n20, 152n28
meaning, 10–13, 113, 116–17, 129n29, 141n41; community and, 45; faith and, 4, 14, 27
Medina, Néstor, 64–65, 112, 141n38, 154n10

Mendieta, Eduardo, 22, 132n4, 133n5, 136nn1–2
mestizaje, 51–52, 54–55, 84–85, 88; universal, 60–64, 66, 141n41, 142n45
Mexican-American community, 52–54, 66
Mignolo, Walter, 111–12
Morse, Donald, 155n28
Mounier, Emmanuel, 40
mujerista theology, 87–88. *See also* feminist theology
Myers, William, 151n22
mysticism, 27, 56–57, 61, 77, 131n38, 144n46
myth, 25–26, 28–31, 34, 71

Nash, Gary, 65
Nava, Alejandro, 129n25, 148n30
nepantla spirituality, 67, 77–78, 84
Neumann, Jacob. W, 137n10
new sense of religion, Mariátegui and, 24–31, 115–16
Niebuhr, Reinhold, 59
Nogueira-Godsey, Elaine, 149n2
North America, 5, 106, 132n5

oppression, 6–7, 40–41, 107; liberation and, 34–35, 44, 71, 81–82, 89–90; power and, 42; religion and, 120–22
Orosco, José-Antonio, 22, 133n5
orthodoxy, 7, 15, 58
orthopraxy, and orthodoxy, 10, 31, 82
Ortiz, Fernando, 142n43

Panotto, Nicolás, 37, 136n3
Pappas, Gregory, 22, 133n5, 136n1, 146n75, 152n26
Parks, Sharon Daloz, 117
patriarchy, 71, 100–101, 104
*Pedagogy of the Oppressed* (Freire), 40–41, 48
Peirce, Charles Sanders, 22, 93, 129n24, 130n30, 132n4
Pérez, Laura E., 84, 145n59
personalism, 38, 40, 138n33
Peru, 32; gamonalismo in, 24, 33, 134n9; Indigenous people of, 23–26
phenomenology, 40–41, 44, 57, 103–4, 131n37
philosophy, 33–34, 36–37; evolution and, 106; feminist, 28, 88–89, 91, 113; God and, 57; theology and, 21–22
Pilario, Daniel, 21
Pineda-Madrid, Nancy, 134n5
Pitts, Andrea, 146n69
pluralism, 61, 114–15; realism and, 68, 80; religious, 5–6, 53, 56, 59, 61–62; spirituality and, 19

the poor, 23; conscientized cotidiano and, 93–94; in Latin America, 102; liberation and, 31; preferential option for, 7, 33–34, 64, 66, 107–8; suffering and, 64, 100, 149n5
popular religion, 33, 96
power, 123; Catholic Church and, 24–26; oppression and, 42
pragmatism, 10, 13, 22, 61, 129n24, 130n30, 132nn4–5; Anzaldúa and, 68, 82, 114, 145n59; experience and, 89, 121–22; feminist theology and, 103–4, 150n17; Freire and, 47–48, 116, 131n36; Gebara and, 103–8, 114; Indigenous people and, 152n26; Isasi-Díaz and, 93–99; liberation and, 112–15; Mariátegui and, 29–30, 35, 114; pragmatic ethos, 112–15, scepsis and, 92–93; spirituality and, 68, 81–85, 121–23; theology and, 152n25
Pratt, Mary Louise, 142n43
Pratt, Scott, 152n26
praxis, 9, 26–27, 49, 51, 67–68; conscientization and, 40, 42, 47–48, 50; creative action and, 82–83; ethical, 42; faith and, 31; Jesus and, 63; spirituality and, 48, 81, 110–11, 116–21; of storytelling, 83–84; theology and, 115–16
preferential option for the poor, 7, 33–34, 64, 66, 107–8
Premawardhana, Devaka, 143n46
Prevot, Andrew, 97, 142n45
problematic situations, 10, 82, 88, 94, 98–99, 107–8; knowledge and, 12, 92–93, 115–16
process thought, 57, 104–6, 152n25. *See also* pragmatism
prophecy, 64, 99, 121
prophetic Christianity, 6–7, 43, 138n25

Quijano, Aníbal, 6, 110

racism, 64–65, 111, 113; education and, 69–70; in social movements, 71; spiritual activism and, 82; in US, 53–55
Rahner, Karl, 31
Raposa, Michael, 22, 133n5, 138n38
realism: imaginal realities and, 68, 75–76, 79–80, 144n46; pluralism and, 68, 80; spirituality and, 72–76, 85–86
rebirth, 46, 48–49, 54–55, 123; violence of, 65–66
reflective thought, 3–4, 16–17, 57–58, 88, 91–92, 115, 140n19
relatedness, 106, 116; ecofeminism and, 102–3; theology and, 104

religion, 26, 36–37, 46; anthropology and, 45, 150n18; lo cotidiano and, 96–97; culture and, 53; experience of, 27–31; gender and, 88; Indigenous people and, 4, 127n2; oppression and, 120–22; popular, 33, 96; revolution and, 27, 34, 62; spirituality and, 3, 8–9, 117–20, 122–23, 137n13, 155n21, 155n23

religious knowledge, 82, 96–97; Mariátegui and, 28–31

religious pluralism, 5–6, 53; Catholic Church and, 56, 59, 61–62

Renan, Ernest, 29

Rensi, Giuseppe, 135n35

revolution, 38–39; Christianity and, 46–47; conscientization and, 34–35; liberation and, 22, 32; religion and, 27, 34, 62

Rivera, Mayra, 112, 130n33, 154n10

Rivera, Omar, 26

Rolheiser, Ronald, 9

Rosario Rodríguez, Rubén, 64–65, 141n38

Ruether, Rosemary Radford, 104, 150n18

salvation, 31; action and, 45; liberation and, 43

scepsis, 92–93

Schneiders, Sandra, 7–8, 128n10, 128n15

Schreiter, Robert, 87, 90, 139n16

Schutte, Ofelia, 26–28, 36,45,132n2

science, 13–14, 28, 72–73, 79, 135n35; theology and, 56–57, 104–5. See also evolution

Seigfried, Charlene Haddock, 113

Seven Interpretive Essays on Peruvian Reality (Mariátegui), 23–26

Shedinger, Robert, 140n19

Shook, John, 135n33

Silva, Grant, 136n2

Sison, Antonio, 129n26

Slabodsky, Santiago, 112, 154n10

Slattery, John, 140n19

Smith, John, 129n22

Smith, Wilfred Cantwell, 117, 155n23

social change, 5–6, 12, 19, 90, 110, 148n2; action and, 37–39, 57–59; dreams and, 60–61; education and, 116; knowledge and, 72; rebirth and, 66; spiritual activism and, 68, 71–72, 82, 84–86

social movements, 5, 7, 81–82, 98; in US, 70–71, 136n5. See also liberation theology

Sorel, Georges, 23, 33–34

South America, 5

Spanish language, 1–2, 71–72

spirit, Anzaldúa and, 67–68, 74–75, 78–79

spiritual activism, 121; Anzaldúa and, 67–68, 76, 80–86; conocimiento and, 15–16,

81–82, 85, 116; racism and, 82; social change and, 68, 71–72, 82, 84–86

spirituality: action and, 9–10, 38, 80–81; anthropology and, 8–9, 120–21, 128n15; Catholic Church and, 66; conocimiento and, 73; conscientization and, 39; critical pedagogy and, 115–22; decolonial, 109–12, 123; dynamism of, 11, 66, 83–85; education and, 116–17; experience and, 5–9, 110, 113, 128n10; faith and, 120; hope and, 109; nepantla, 67, 77–78, 84; pluralism and, 19; pragmatism and, 68, 81–85, 121–23; praxis and, 48, 81, 110–11, 116–21; realism and, 72–76, 85–86; religion and, 3, 8–9, 117–20, 122–23, 137n13, 155n21, 155n23; theology and, 137n13, 156n42

Stehn, Alexander, 22, 37, 133n5, 136n3

storytelling, 69, 75, 144n27, 148n35; praxis of, 83–84

struggle, 26, 92–93, 98–99; collective, 73, 141n41, 153n15; gender and, 101–2, 107, 149n5

subversive knowledge, 90–91, 93–96, 107–8

suffering, 18–19, 44, 55, 121–22; the poor and, 64, 100, 149n5

Taves, Anne, 75–76

teachers, 44; Christ as, 42–43

Teilhard de Chardin, Pierre, 56–57, 141n32; Elizondo and, 51, 58–66, 114, 140n19; Vasconcelos and, 65–66

teleology, evolution and, 140n19

theology, 14–15, 132n5; ethnographic, 55, 87, 89; evolution and, 51; feminist, 87, 89–90, 103–4, 150n17; Latine, 7–8, 51, 87–88, 97, 128n11; mujerista, 87–88; philosophy and, 21–22; pragmatism and, 152n25; praxis and, 115–16; relatedness and, 104; science and, 56–57, 104–5; spirituality and, 137n13, 156n42. See also liberation theology

Theology Institute of Recife (ITER), 100, 149n3

A Theology of Liberation (Gutiérrez), 31–35

Tillich, Paul, 21, 59, 128n18, 137n13

Tinker, George, 127n2

Tisdell, Elizabeth, 117

transcendence, 9, 104, 111, 155n23; experience and, 19, 45, 77–78

transculturation, 65, 142n43

truth, 82, 92, 104, 107, 113; creativity and, 30–31

United States (US): immigrants in, 1–4, 16–18, 52–53, 109; Latin America and, 51; racism

in, 53–55; social movements in, 70–71,
136n5
universal mestizaje, of Elizondo, 60–64, 66,
141n41, 142n45
US. *See* United States

Vaihinger, Hans, 29, 135n35
Vasconcelos, José, 64–65, 141n41; Teilhard de
Chardin and, 65–66
Vatican II, 39, 61–62
Vieira Pinto, Álvaro Borges, 41
violence: conocimiento and, 67–68; in Latin
America, 2; of rebirth, 65–66
Vizcaíno, Rafael, 112, 154n9

Watkins, Mary, 79
West, Cornel, 7
White, Carol Wayne, 112, 154n11
Wilshire, Bruce, 152n26
witness, in Christianity, 42–43
women religious, 1, 100, 148n2
Women's Ordination Conference, 97–99
Word of God, 42–43

Yountae, An, 112, 154n10
Yuasa, Yasuo, 83

Zegarra, Raúl, 133n5, 135n38
Zubiri, Xavier, 13–14, 130n30

**Christopher D. Tirres** is the Michael J. Buckley Endowed Chair at Santa Clara University. He is the author of *The Aesthetics and Ethics of Faith: A Dialogue Between Liberationist and Pragmatic Thought* and coeditor of *Religion in the Américas: Trans-hemispheric and Transcultural Approaches*.

Printed in the USA
CPSIA information can be obtained
at www.ICGtesting.com
JSHW020851161124
73718JS00001B/1